[TMP VOLUME I]

Spoke Art gallery exists because of Rod Luff and our last six years of success are all the result of his very first Moleskine Project.

Let me back up.

In 2010, I was managing the online content for a popular art magazine during the day and working a restaurant job at night. Like many art writers, I got a curatorial itch and was soon putting on pop-up group shows around San Francisco.

In early 2011, I learned that Rod Luff was coming to the U.S. for a solo show in Los Angeles. I immediately contacted him to see if he'd like to make the most of his trip and do a second solo show with me in SF. Rod cordially agreed and soon mailed me the deconstructed contents of his sketchbook as he had been documenting it's progress online with his "Moleskine Project" blog.

Rod booked his flight, I custom framed the pages, and soon thereafter the gallery I had rented went out of business, leaving Rod and I with a body of work but no place to show it.

I scoured SF for a new venue, but couldn't find anything on such short notice. Eventually I came across a small retail storefront on Sutter street, and, with no other options, decided to sign a two-year lease.

Rod arrived soon thereafter, his solo show sold out, I quit my day job and the rest is history.

This book is not just a compendium of the past two Moleskine Project exhibitions, but also a culmination of six years of hard work, unbridled passion, and a true love for the art and artists we've had the honor to show...I hope this becomes the first in many volumes to come, enjoy!

–Ken Harman, Curator & Gallerist,
Spoke Art/Hashimoto Contemporary, San Francisco

22 Jan '16

The Moleskine Project began as a solitary mission to fill my new sketchbook cover to cover, and was then exhibited at Spoke Art Gallery in 2011. For the second show, Ken Harman and I decided to invite artists from around the world to complete their own double page of art to display on the gallery walls.

We started an annual, collective sketchbook exhibition full of art that stemmed from a variety of creative backgrounds like film, comics, fine art, illustration and more. Each double page became a gateway to experience the personal realm of each artist and appreciate the seemingly infinite creative possibilities within that omnipresent blank page. The ubiquitous sketchbook became a common ground that linked this diverse group of artists into a network, reflecting our interconnected, online world.

Now in it's fifth year, the Moleskine Project returns as a single book. However, it's no longer a solitary mission! It has grown into a bigger and better project than I ever could have achieved on my own and I couldn't be more thrilled about the incredible artists that have filled this new book cover to cover.

I'm very thankful to Ken Harman and Ryan Graff for their support and dedication in making this happen, to the artists who brought our idea to life and lastly, a huge thanks to <u>you</u> for picking up this book. I hope it inspires you to fill up a book of your own!

Rodrigo Luff, co-curator of the Moleskine Project

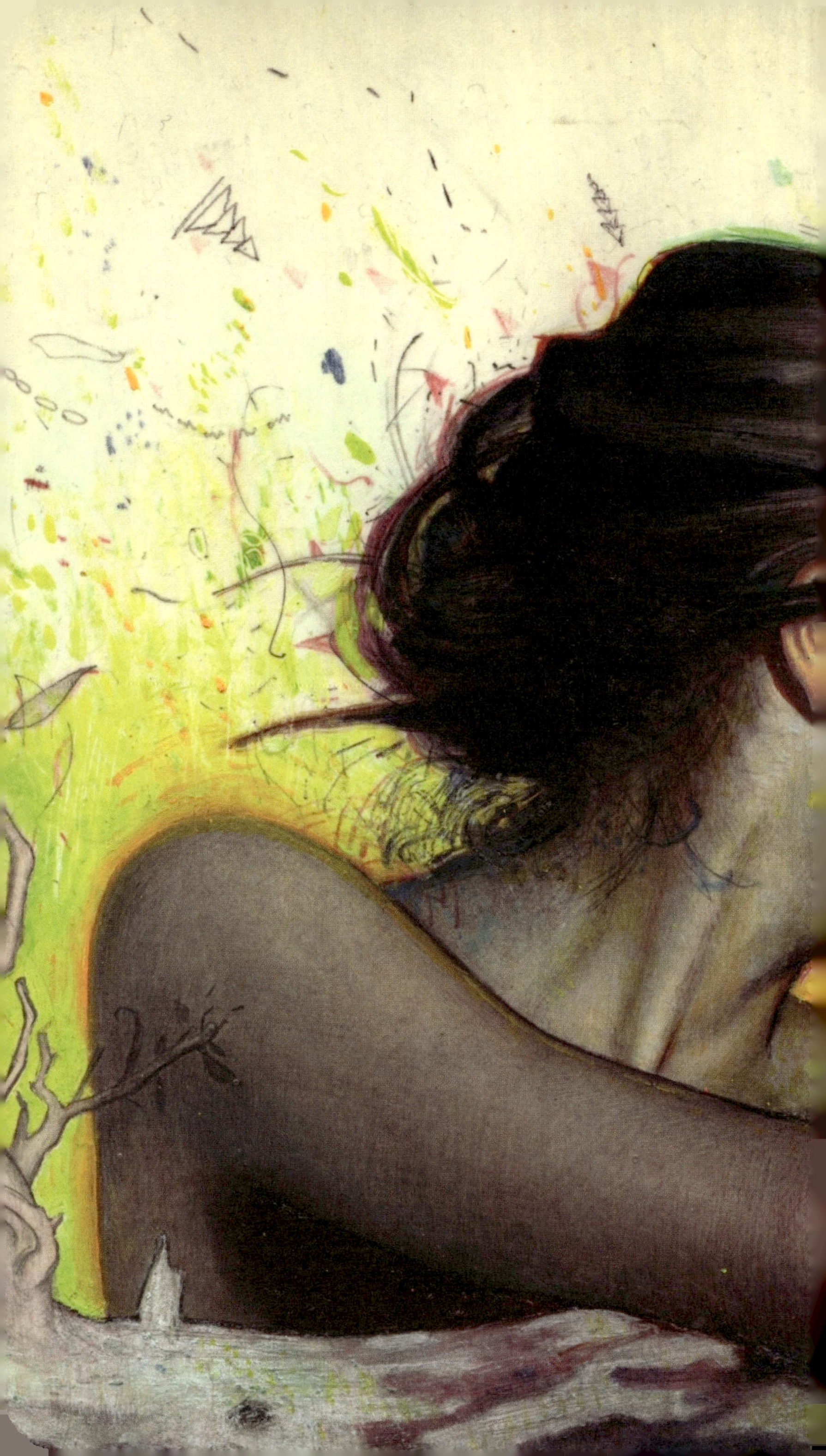

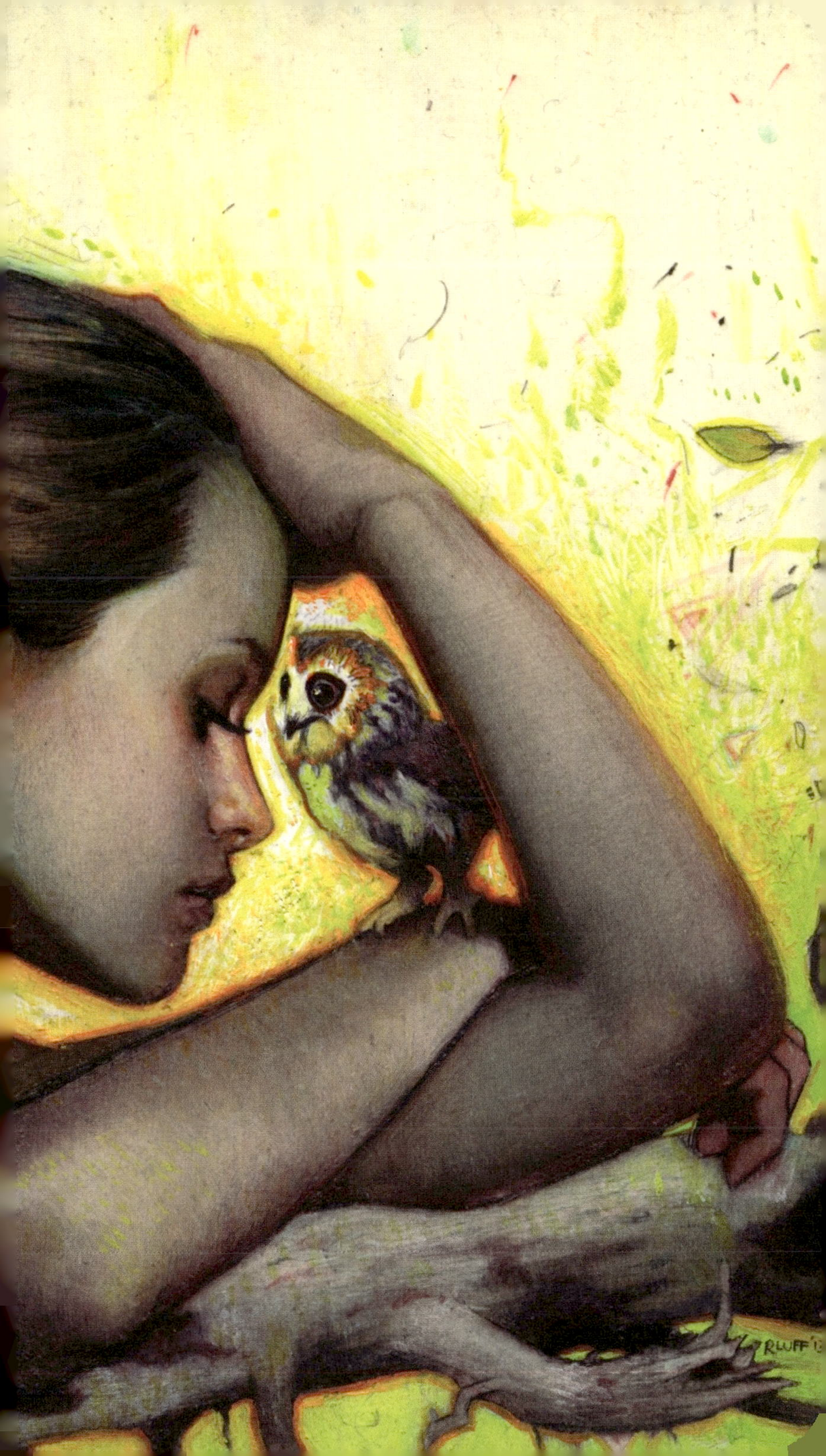
RLUFF

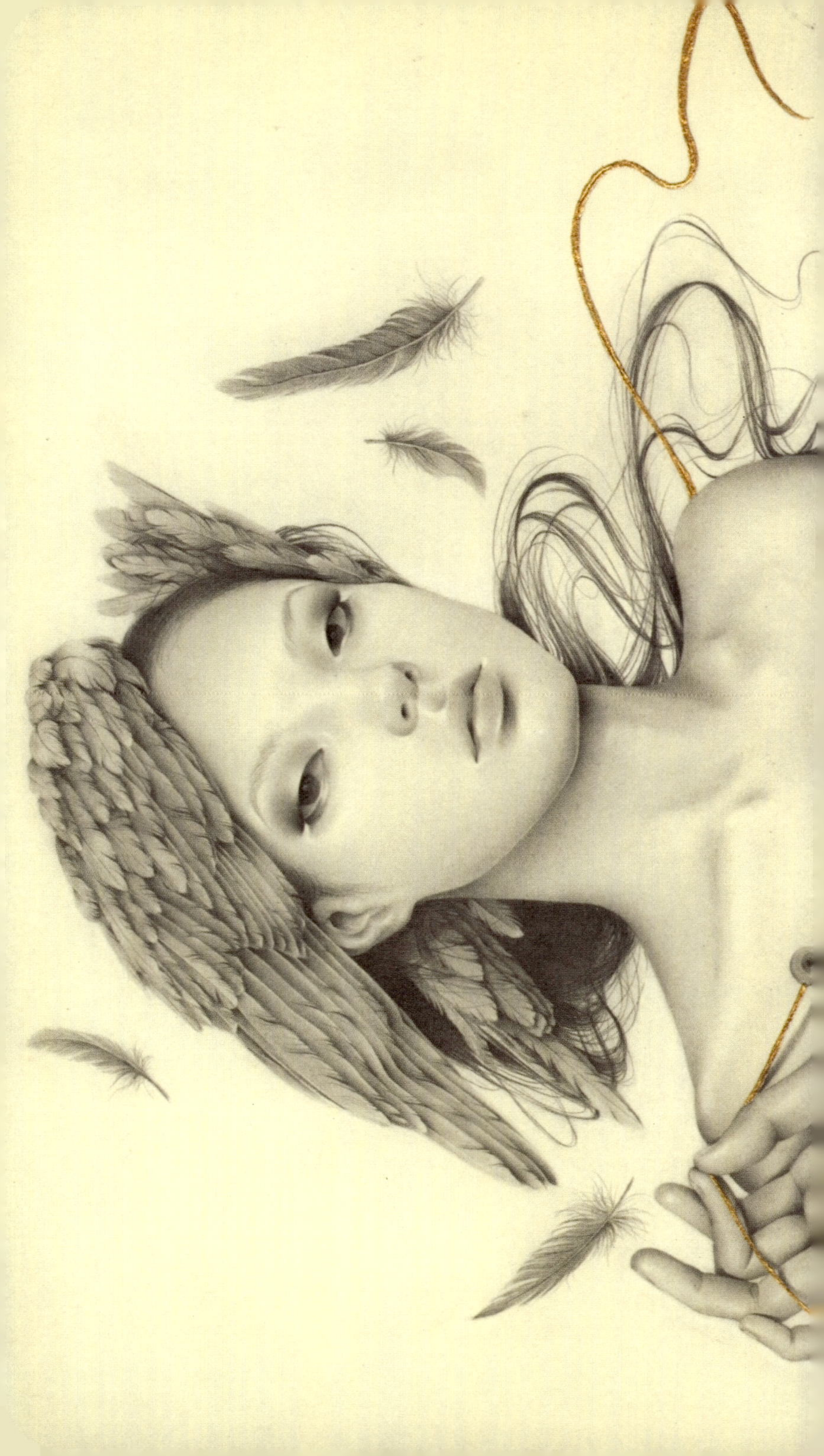

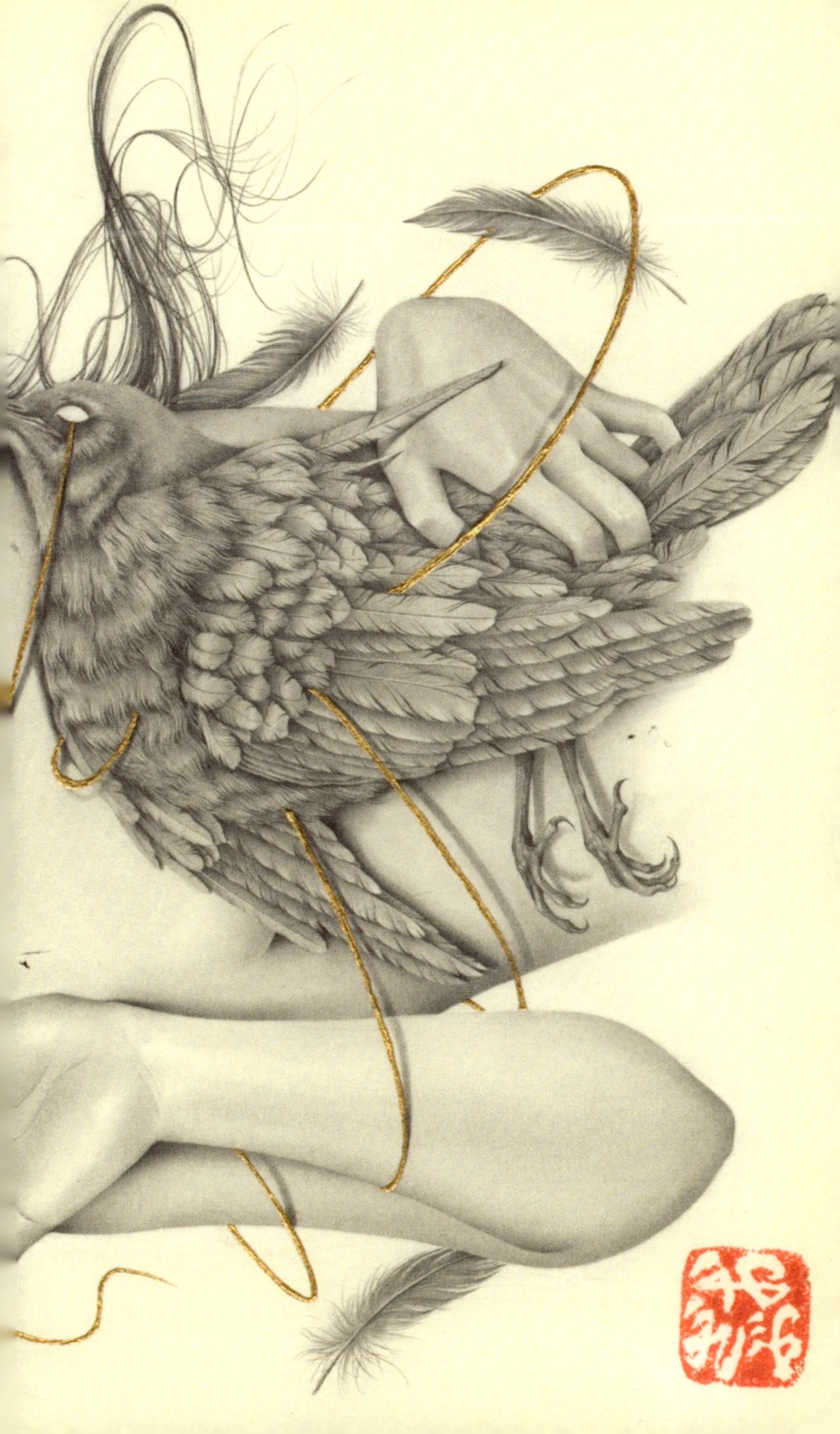

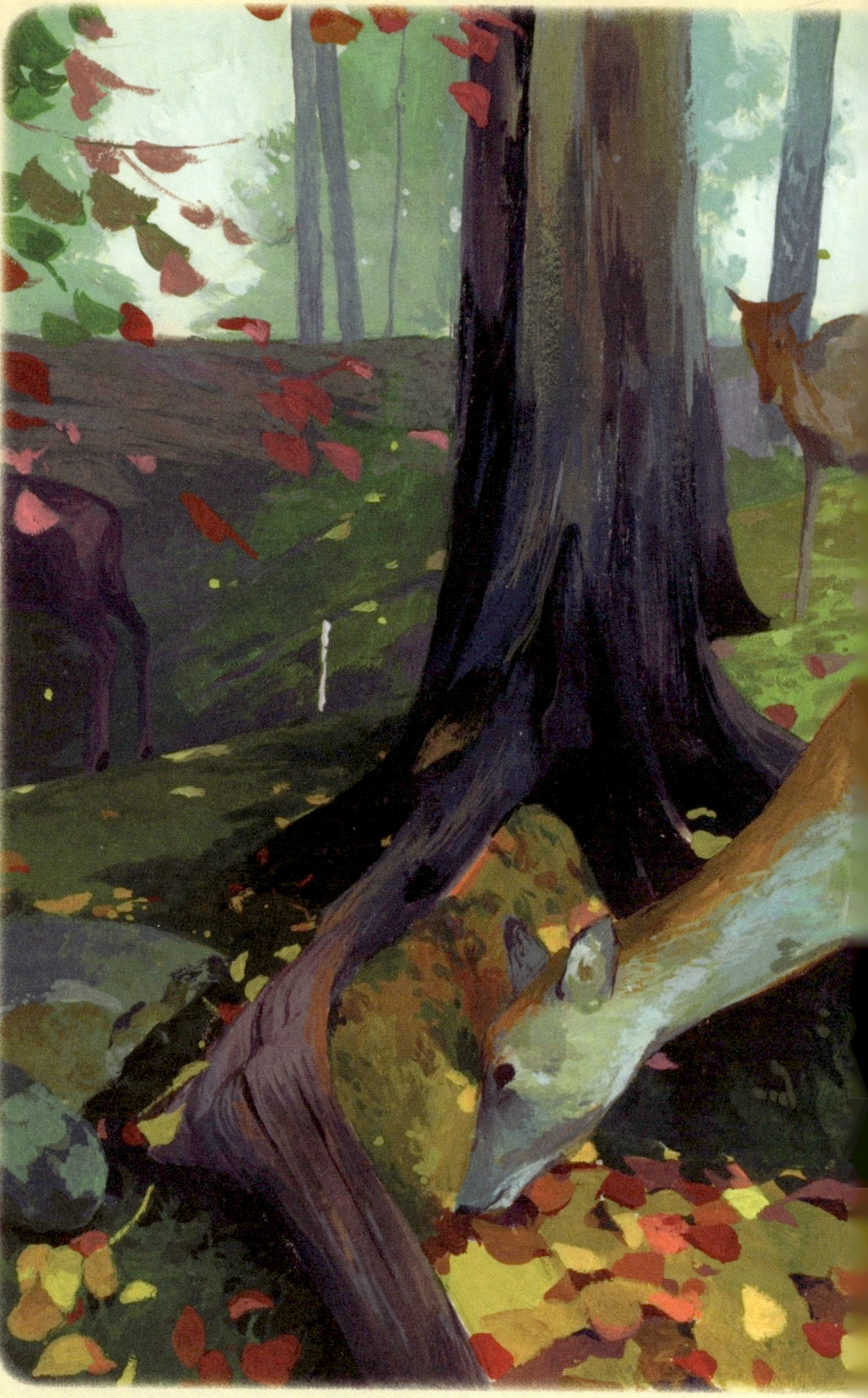

Make it Rain!

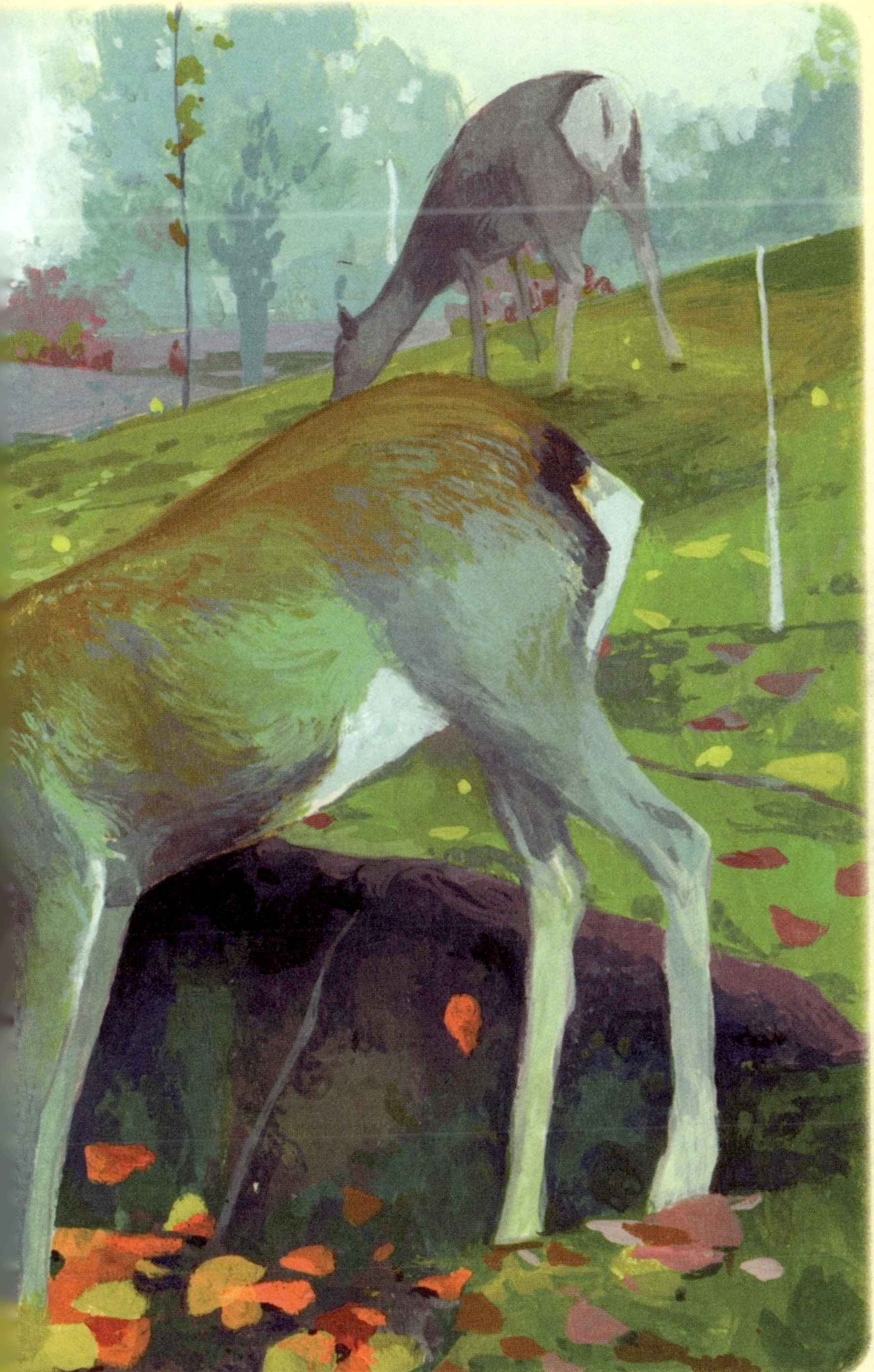

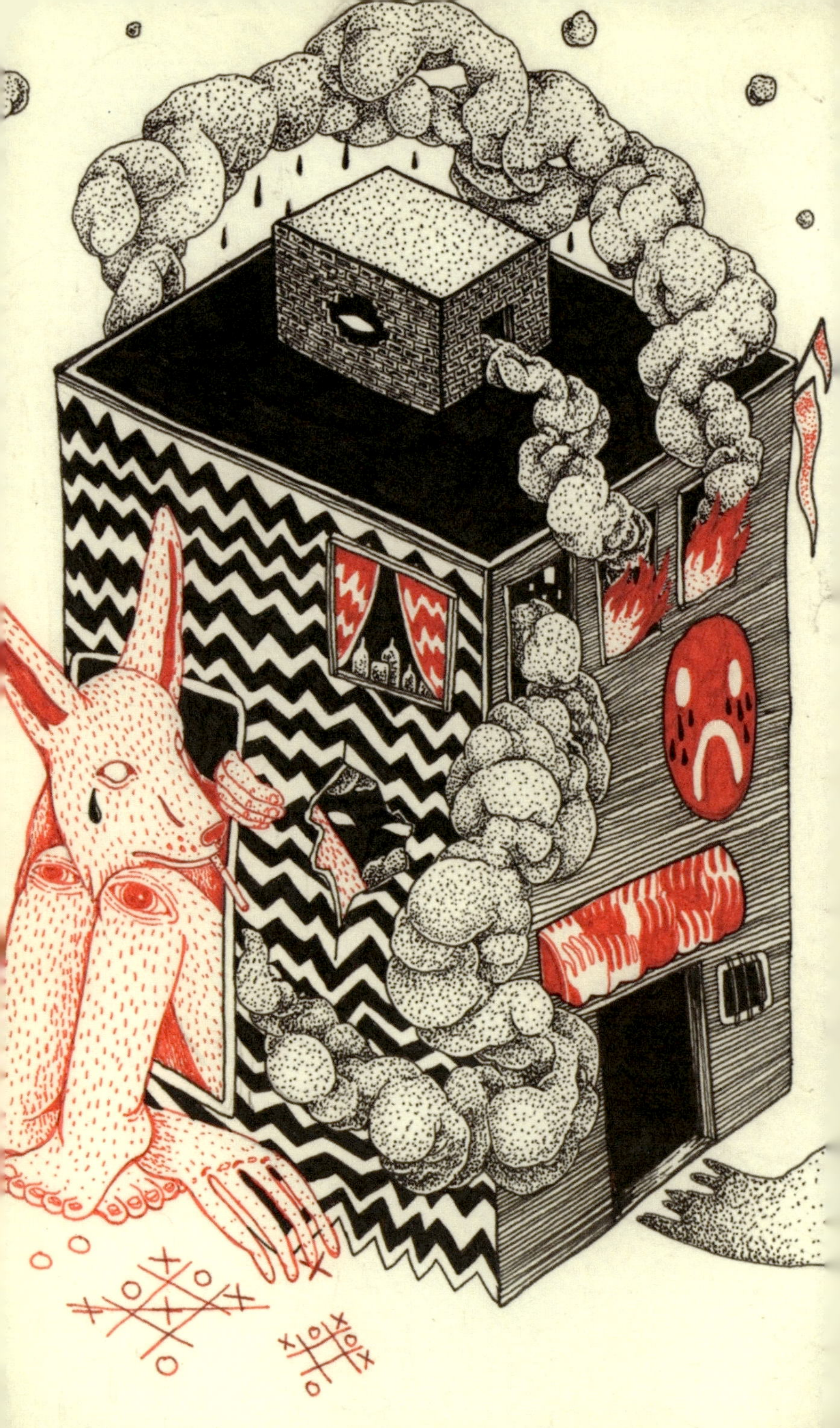

3·1

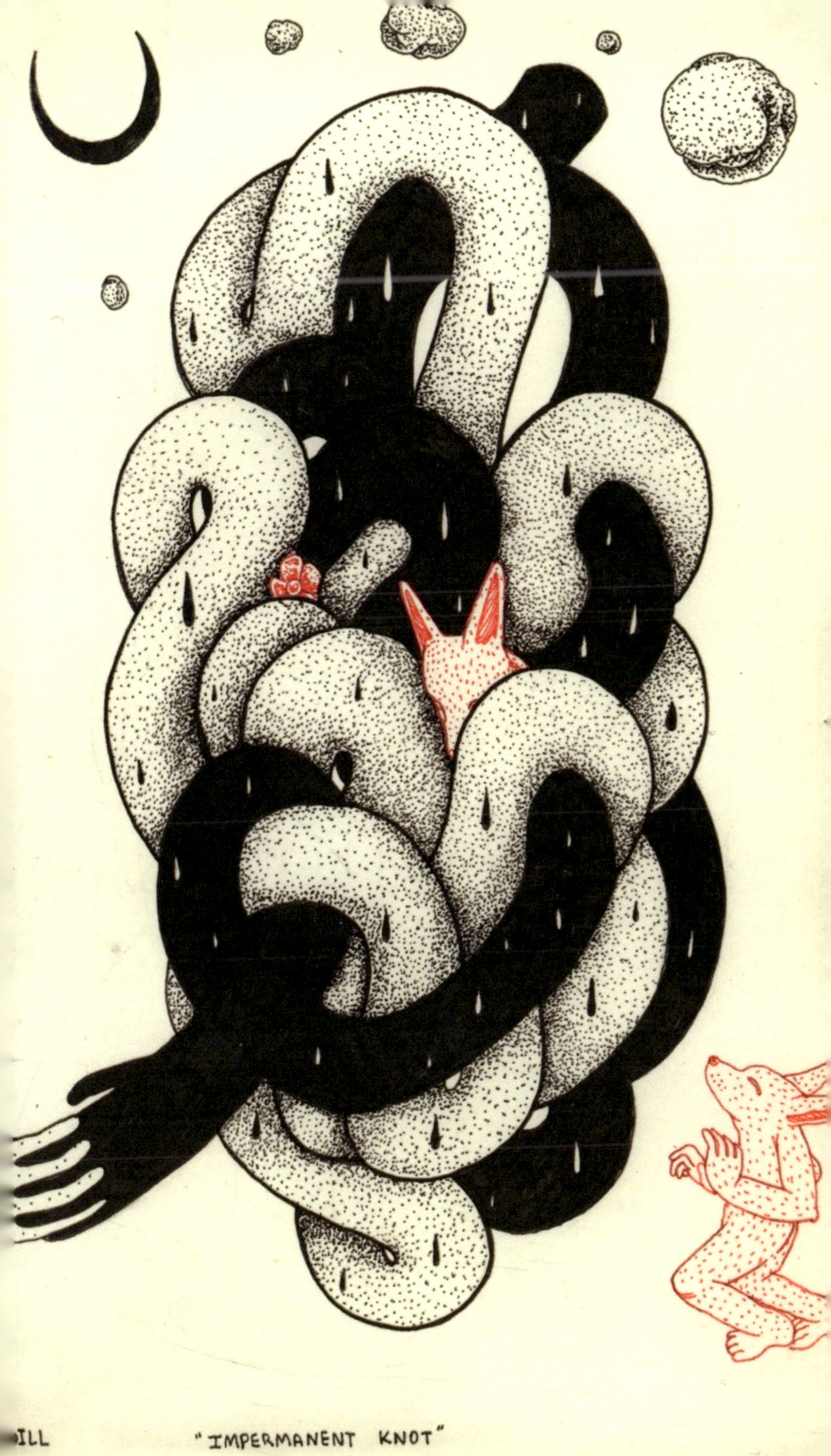

ILL "IMPERMANENT KNOT"

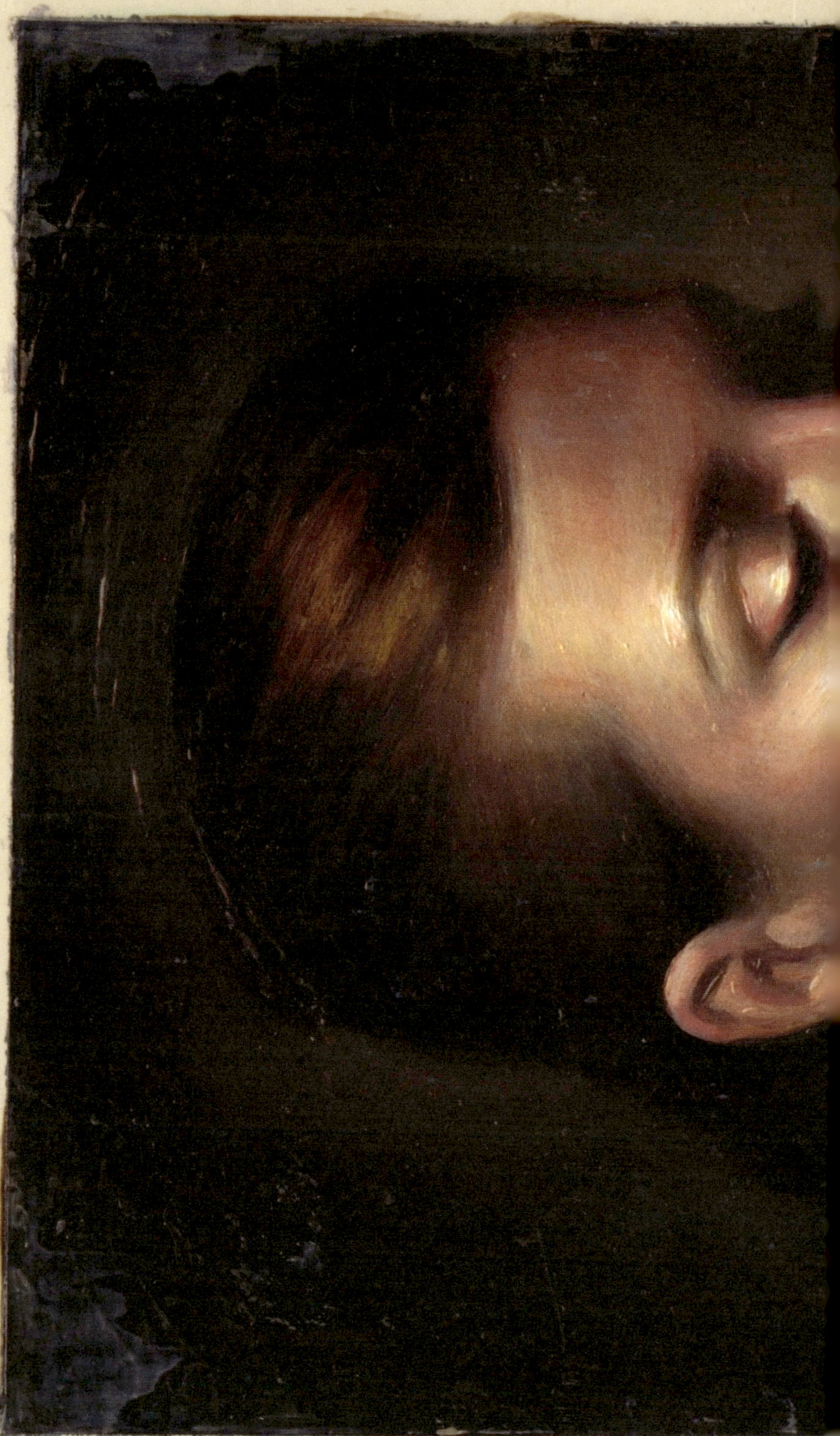

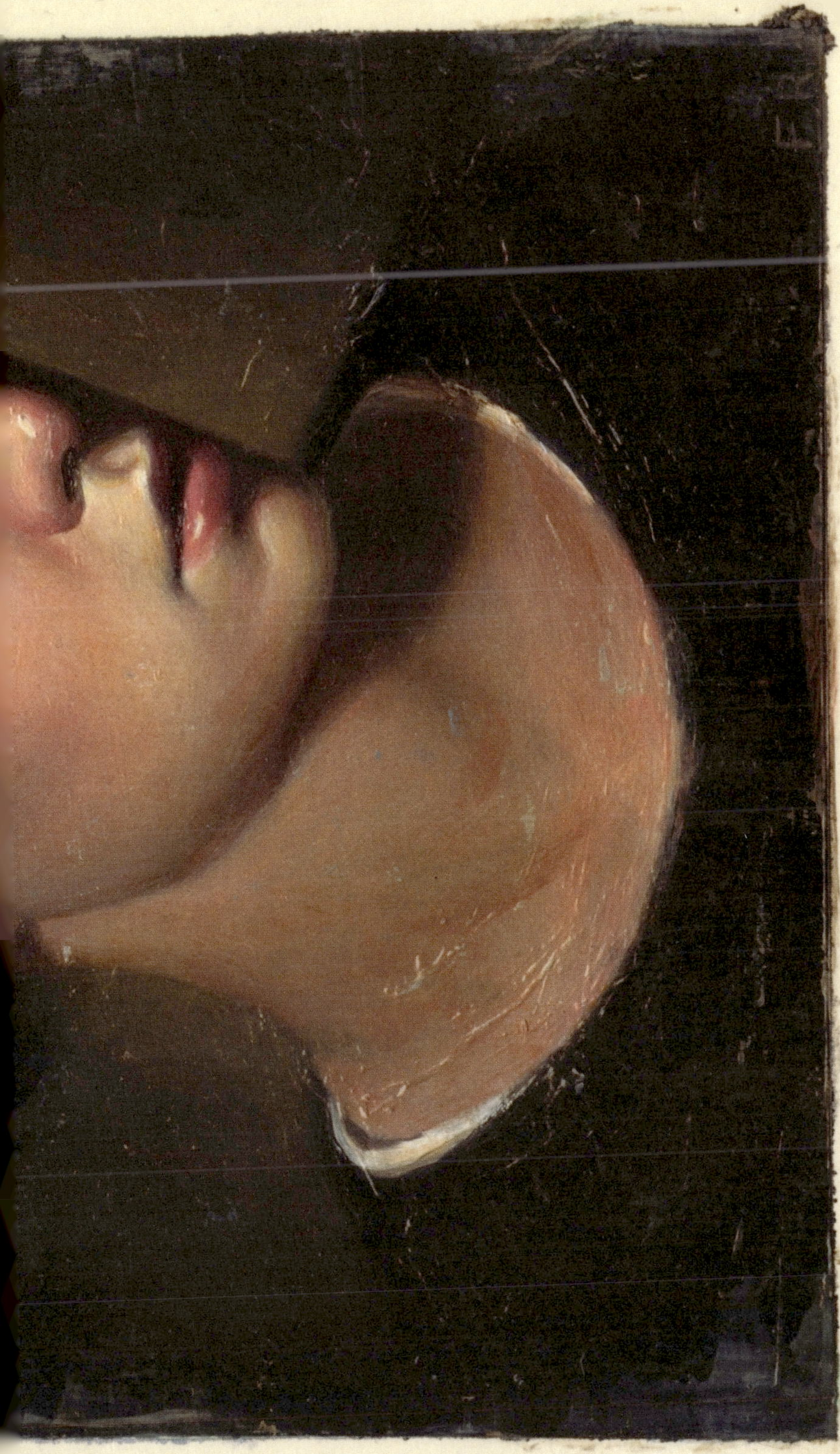

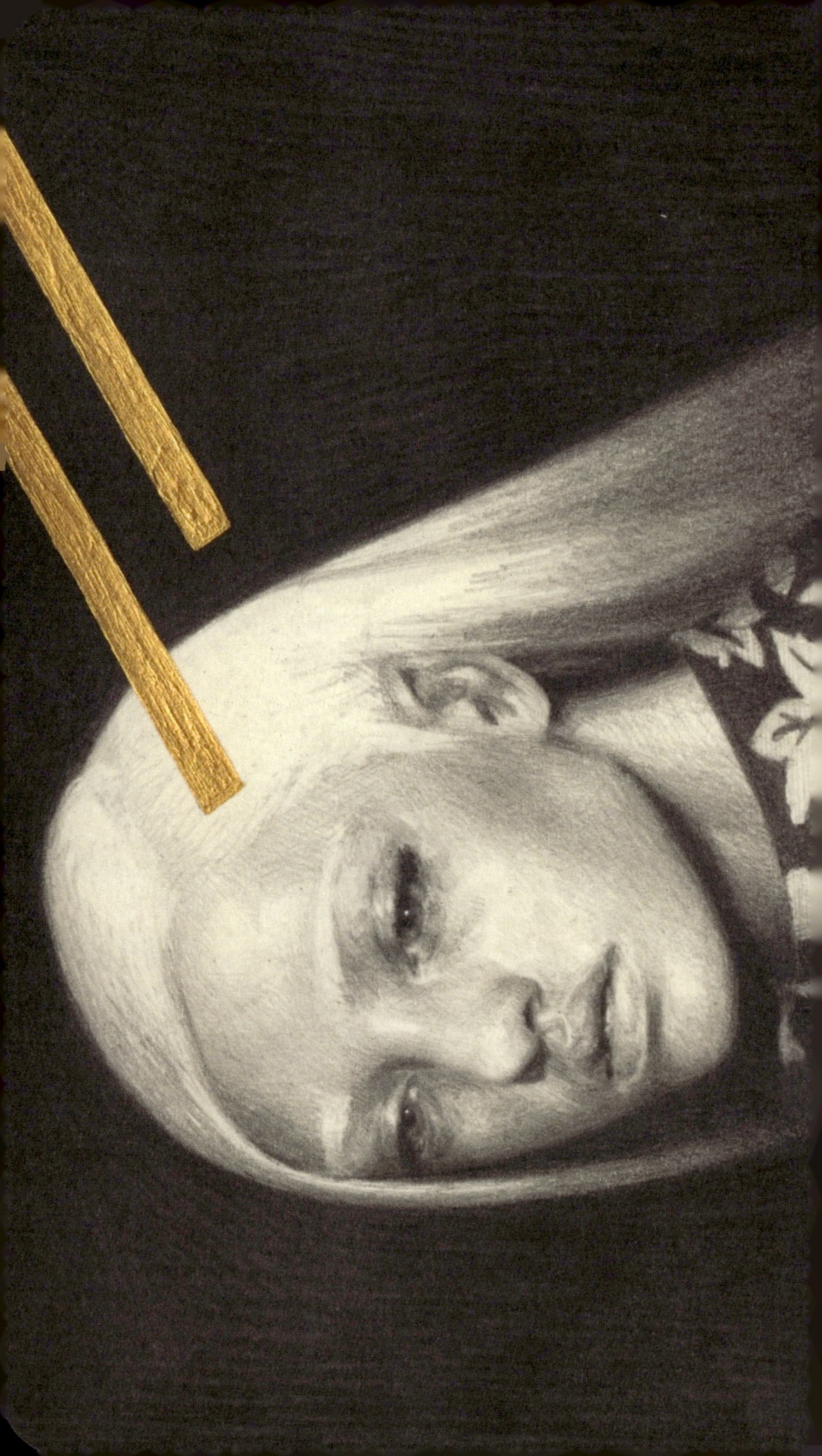

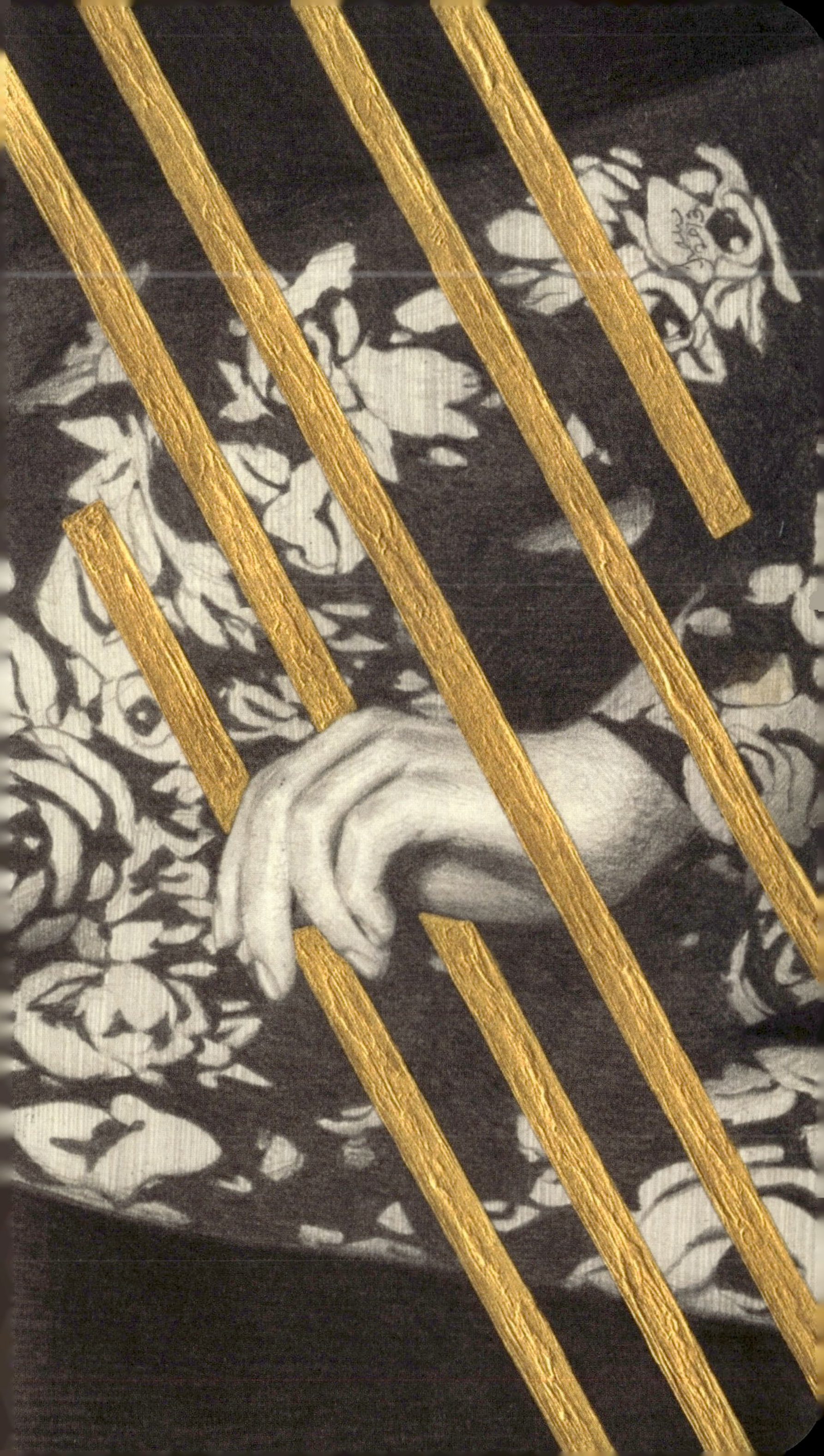

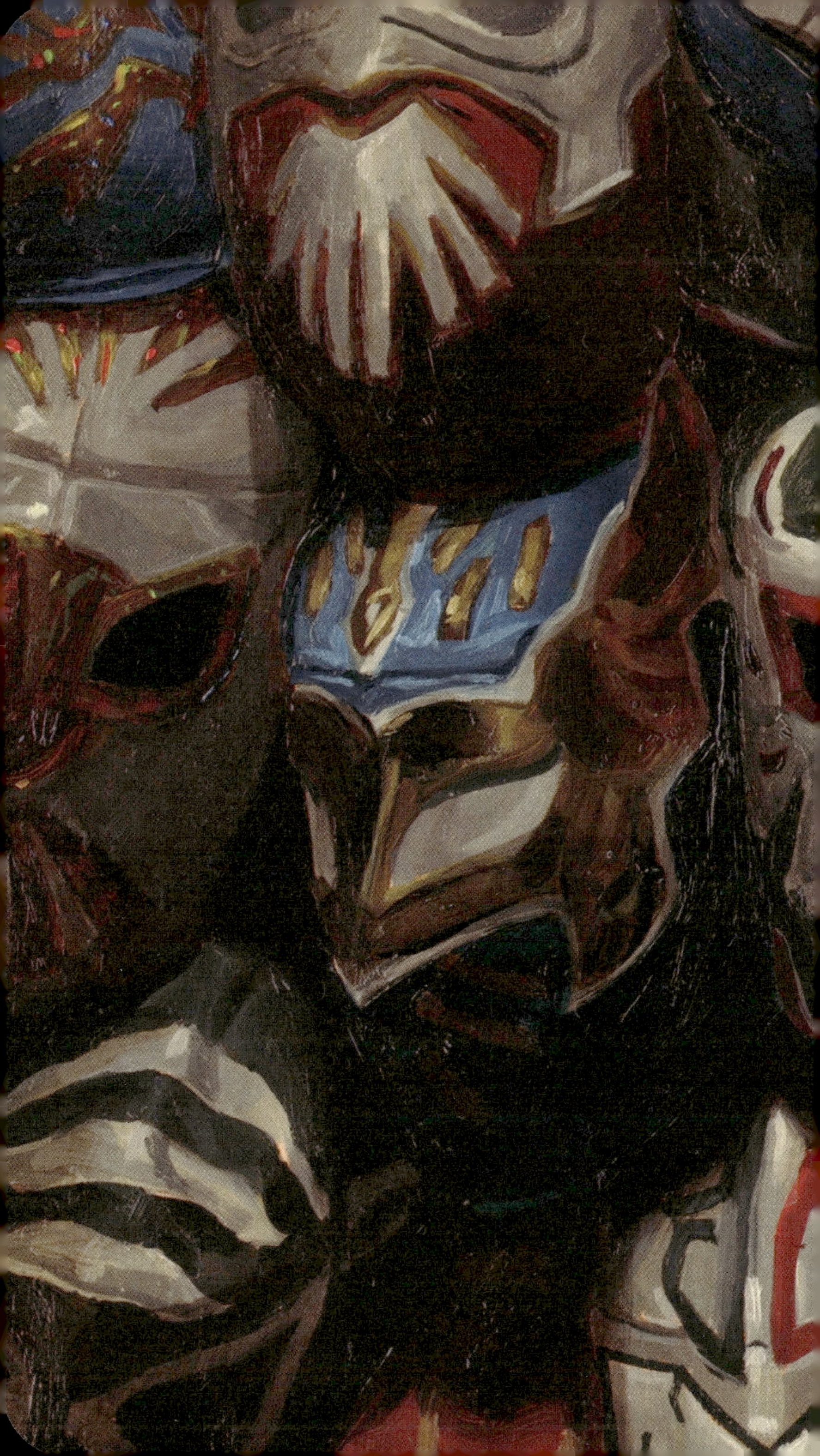

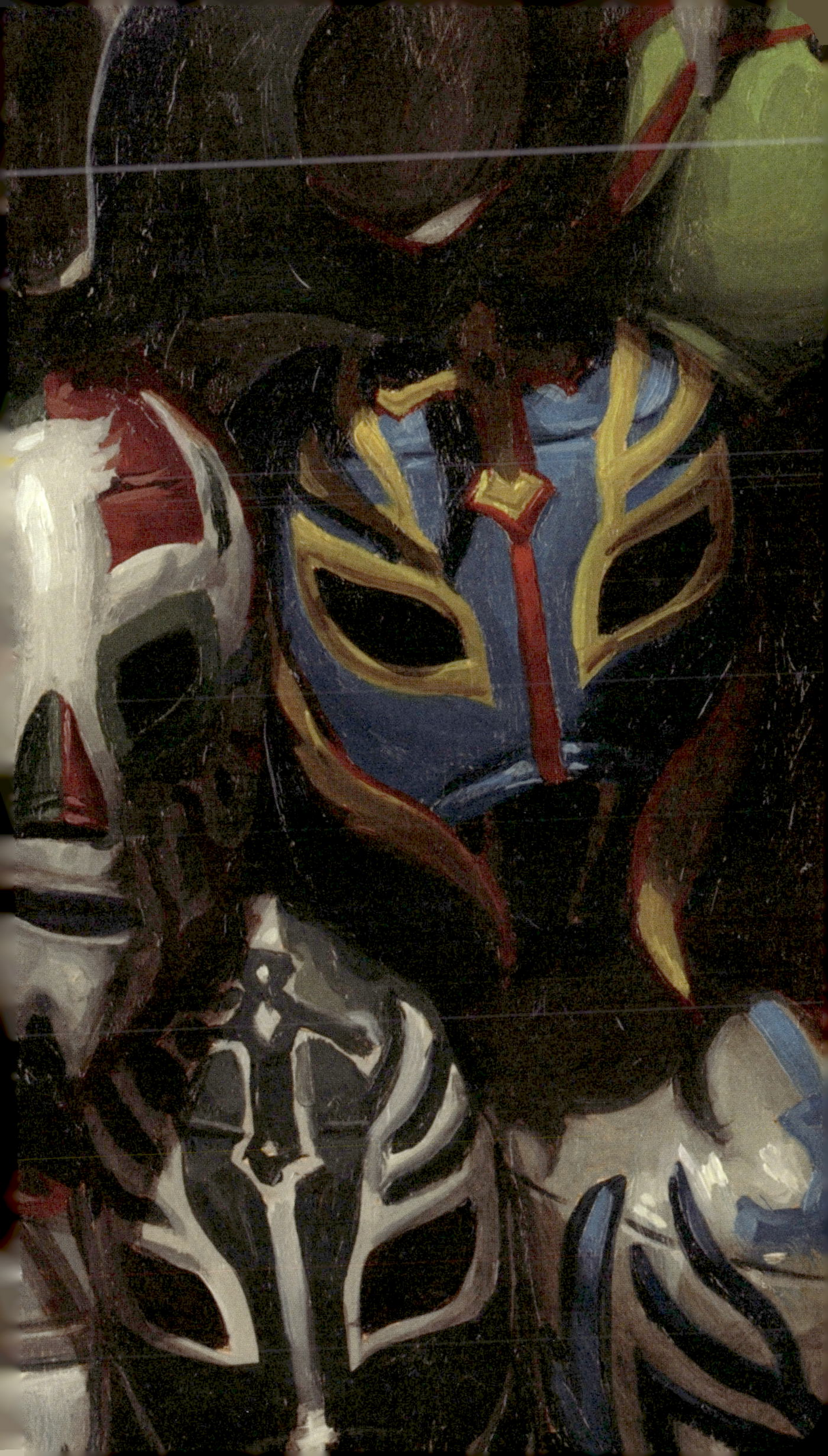

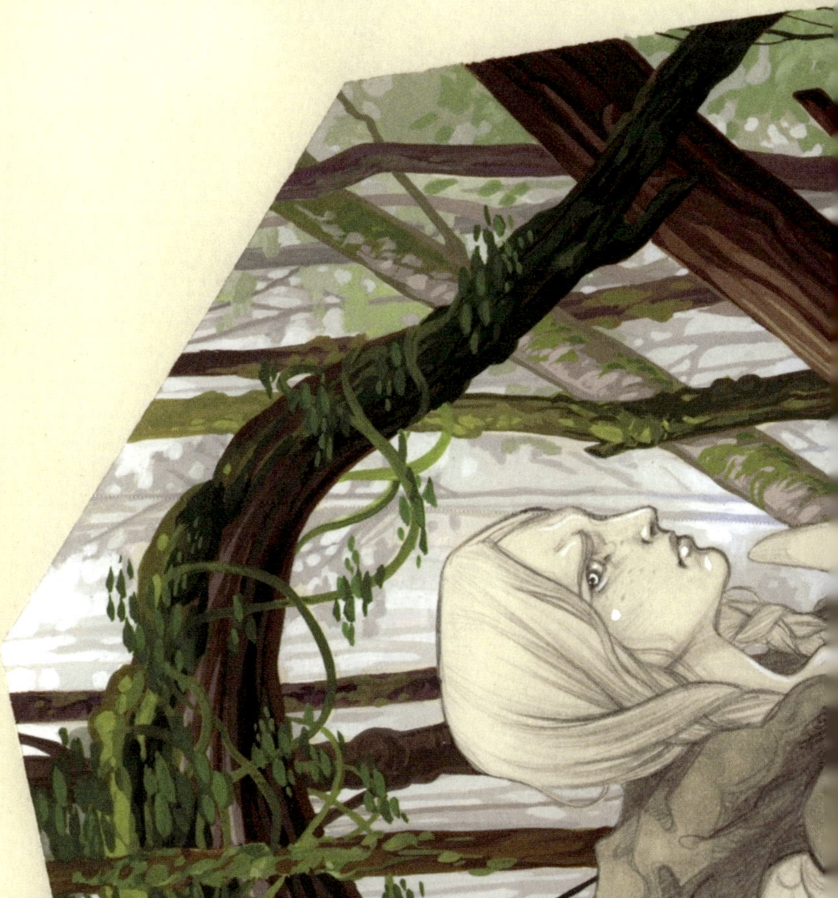

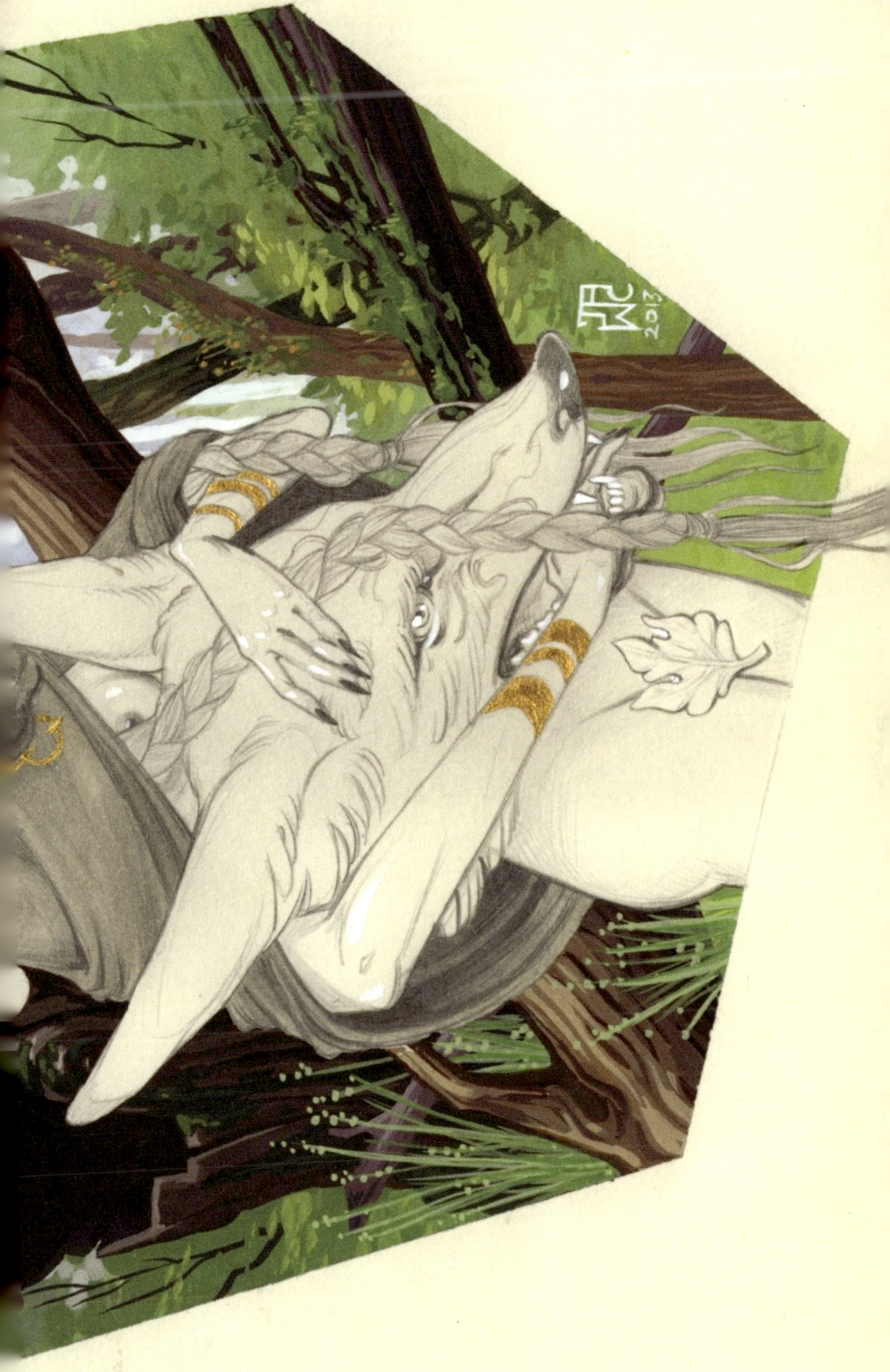

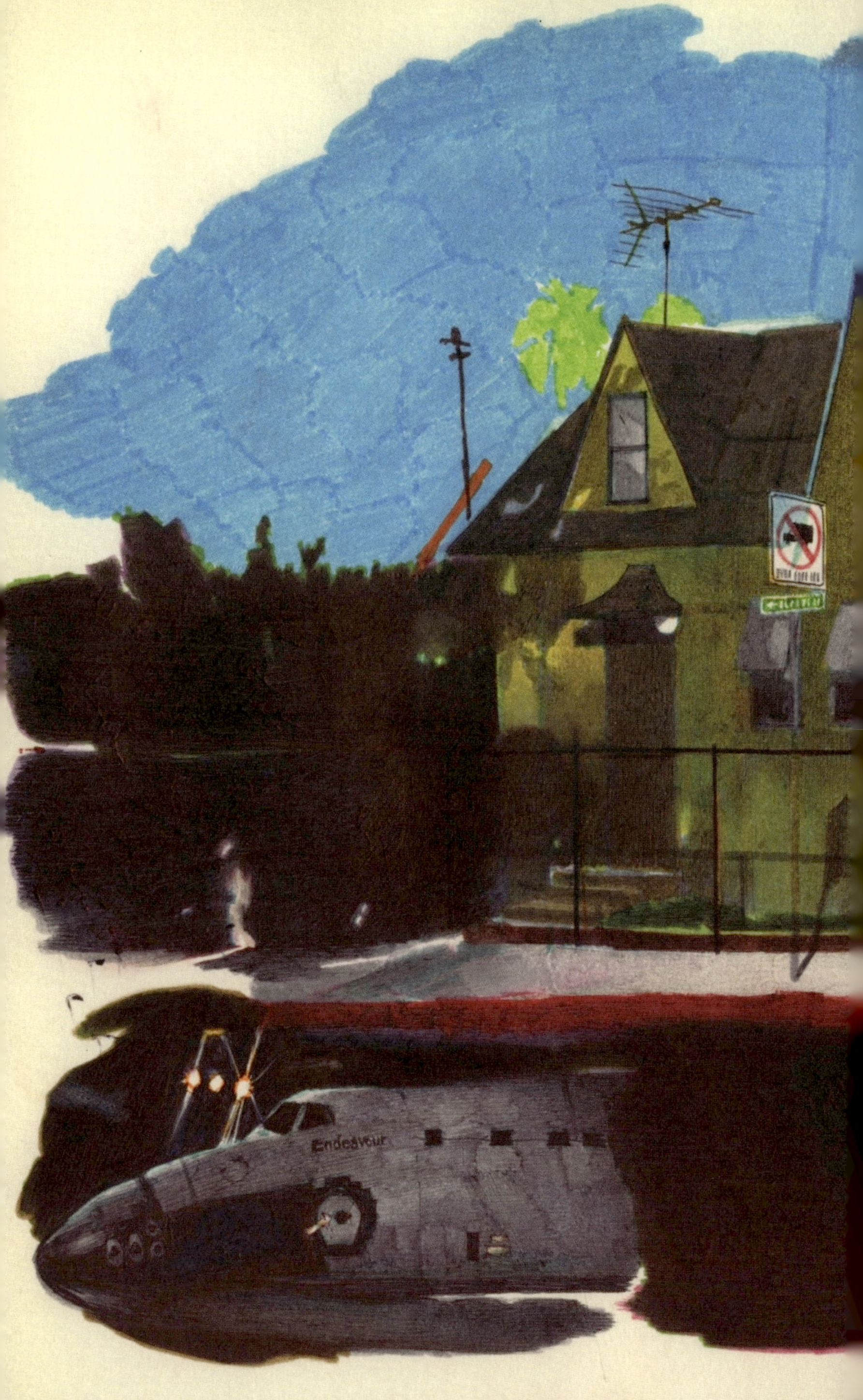

* 534 PM, THURSDAY, OCTOBER 10, 2013 I AM SO COMPELLED TO DRAW THIS HOUSE. IT'S ON HIGUERA / WESLEY IN CULVER CITY, CALIFORN
ARM – UDE / FAT – FUTOTTA / THIN – HOSOI / BODY – KARADA / SHOULDER – KATA / ANY QUESTIONS? – SHITSUMON GA ARIMASUKA / ANOT
KNOWN AS THE "JEWEL OF THE FLEET," WAS BUILT AS A REPLACEMENT FOR CHALLENGER, WHICH WAS DESTROYED SHORTLY AFTER LAUNCH IN JANUARY 1986.

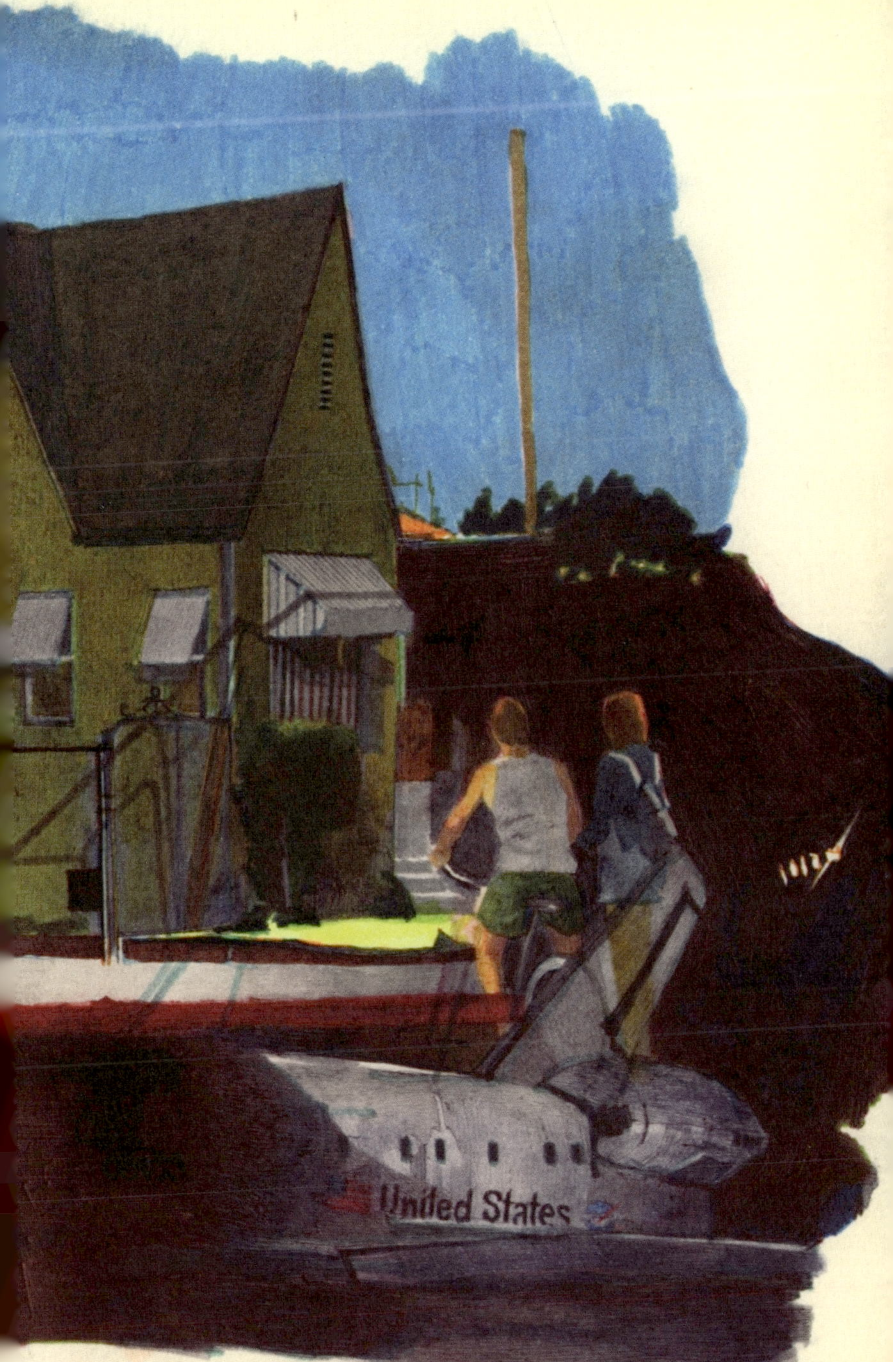

THIS DAY I BUMPED INTO MARY ON HER DRIVE BACK HOME. LEARNED SOME JAPANESE. ADULT - OTONA / SHADE - KEIJO / SHORT - MIJIKAI /
M FASCINATED WITH IS THE SPACE SHUTTLE ENDEAVOR @ THE CALIFORNIA SCIENCE CENTER LAUNCHED IN MAY 7, 1992, THE NEWEST OF THE ORBITERS AND
A TOTAL OF 25 MISSIONS. MONDAY, OCTOBER 14, 2013 4:36 PM SHORTLY AFTER DAN CALLS AND I CATCH THE EXPO LINE BACK HOME, RUNNING TO GET TO SEE HER.

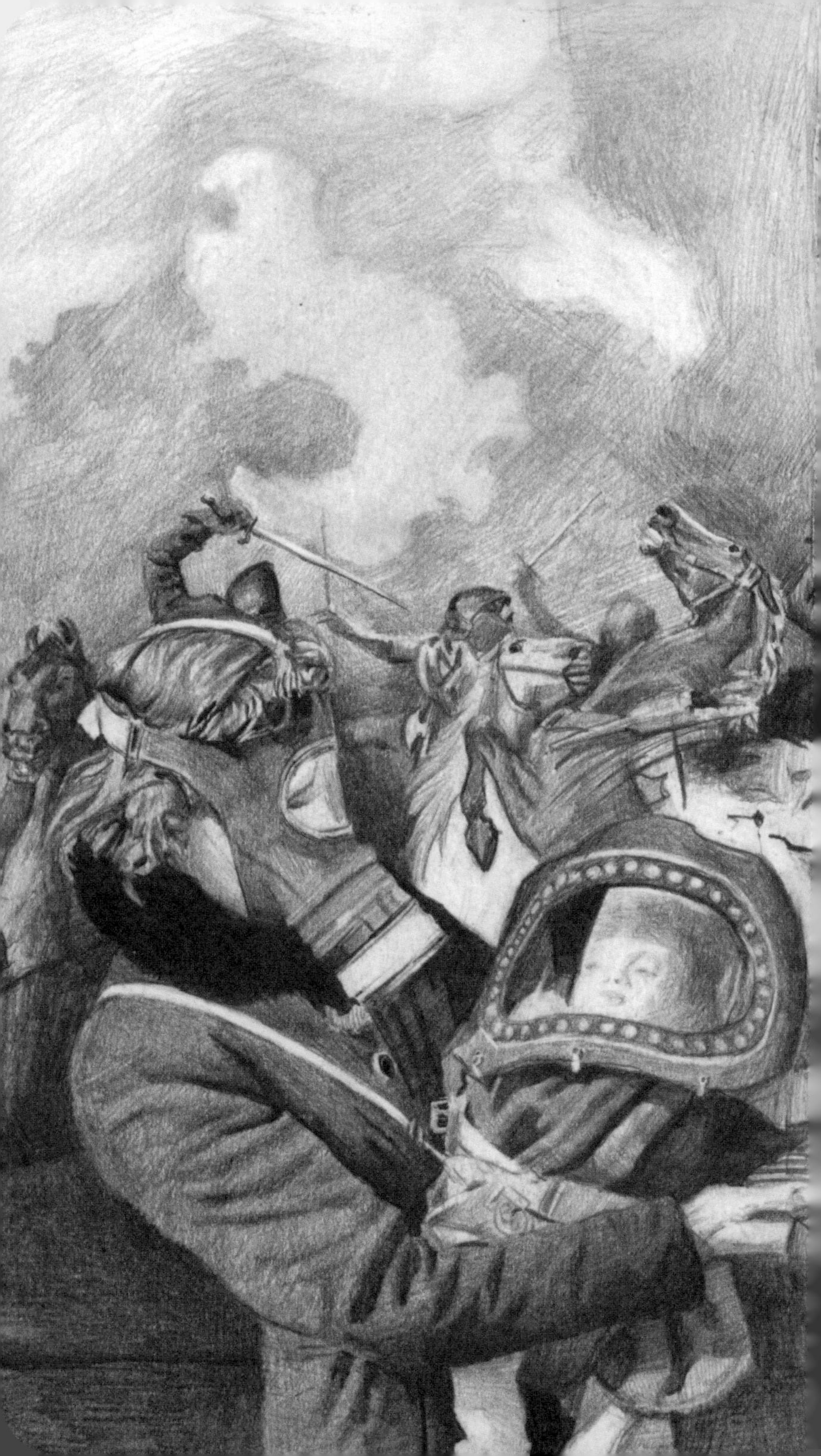

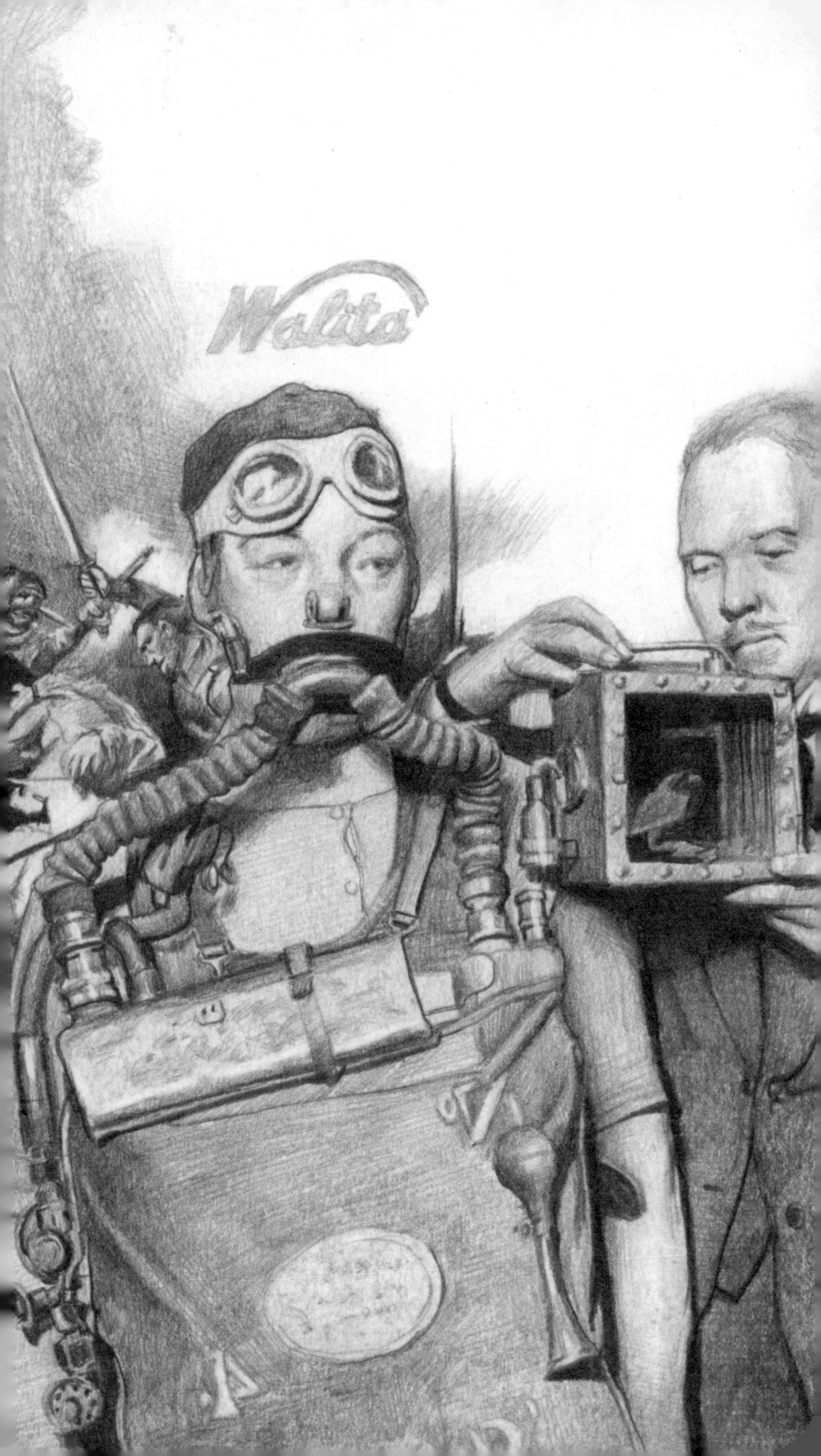
Walita

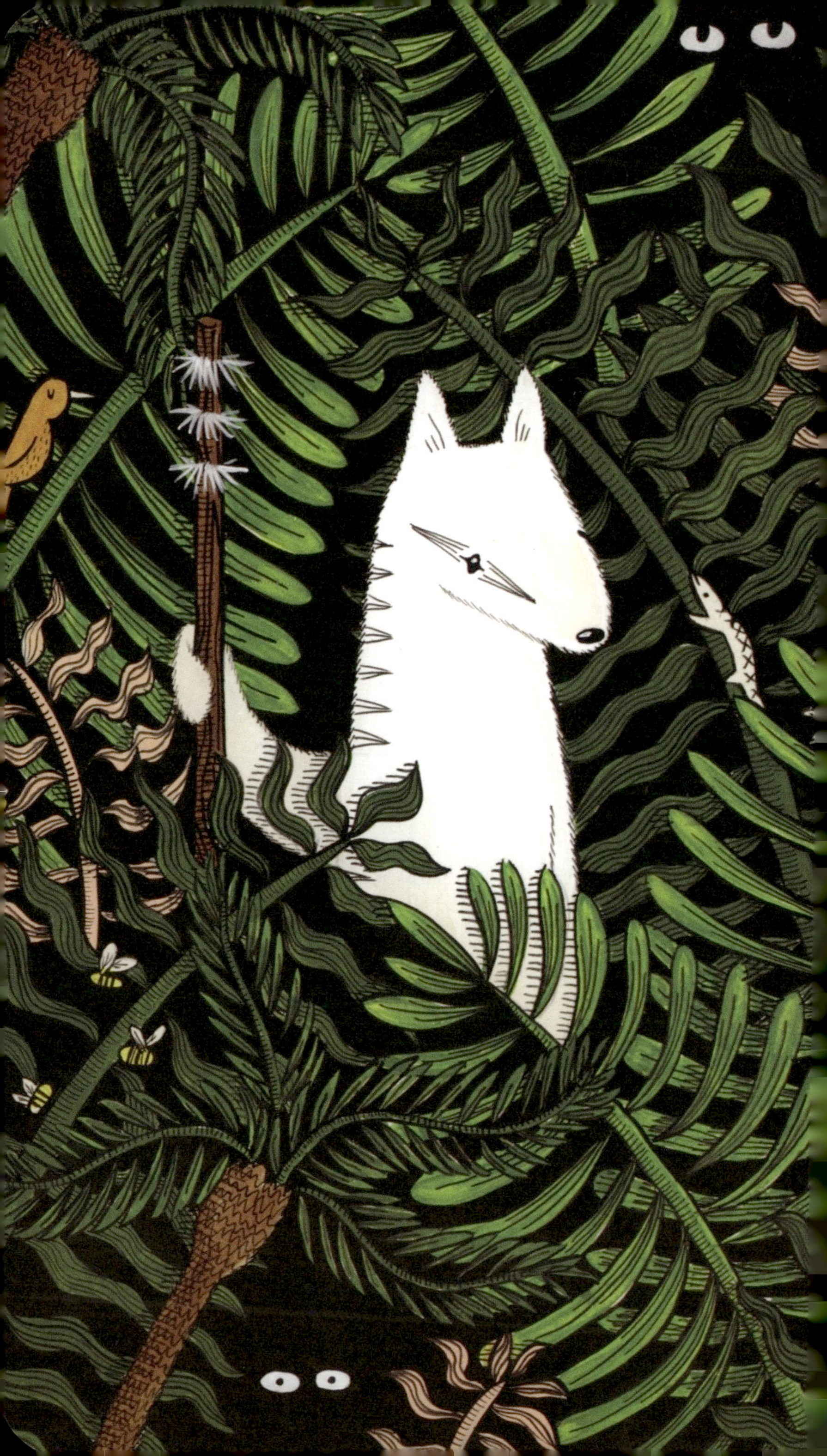

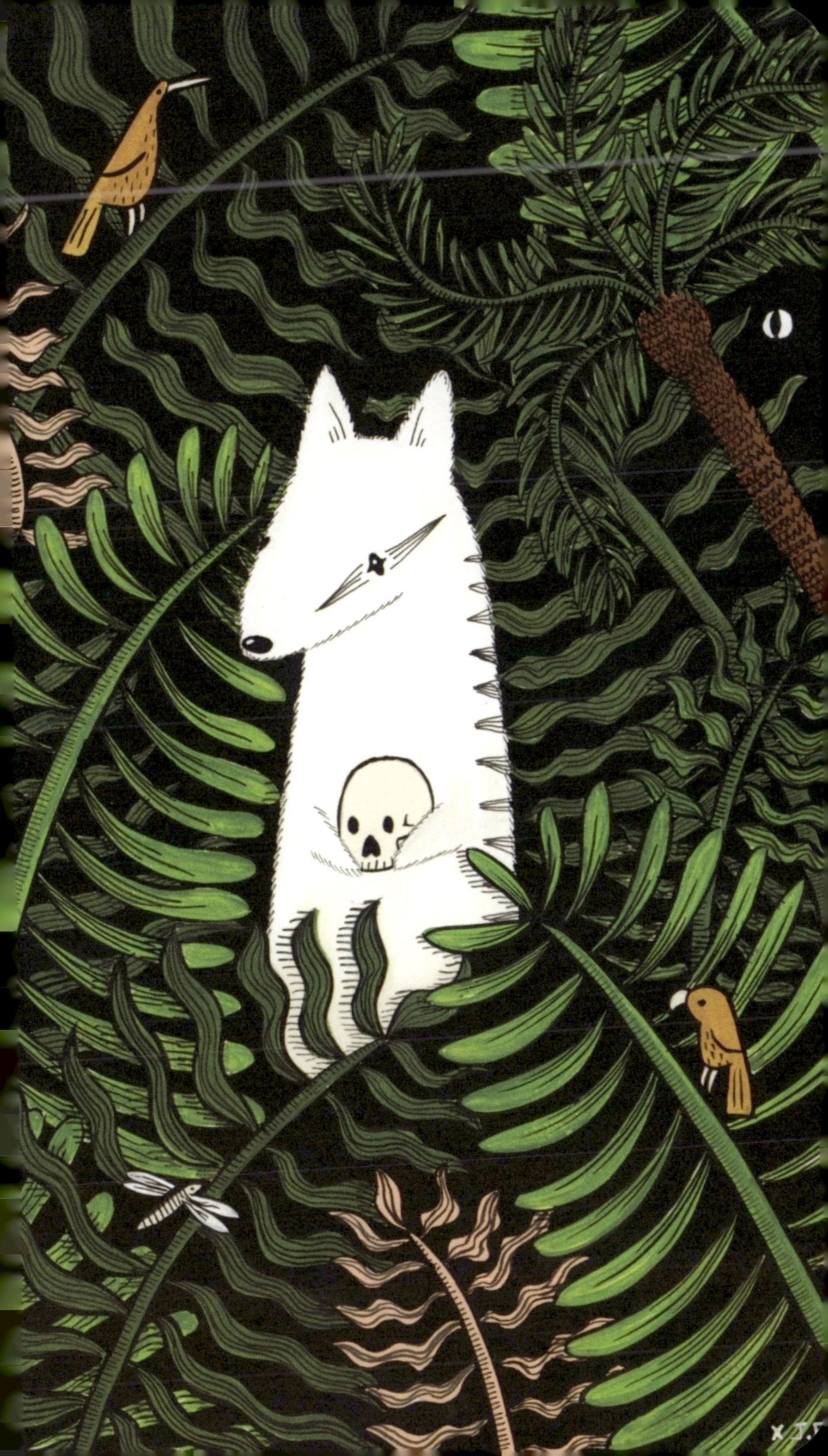

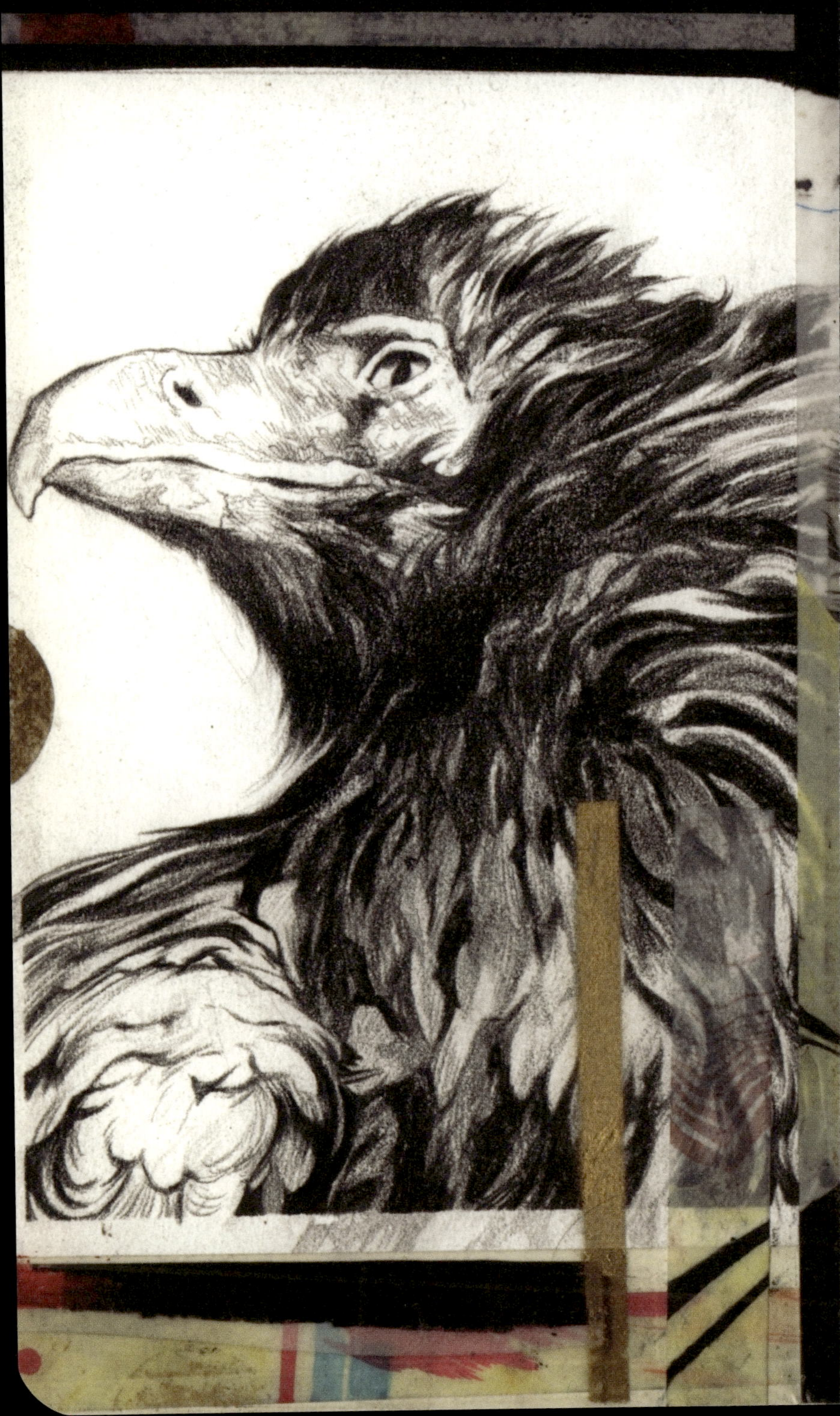

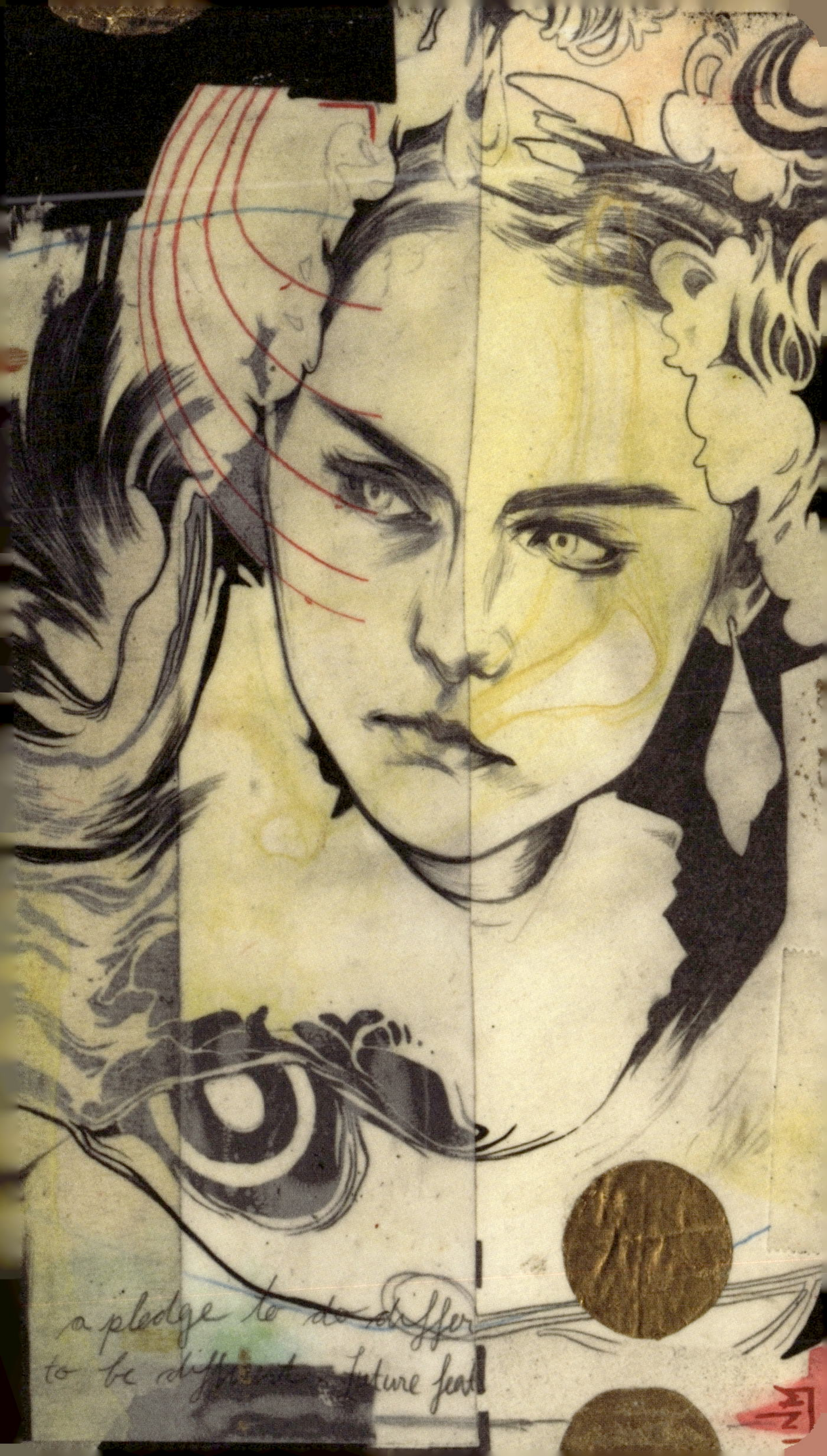
a pledge to do differ
to be
future fea

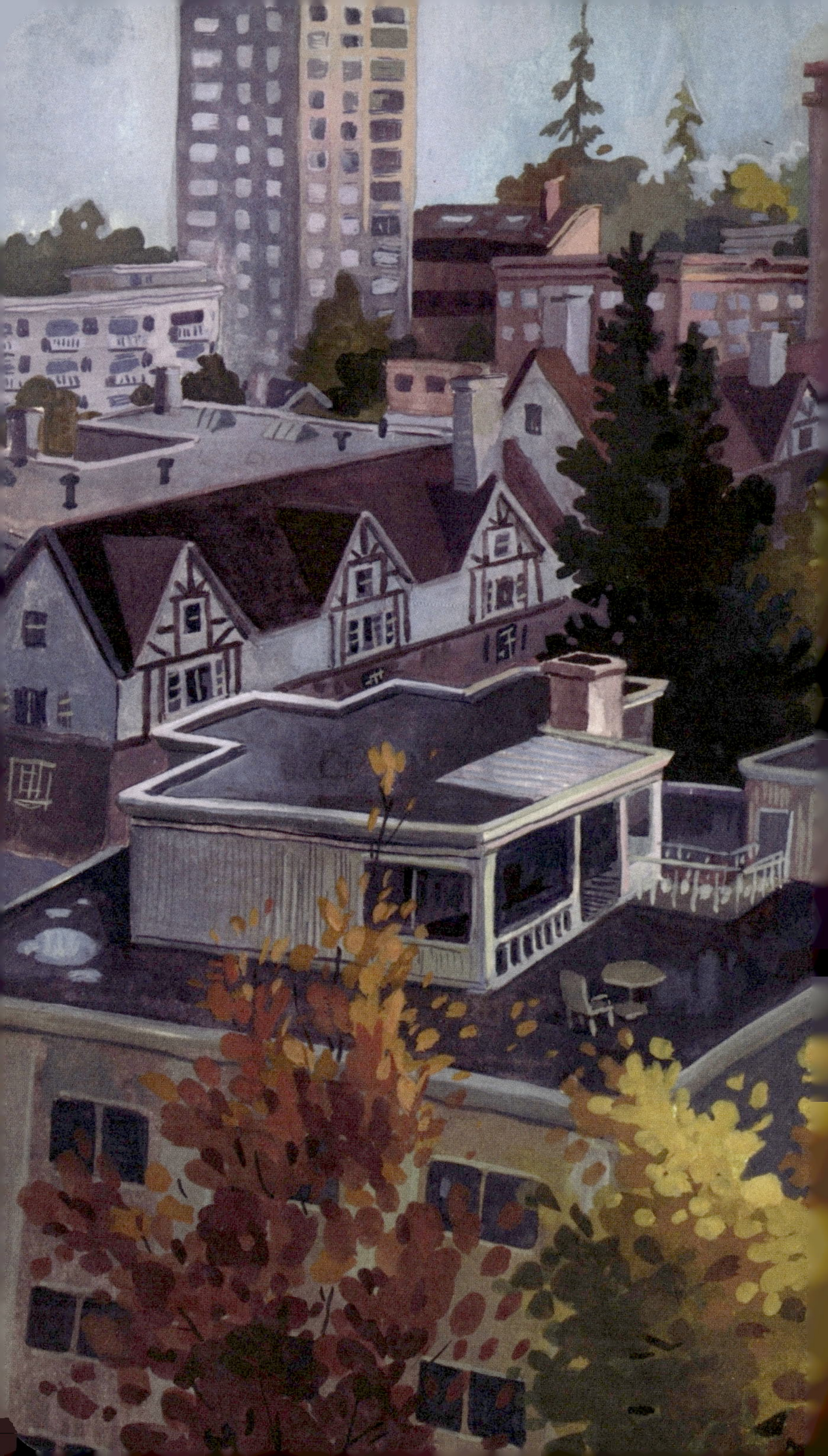

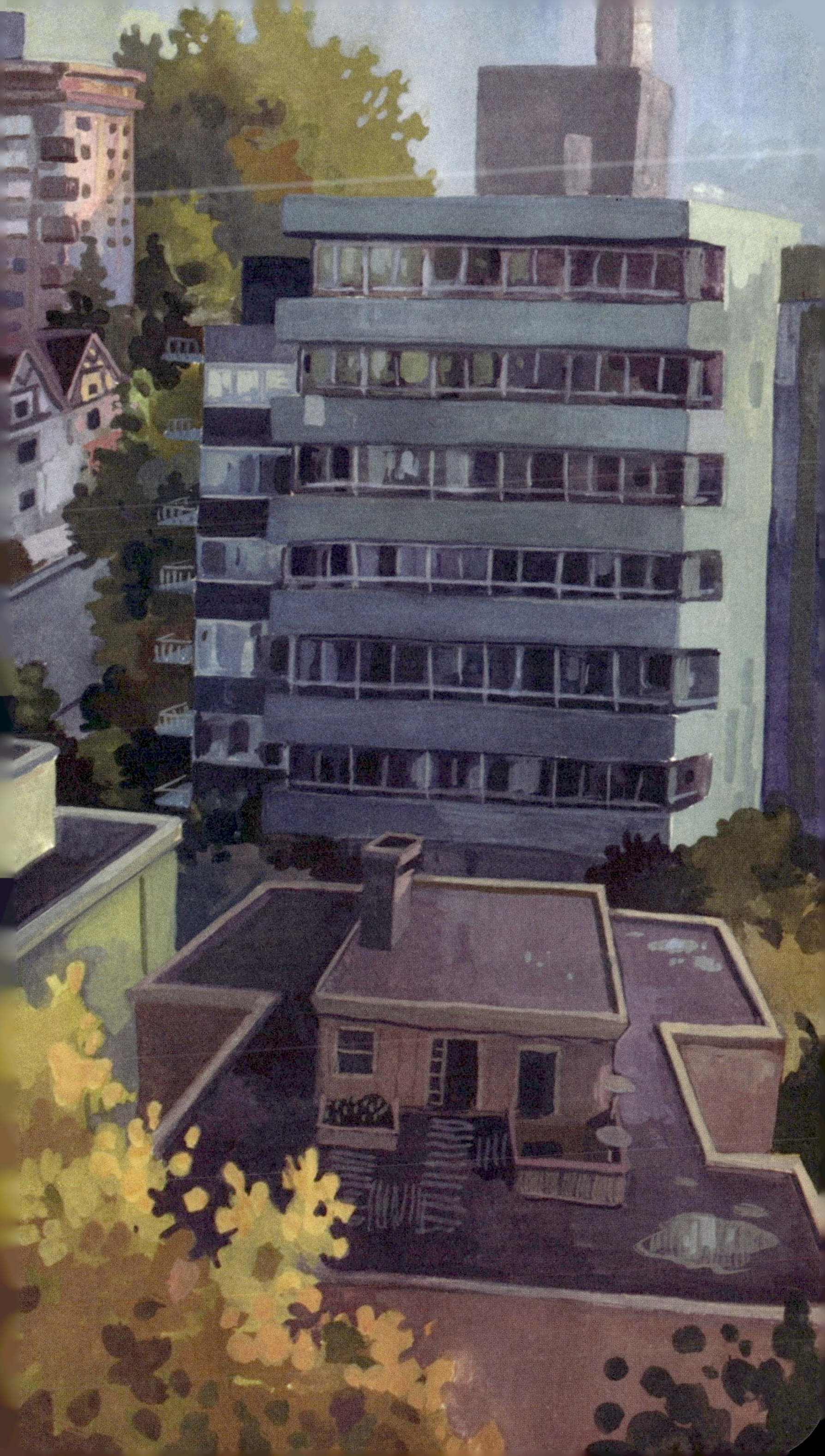

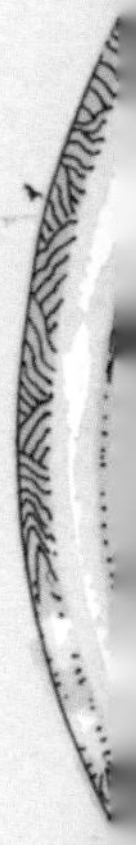

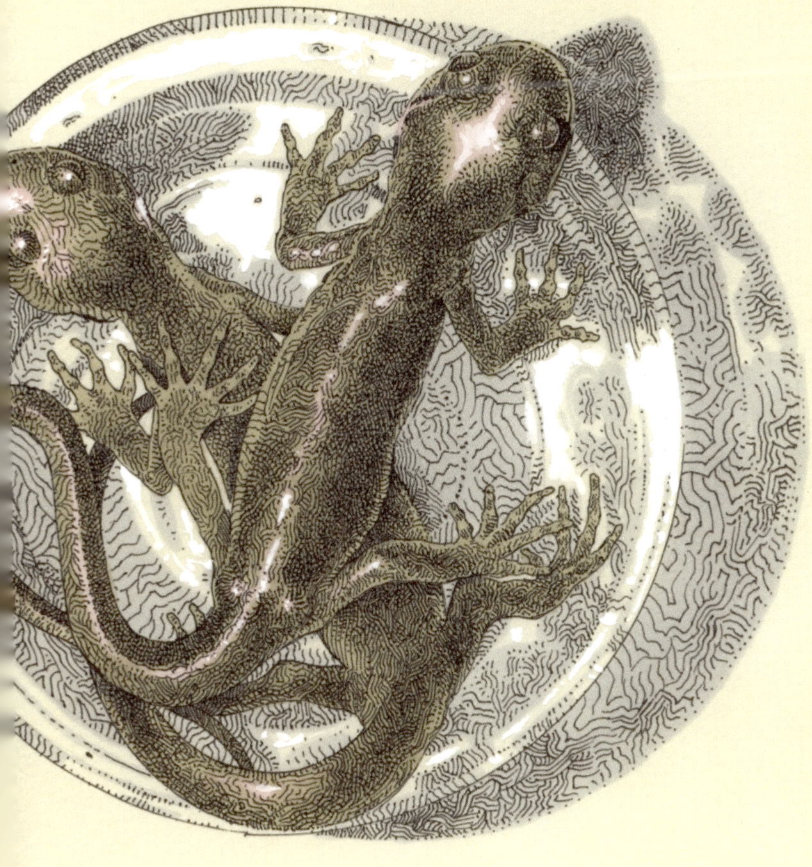

CORO
2015

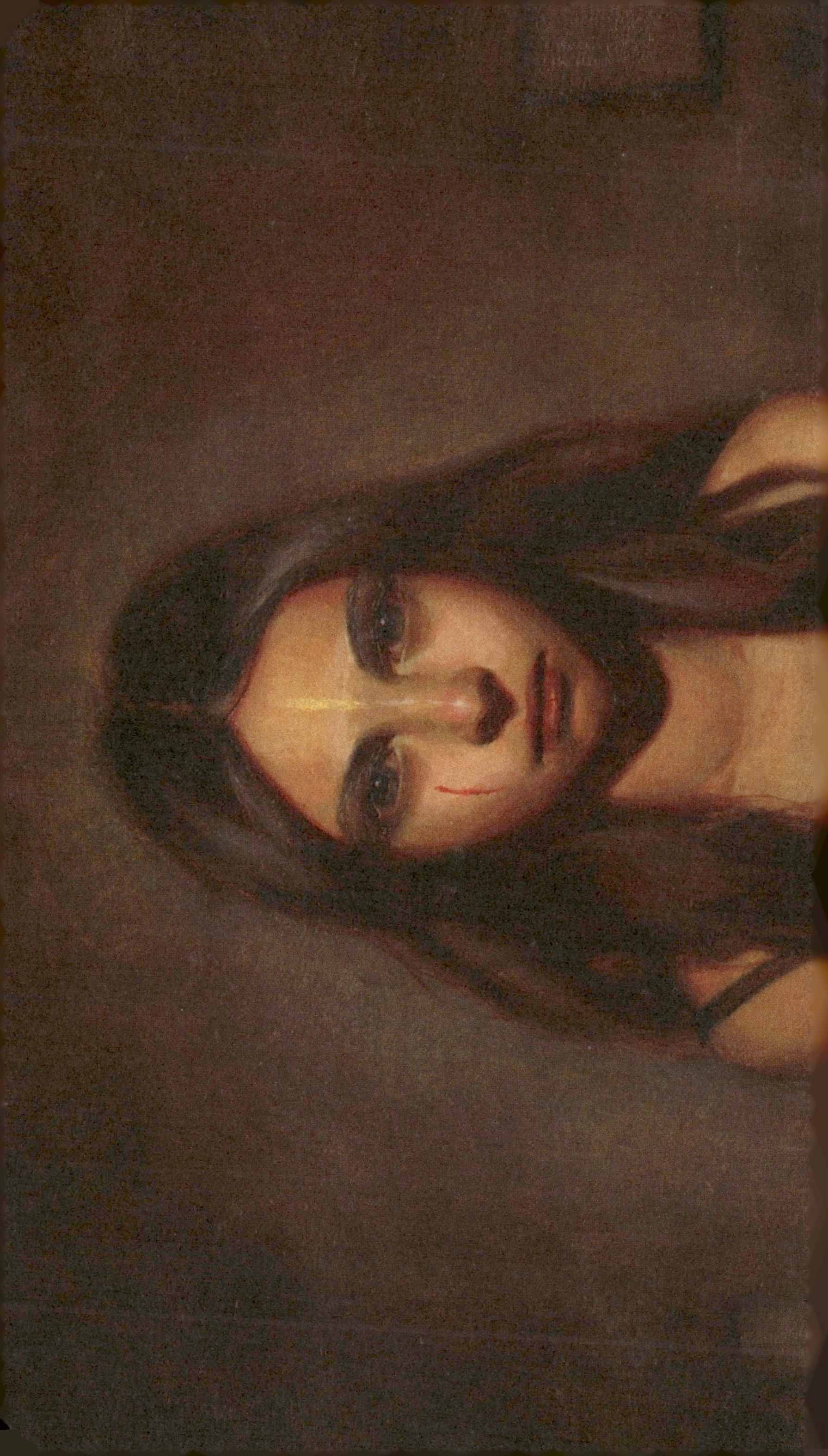

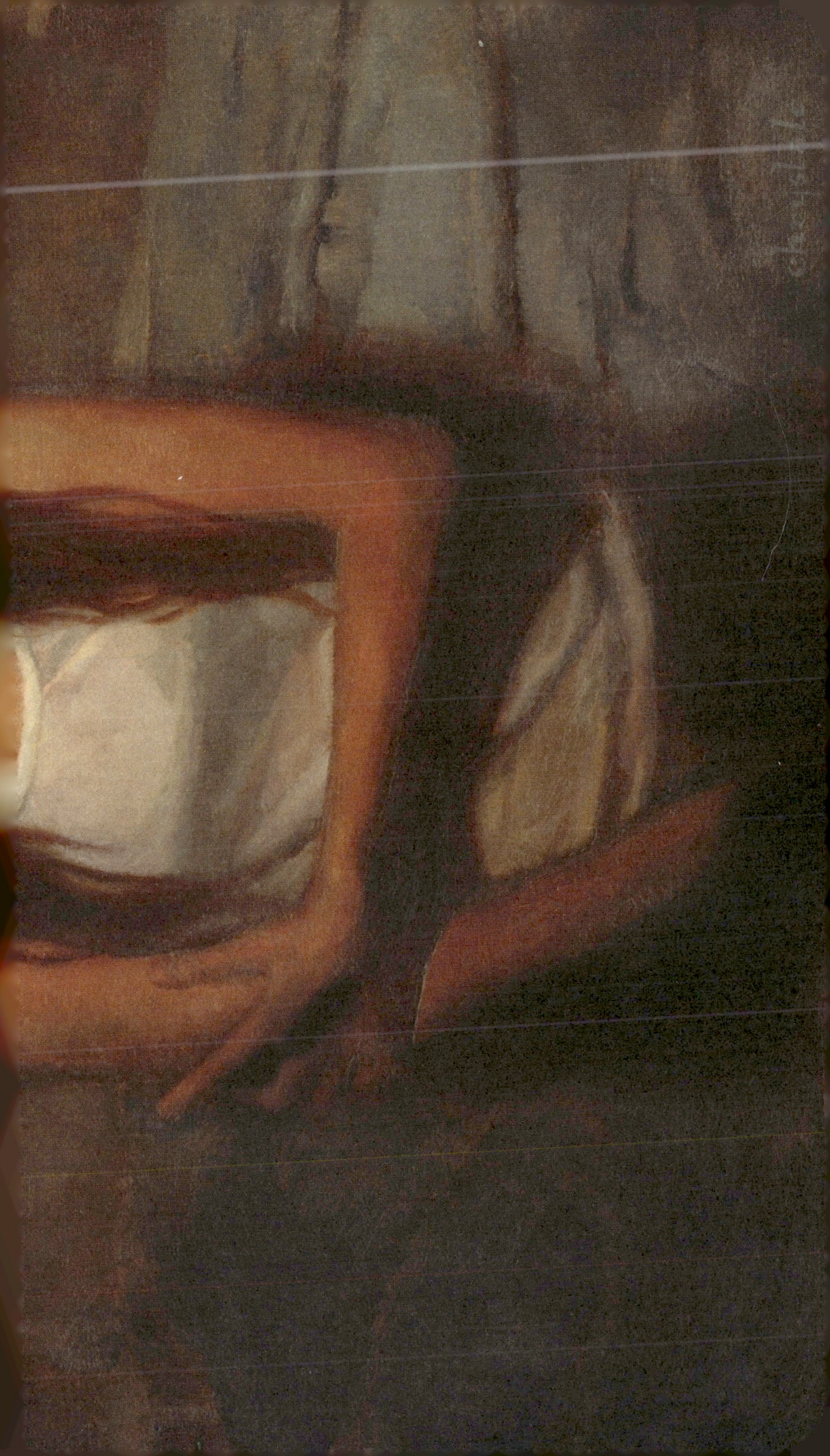

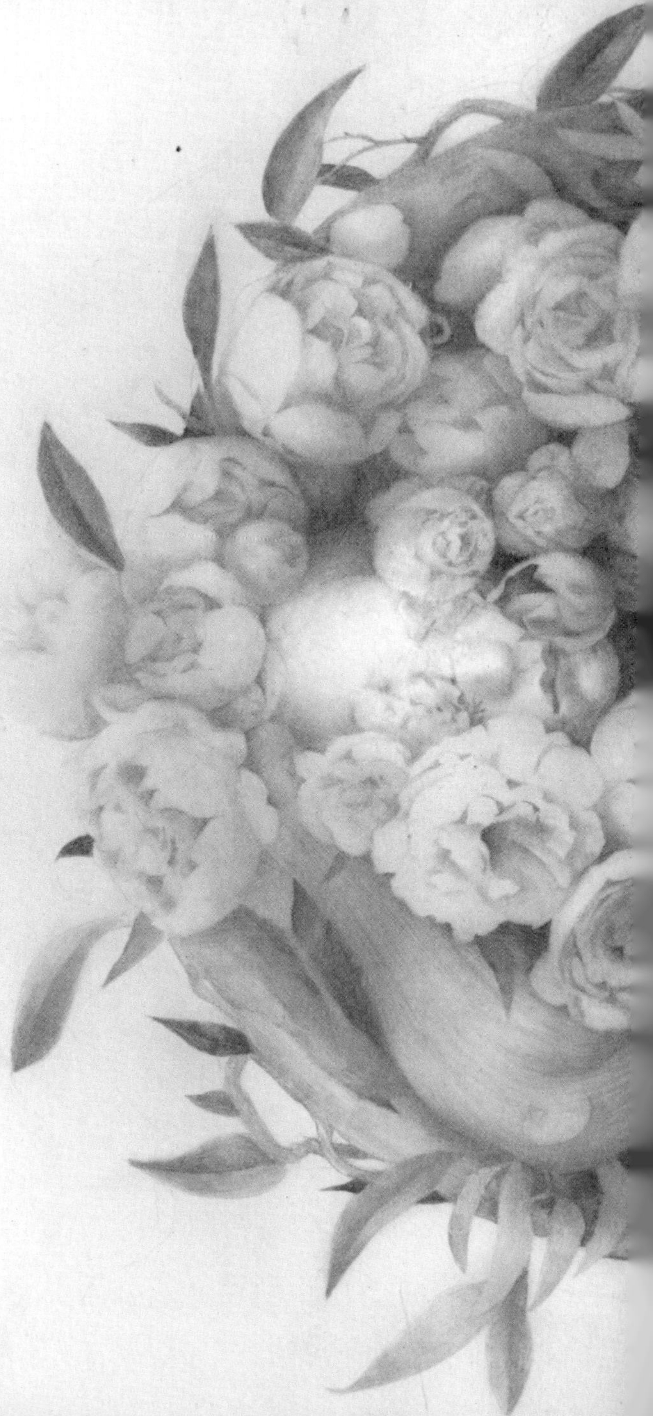

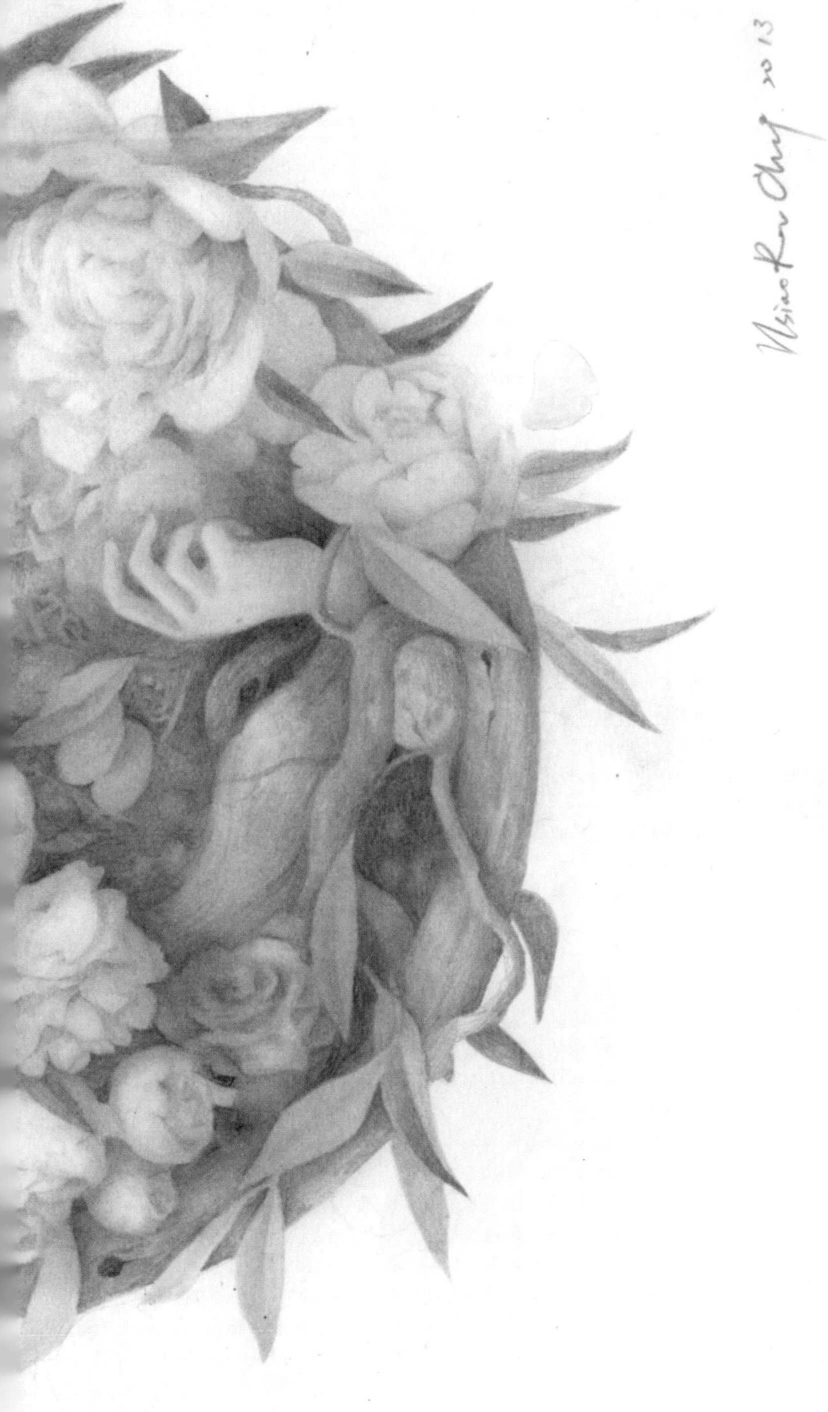

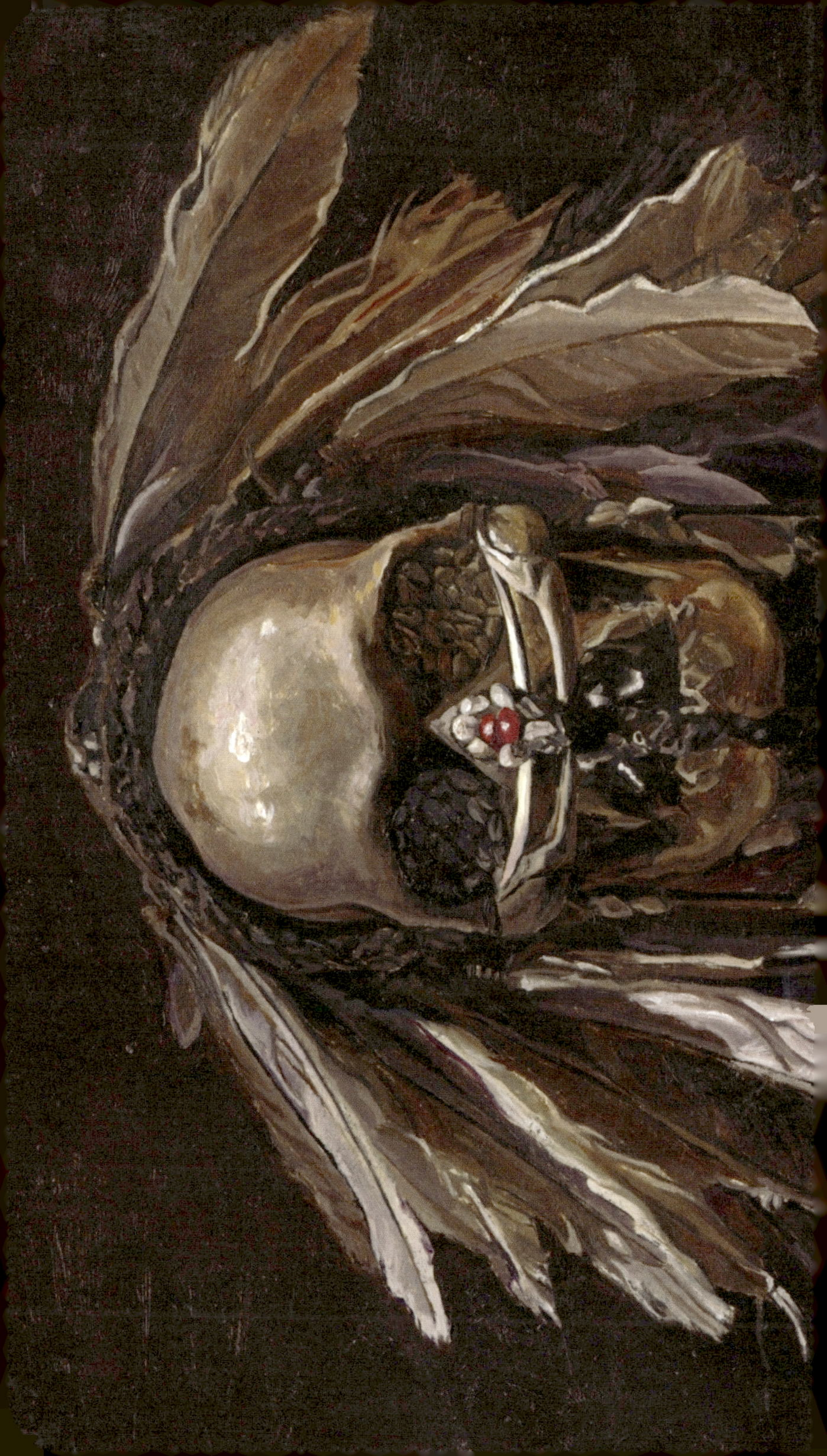

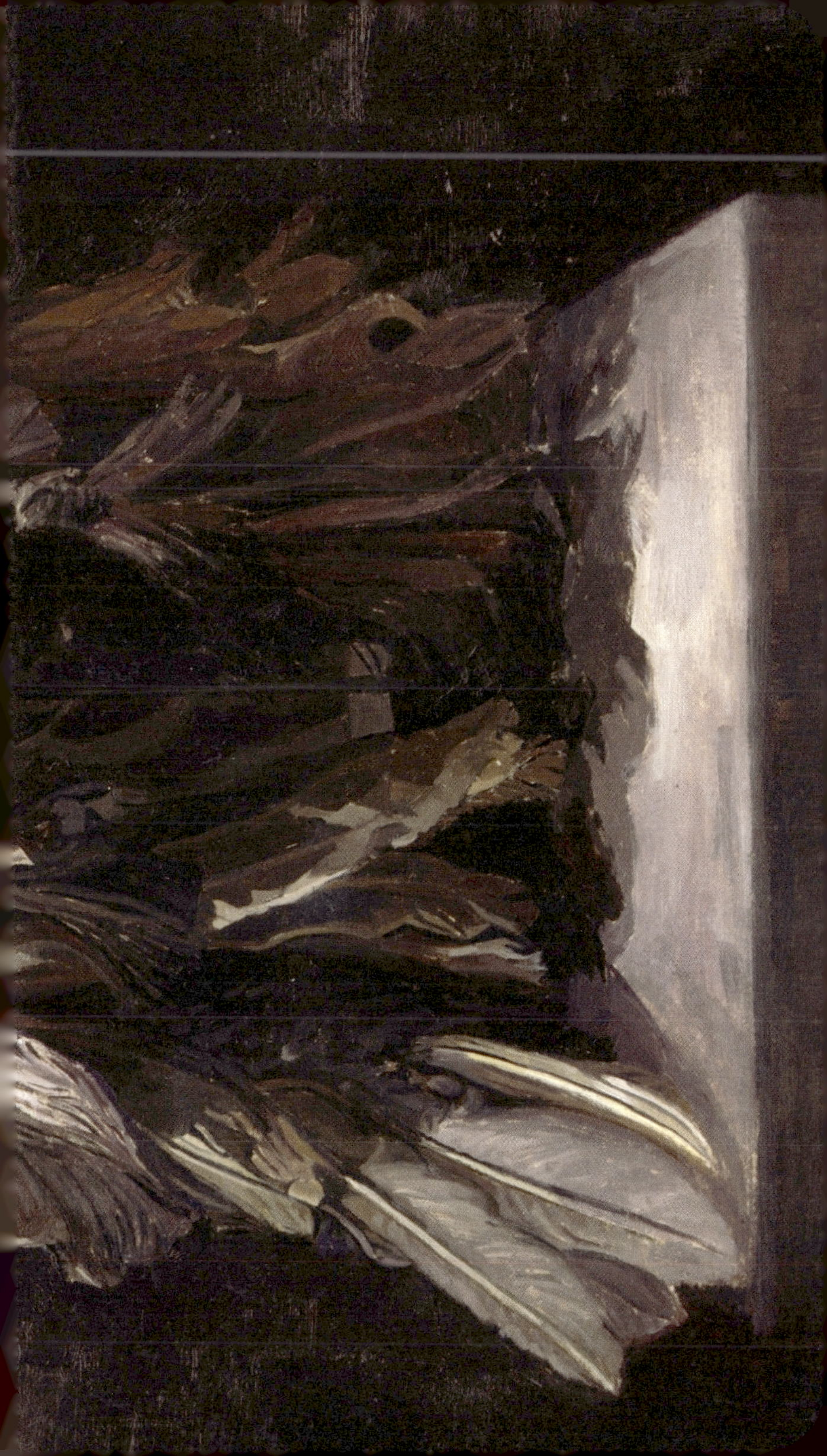

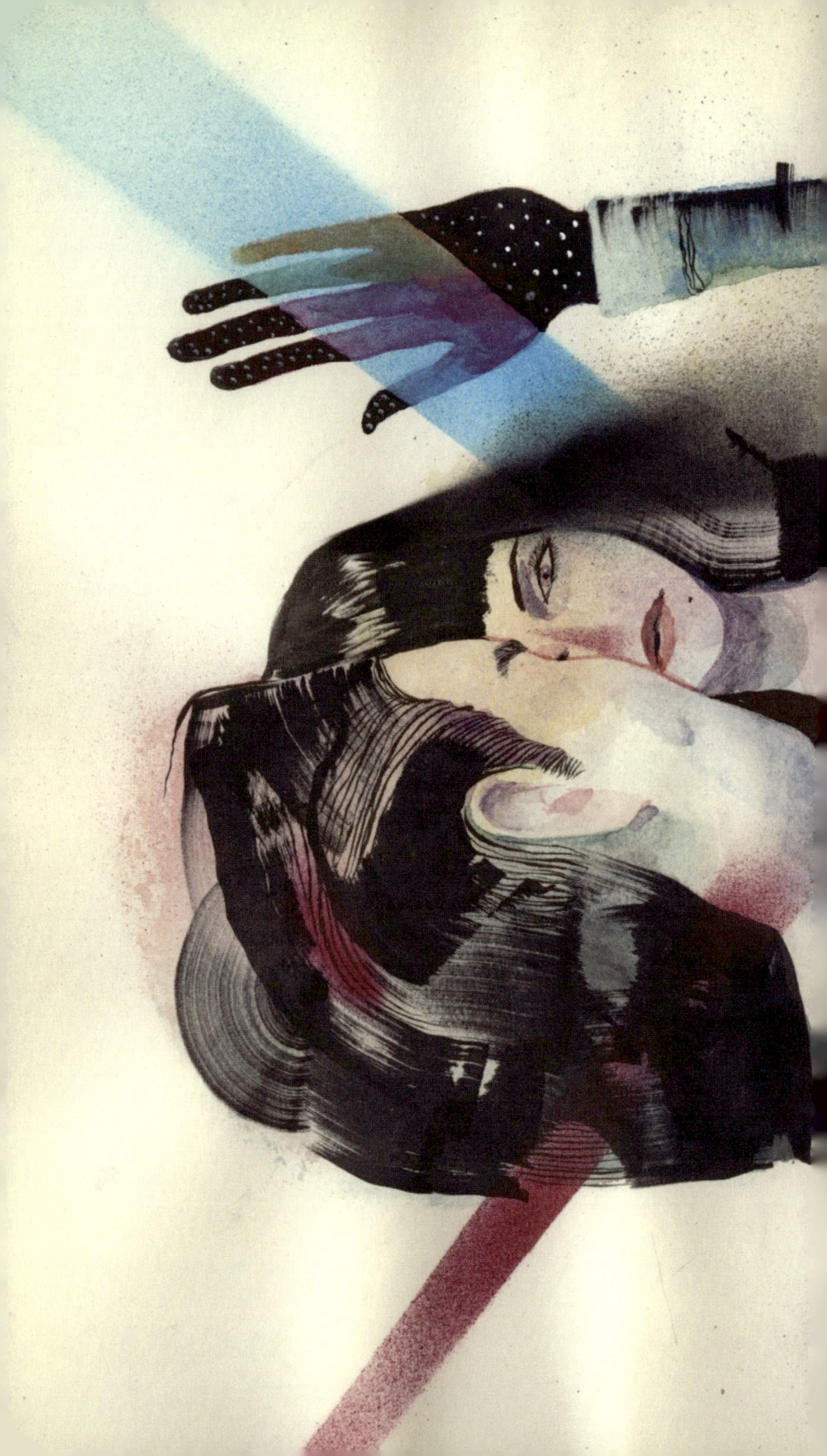

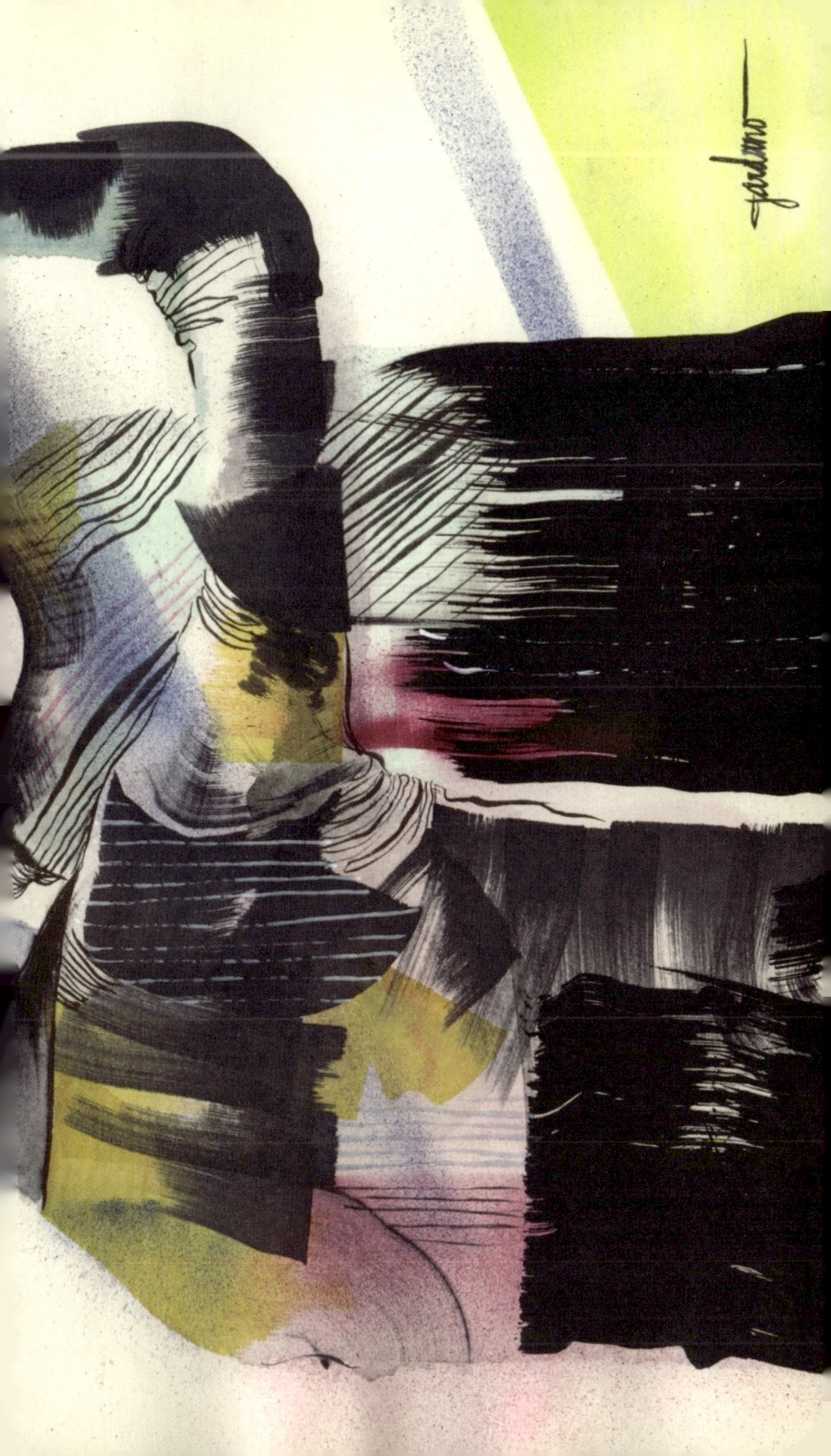

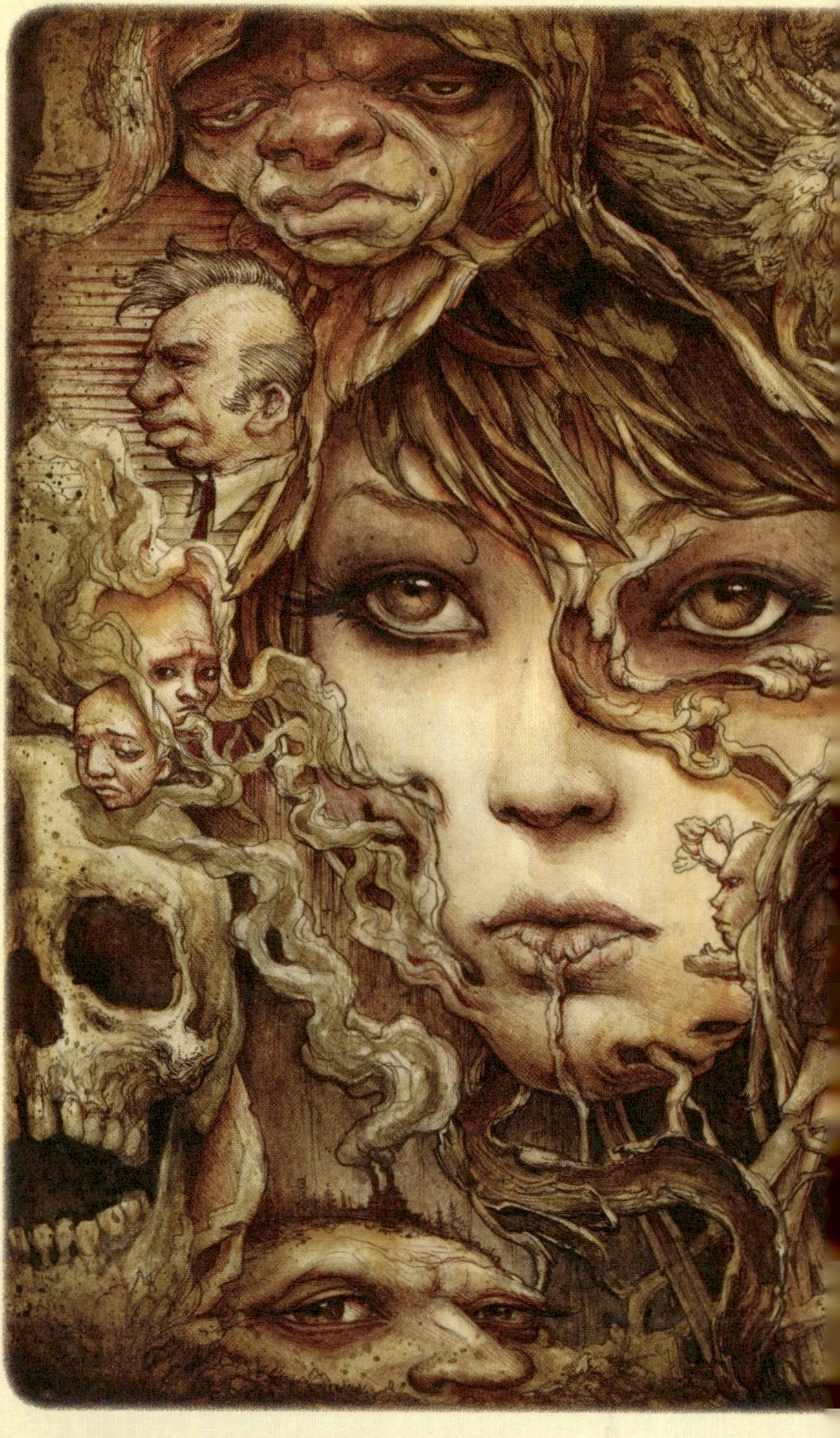

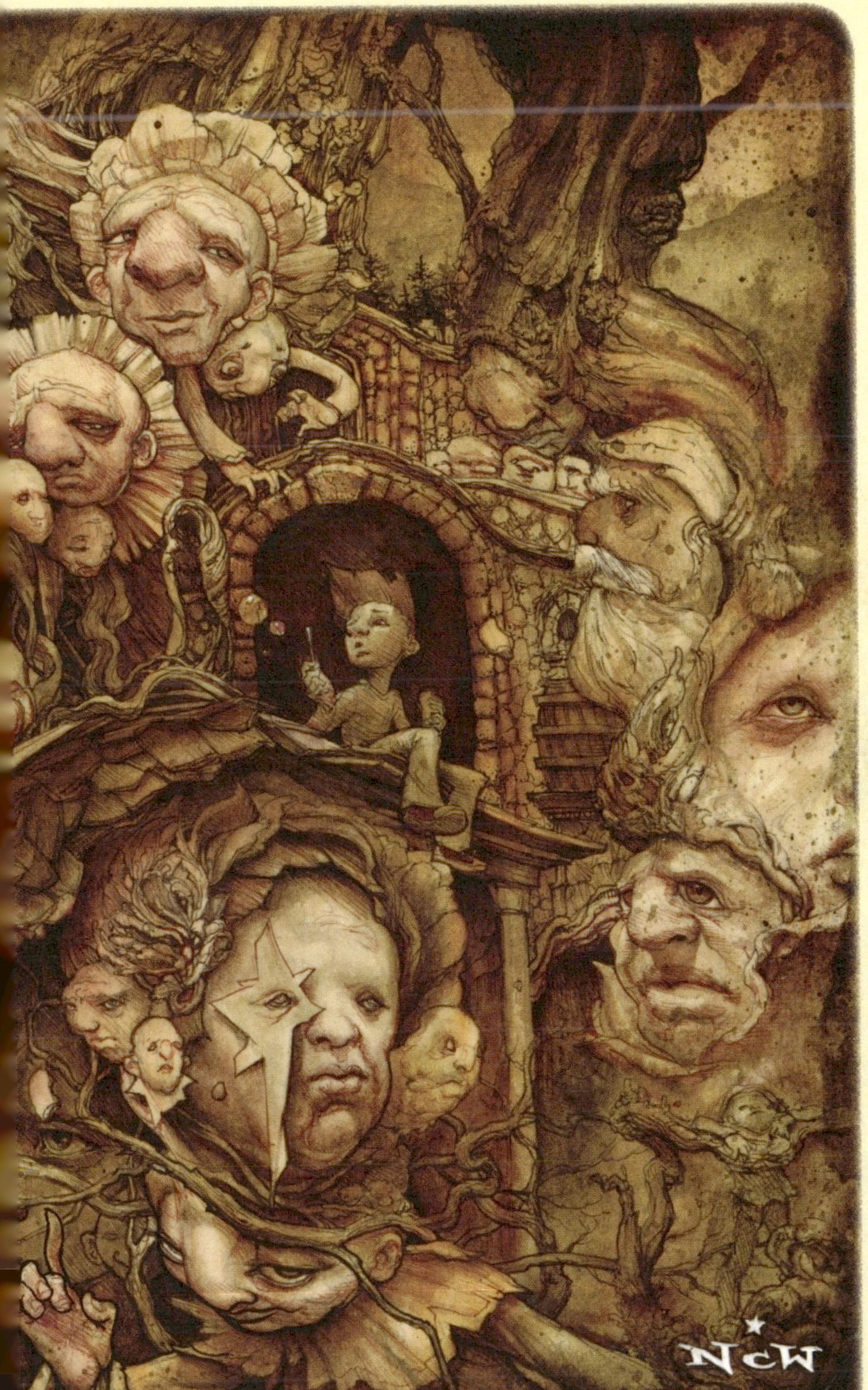
NcW

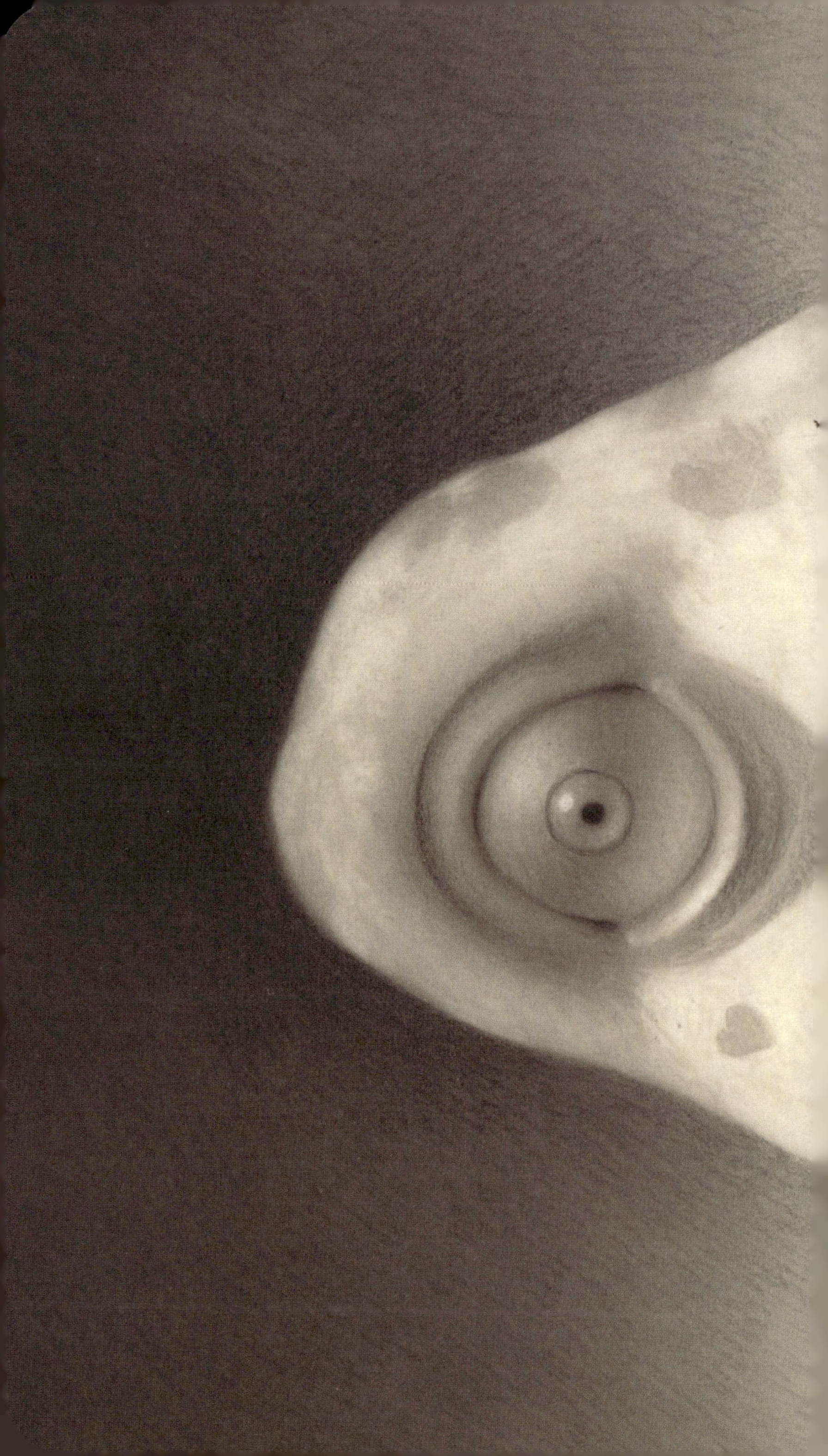

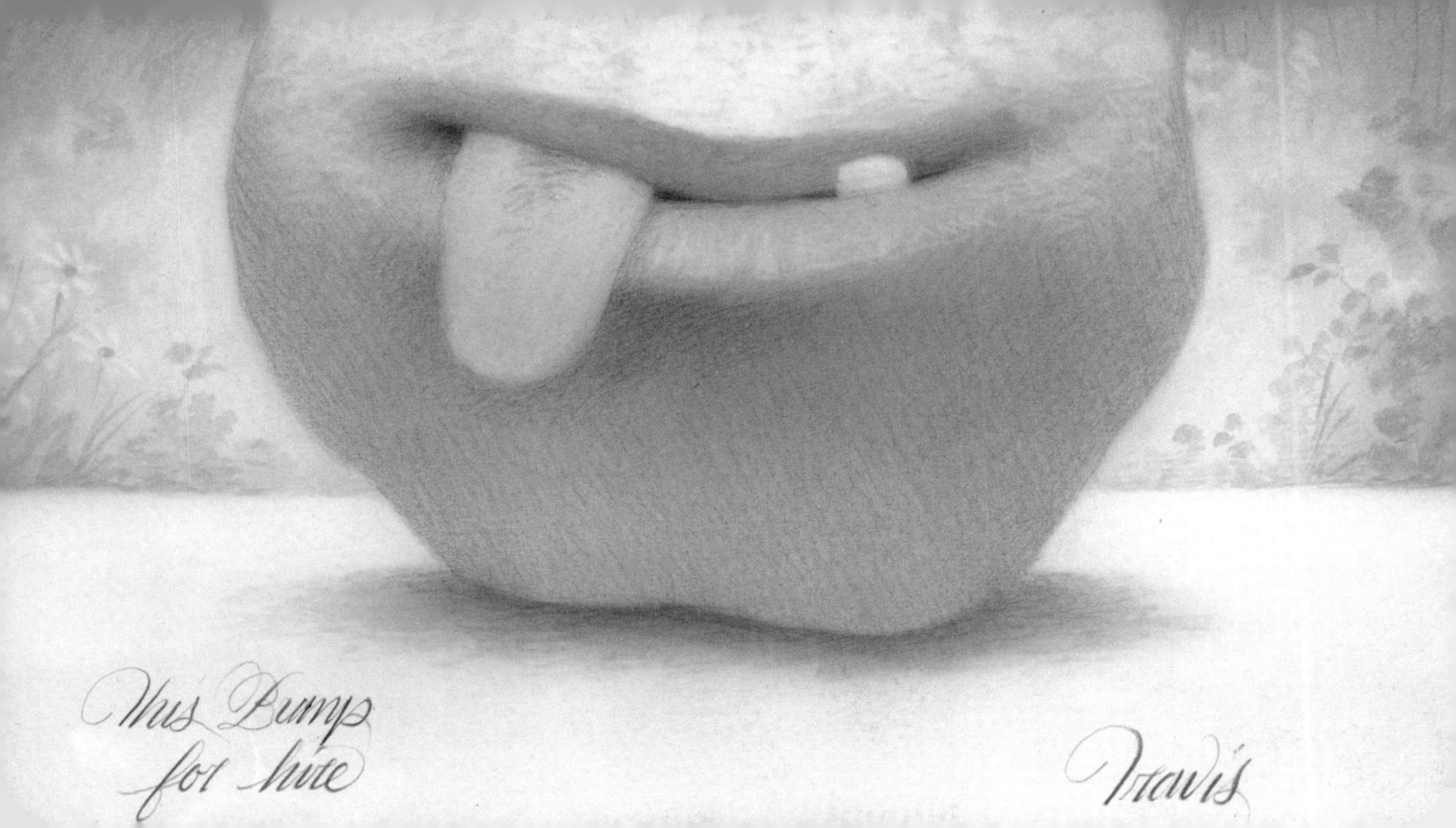
This Bump for hire
Travis

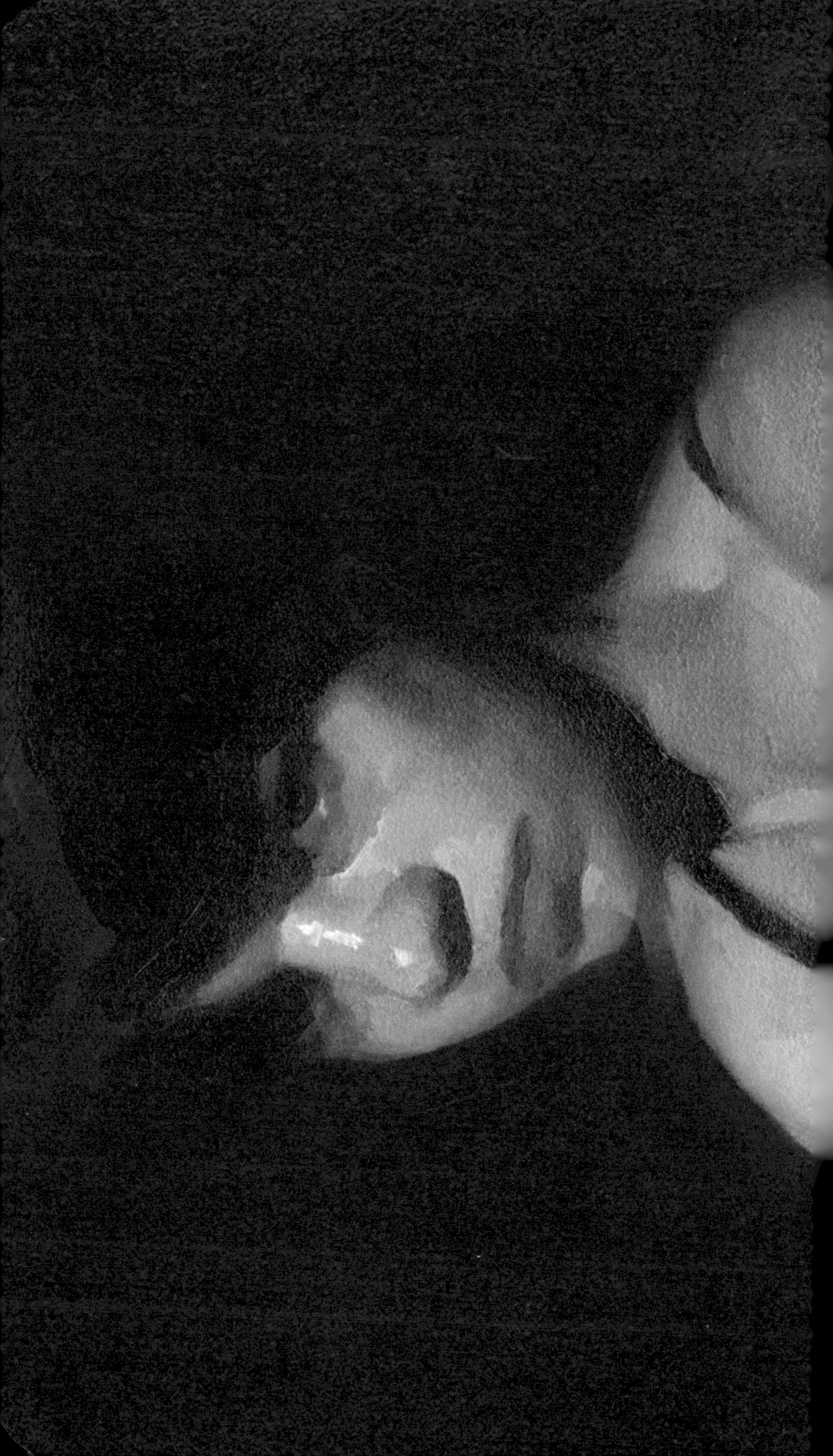

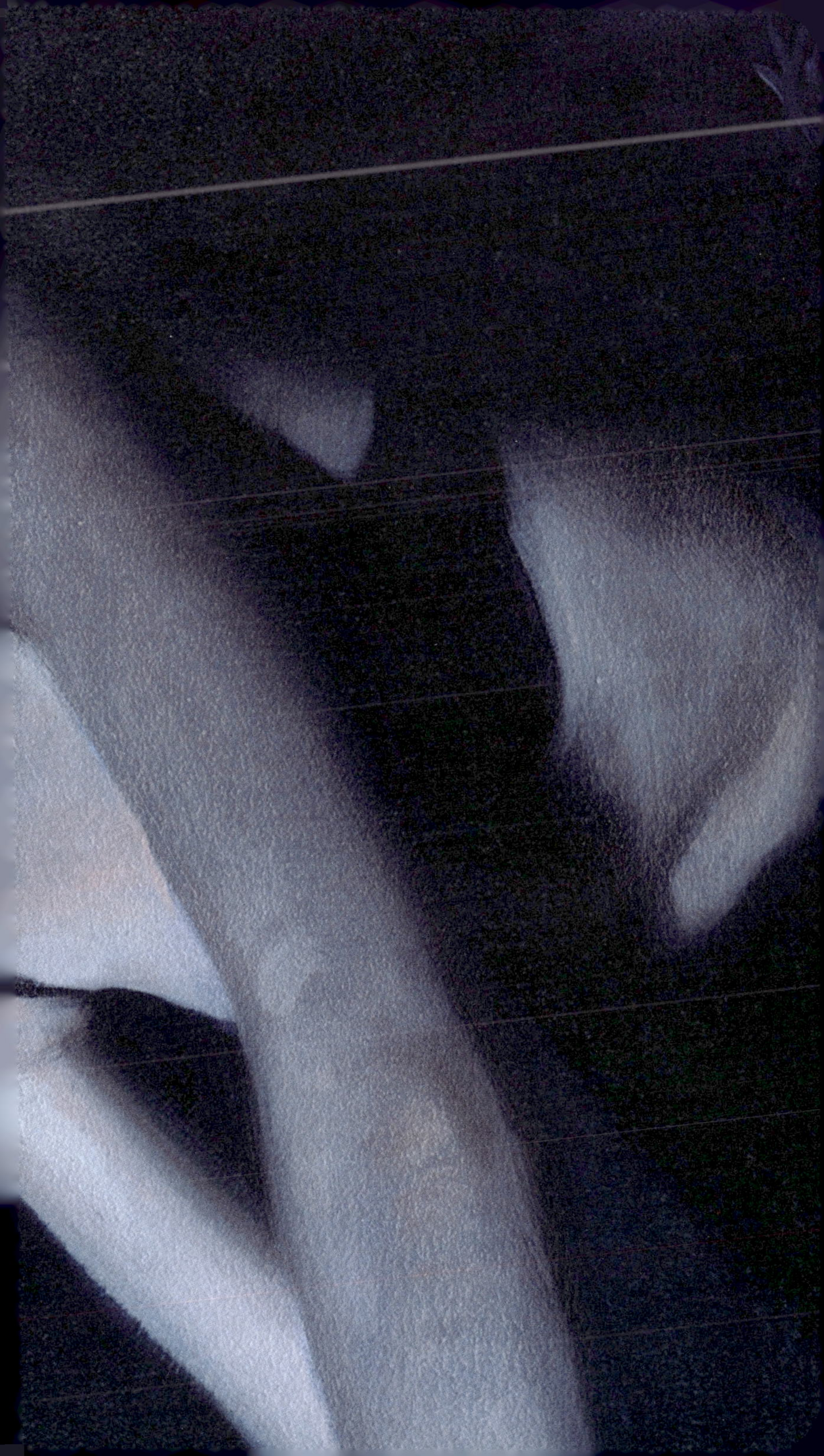

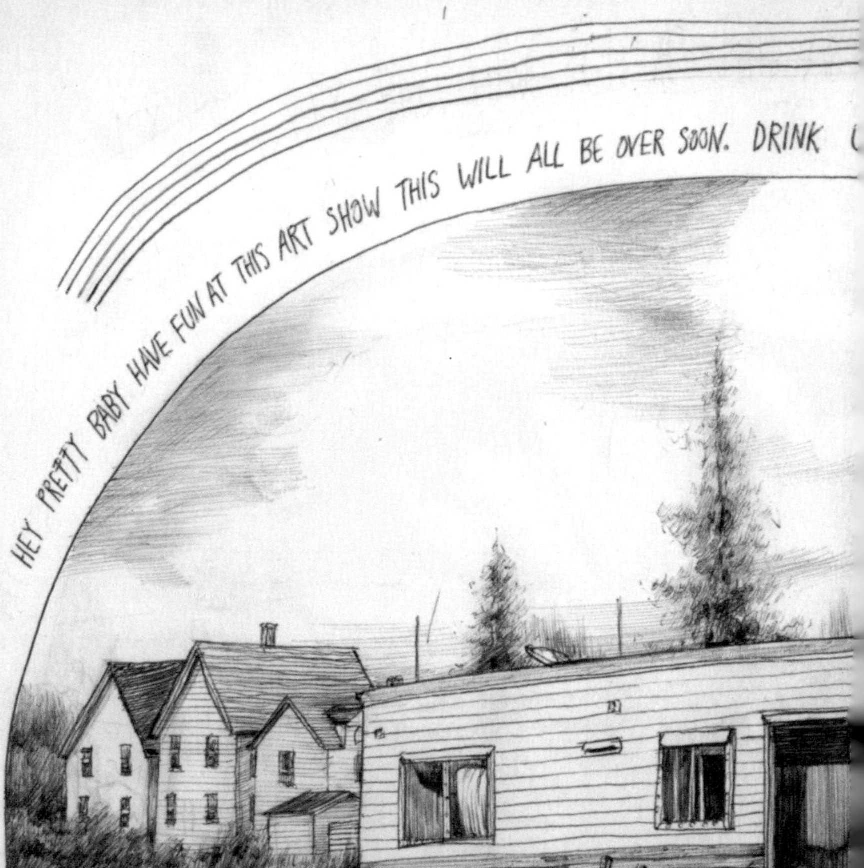
HEY PRETTY BABY HAVE FUN AT THIS ART SHOW THIS WILL ALL BE OVER SOON. DRINK
THINK OF YOUR MOM AND REMEMBER THAT THE WINDS ARE TURNING.

LOOK AT THE ORANGE IN THE SKY WHEN YOU GET BACK OUTSIDE STAND IN THE STREET

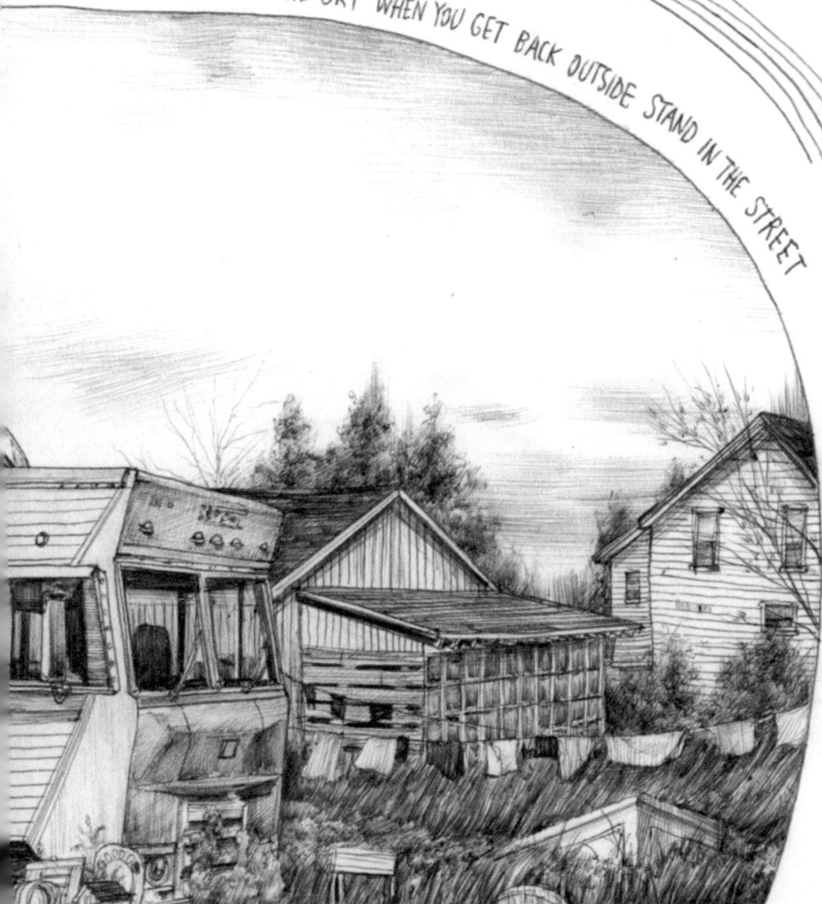

GS FROM THE ROTTING RUST BELT. GREETINGS FROM EVERYWHERE BUT HERE.

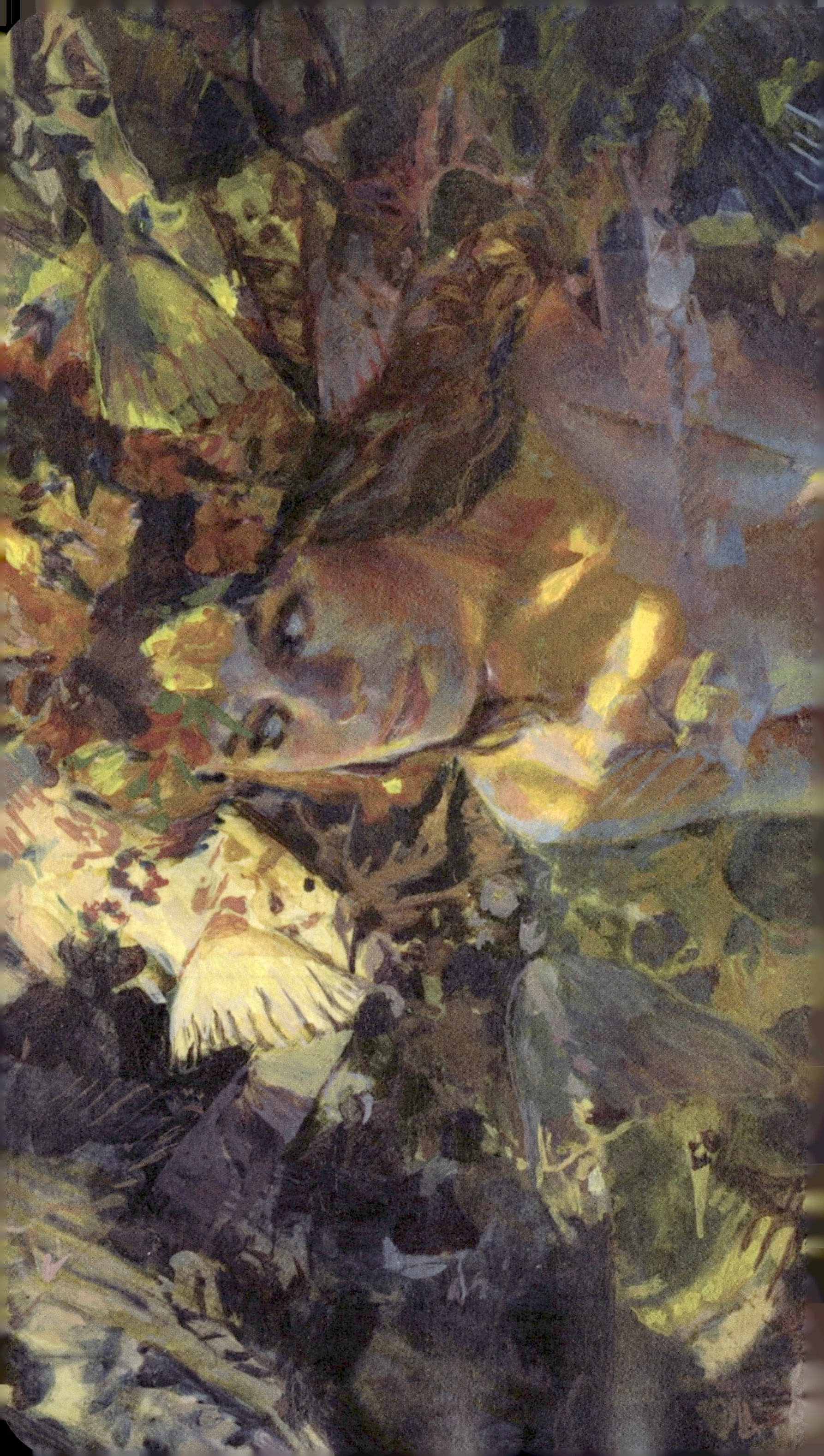

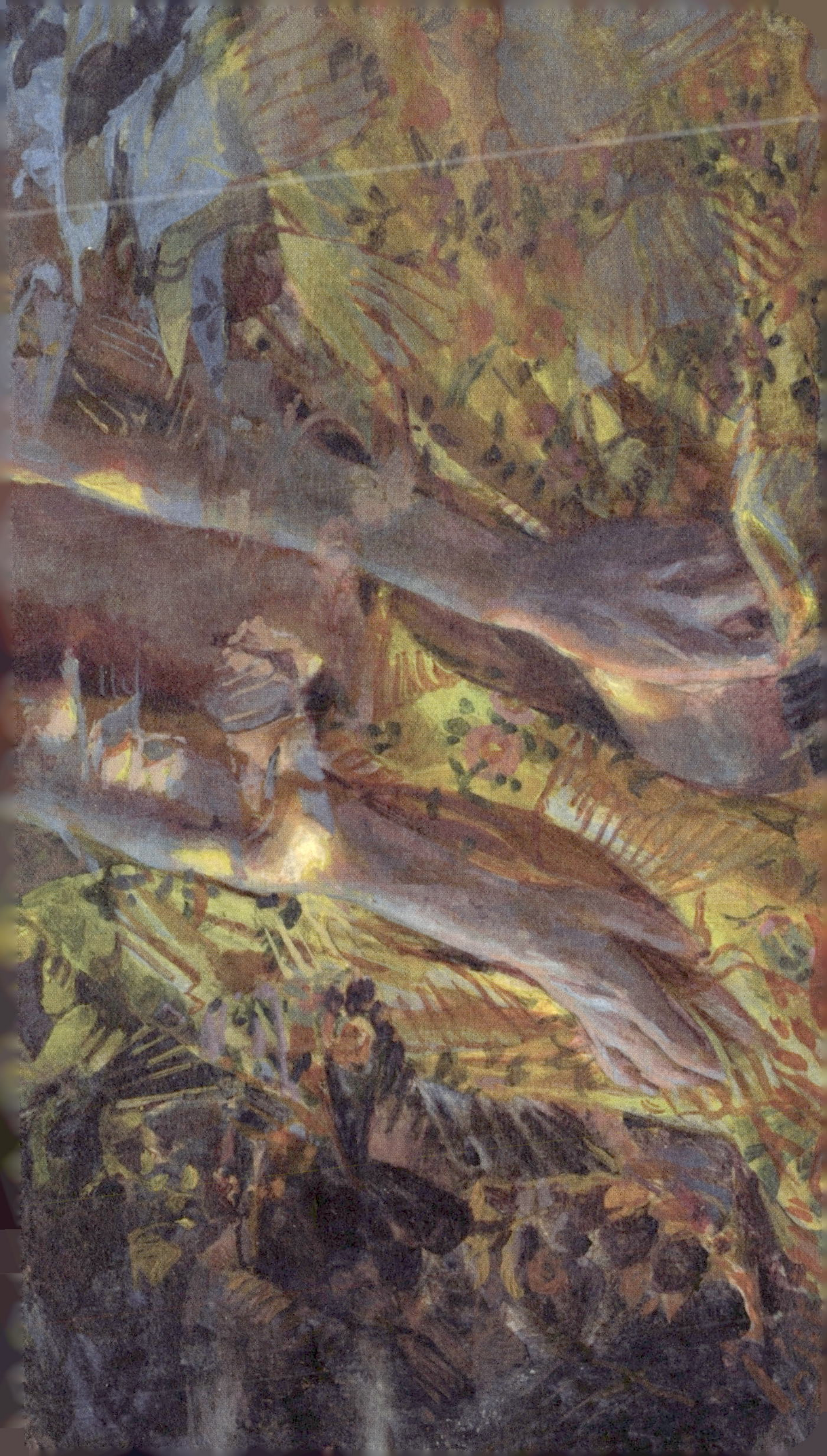

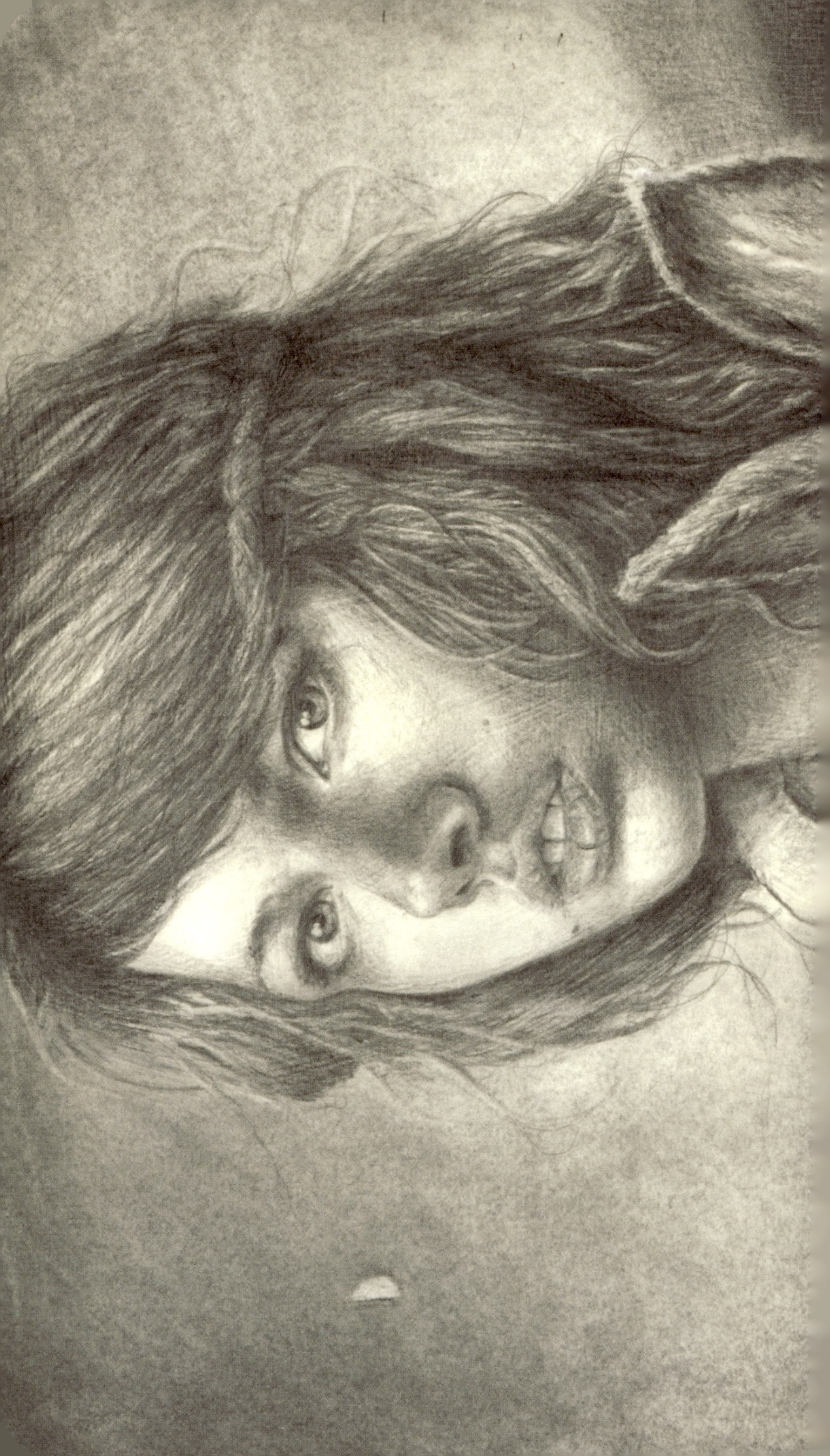

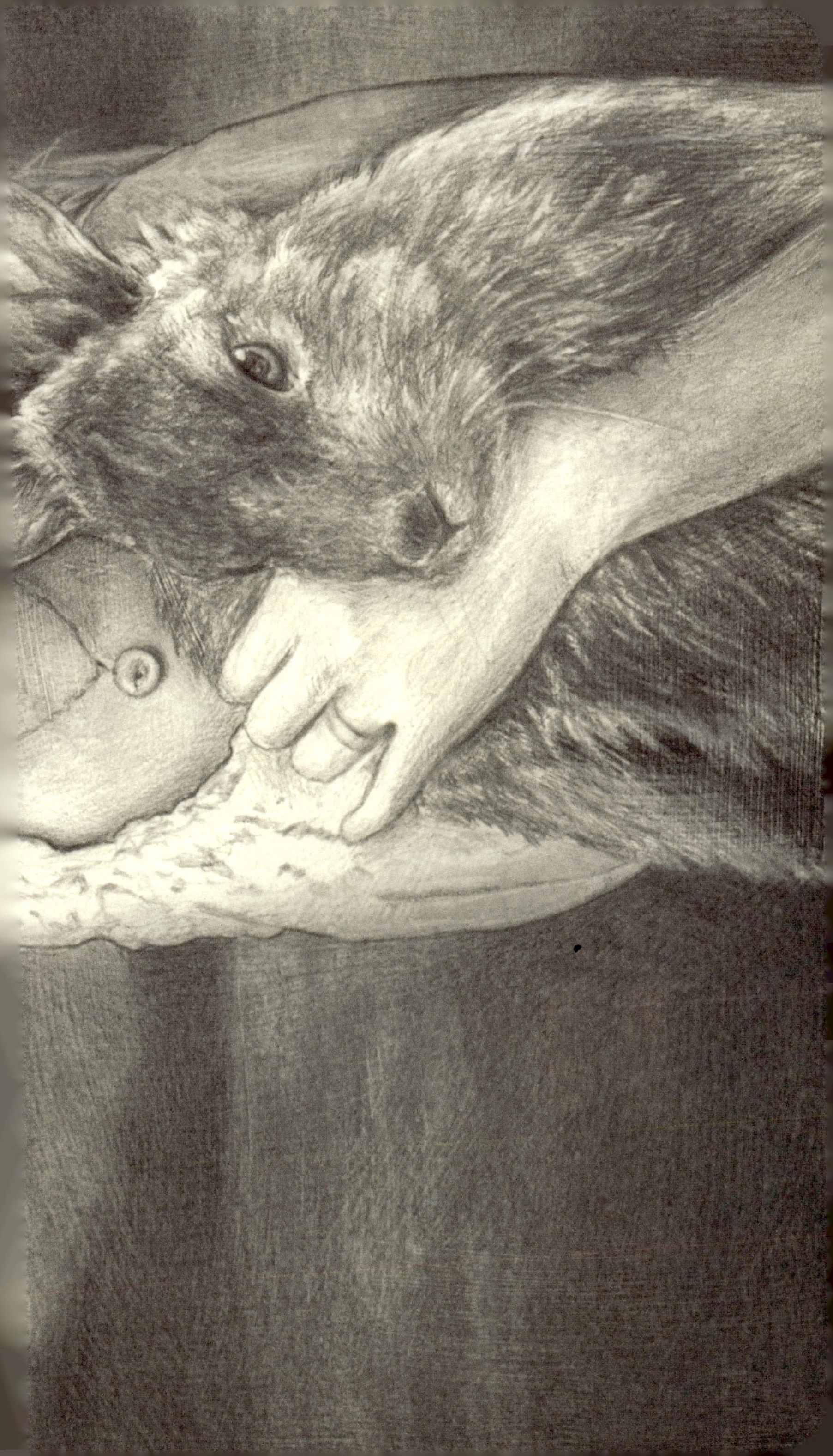

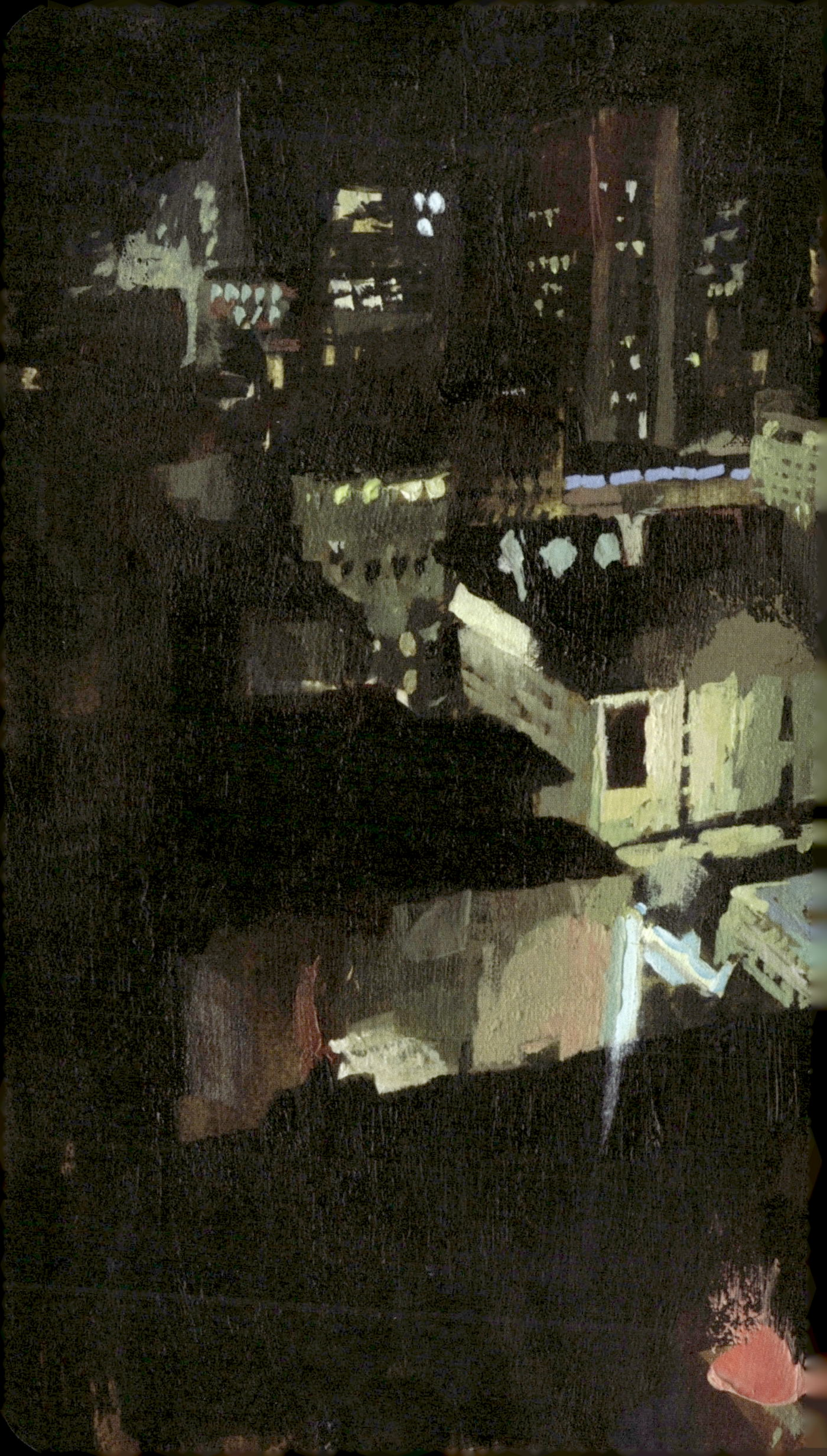

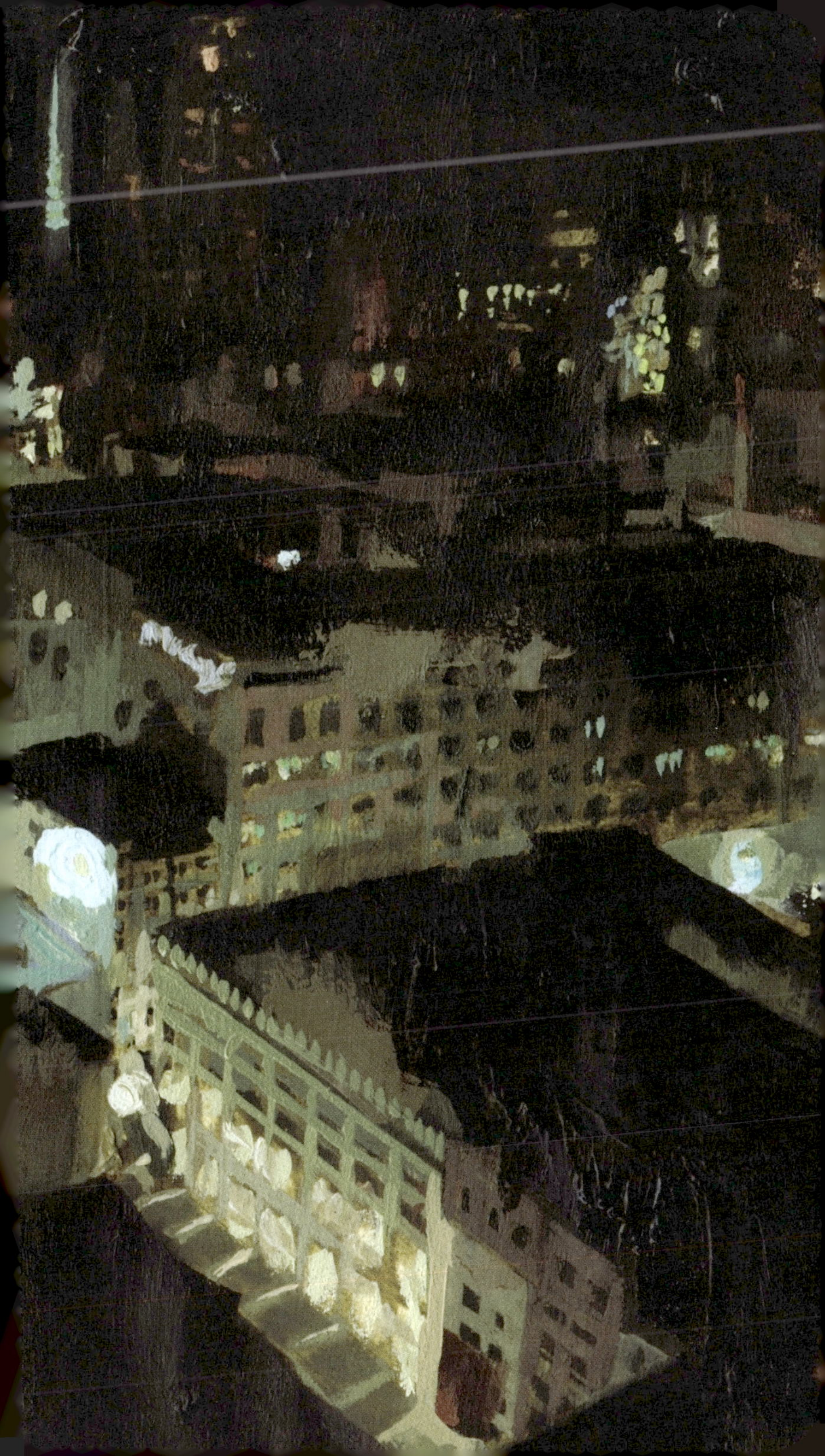

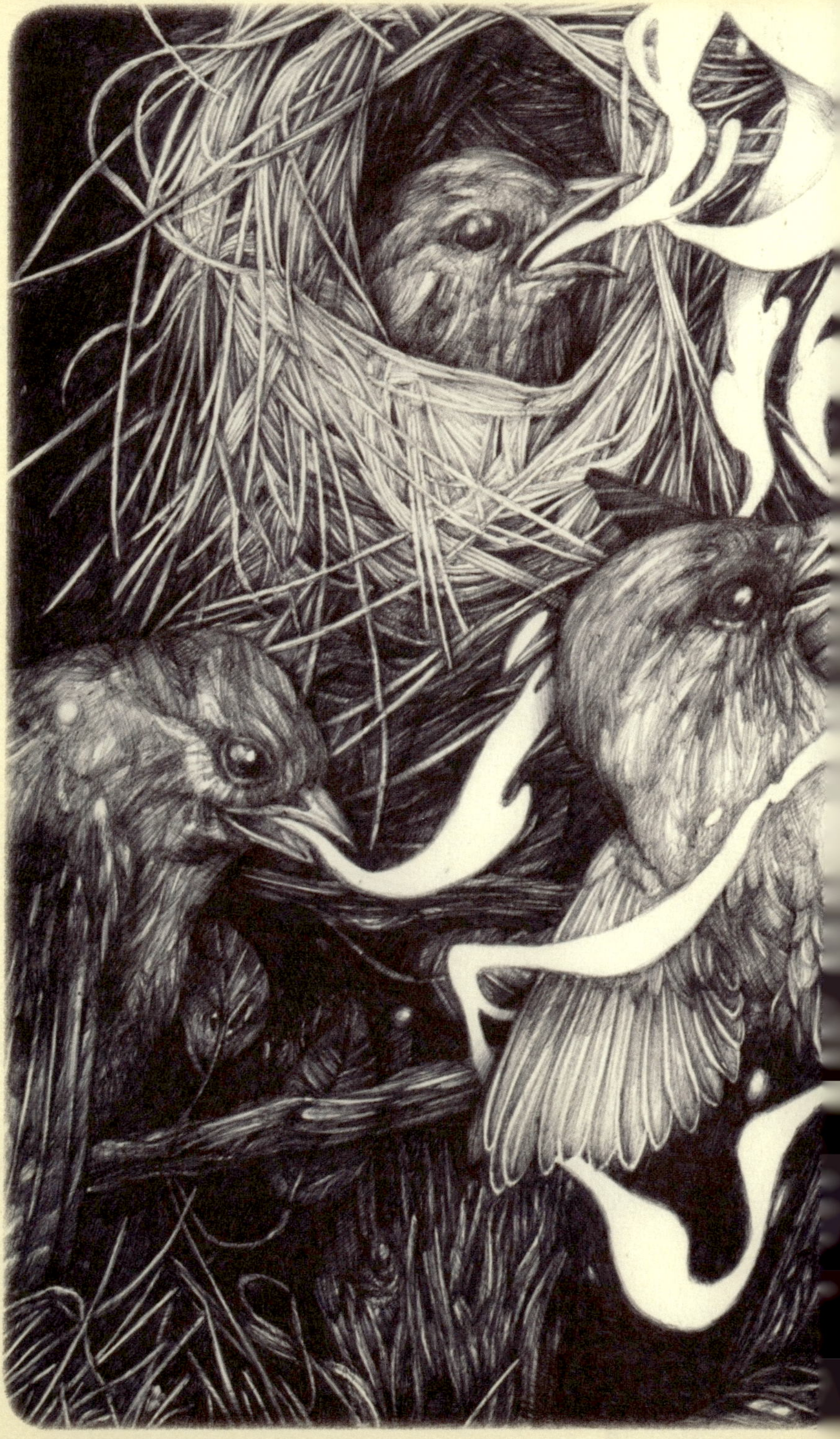

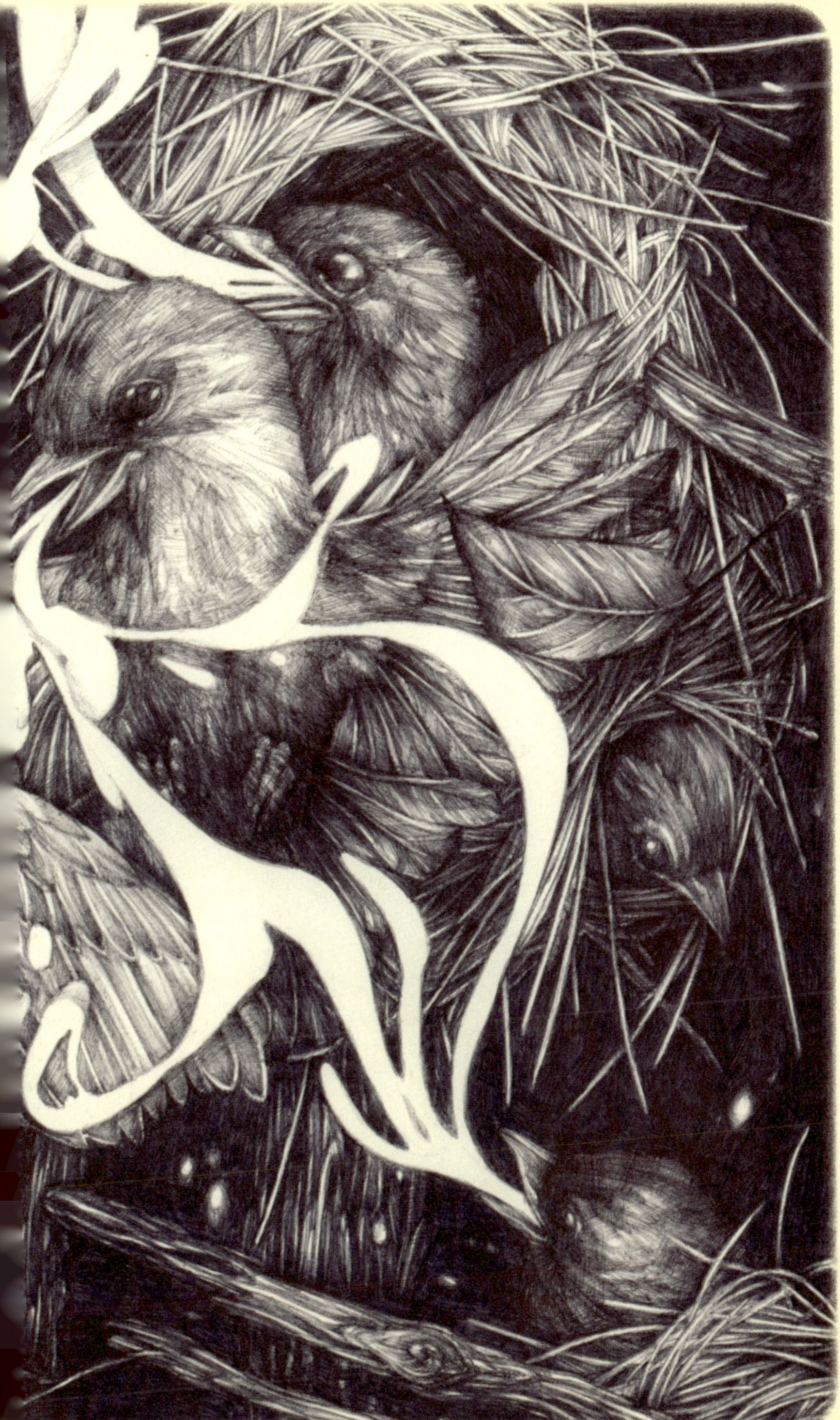

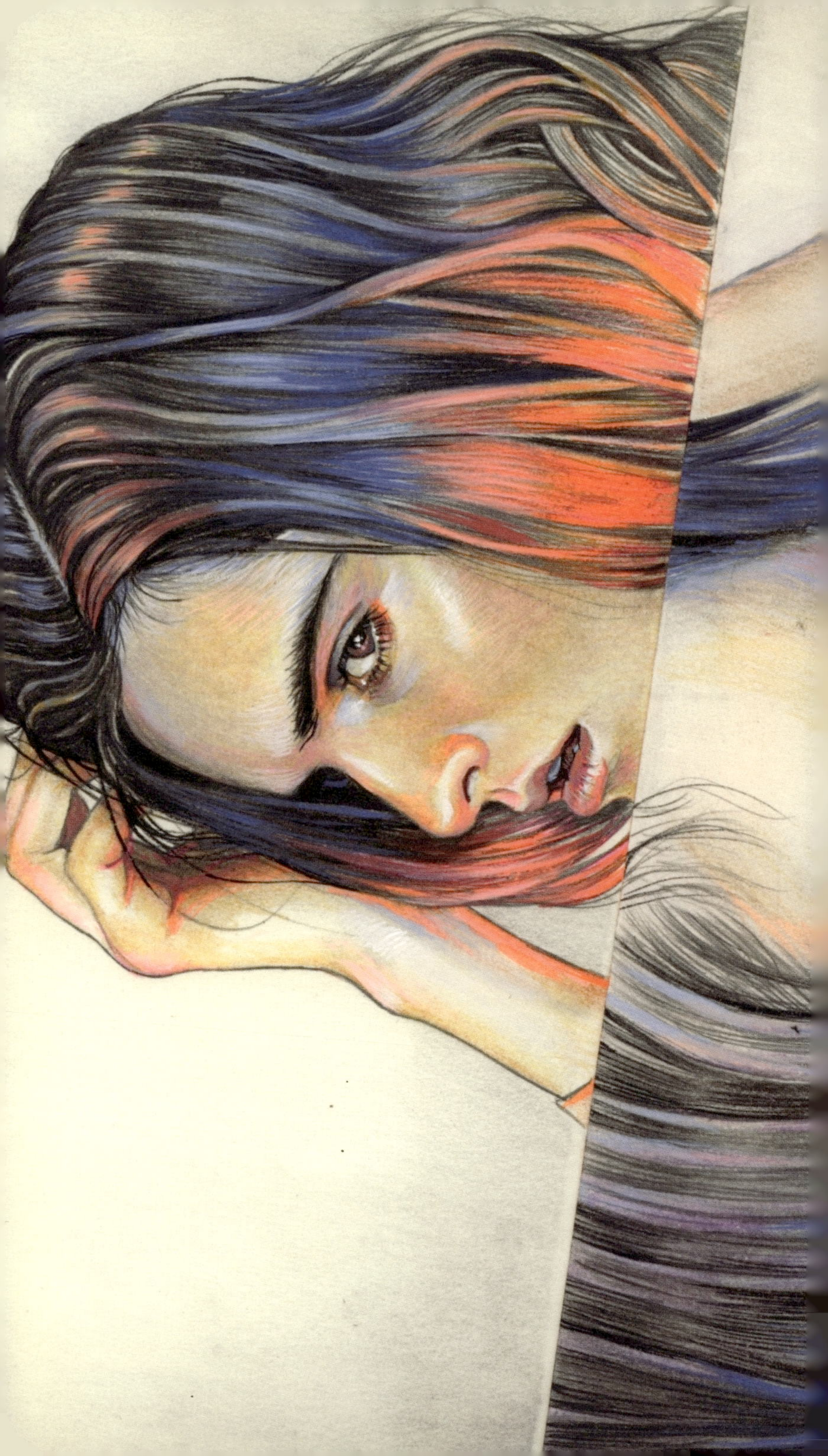

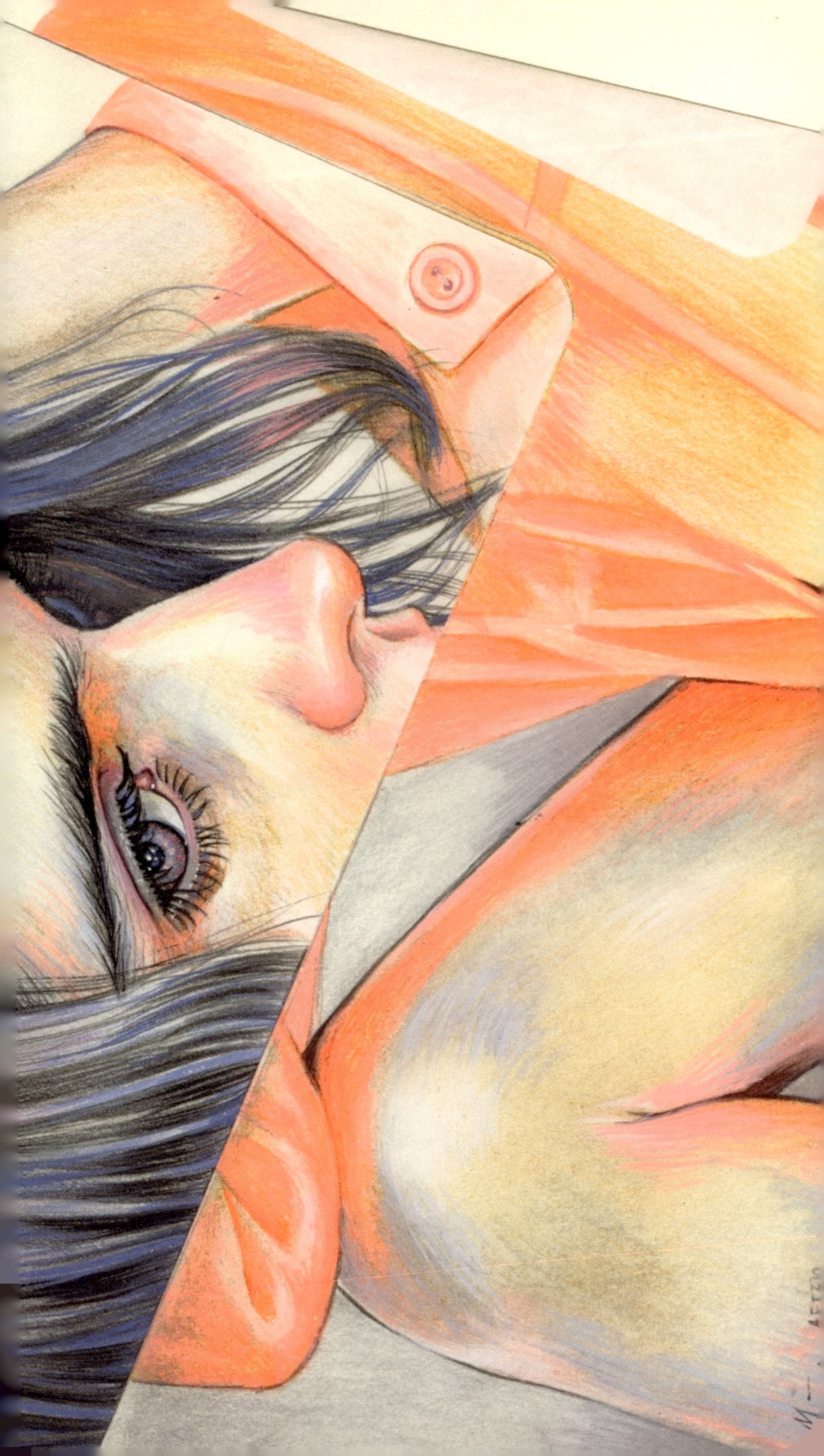

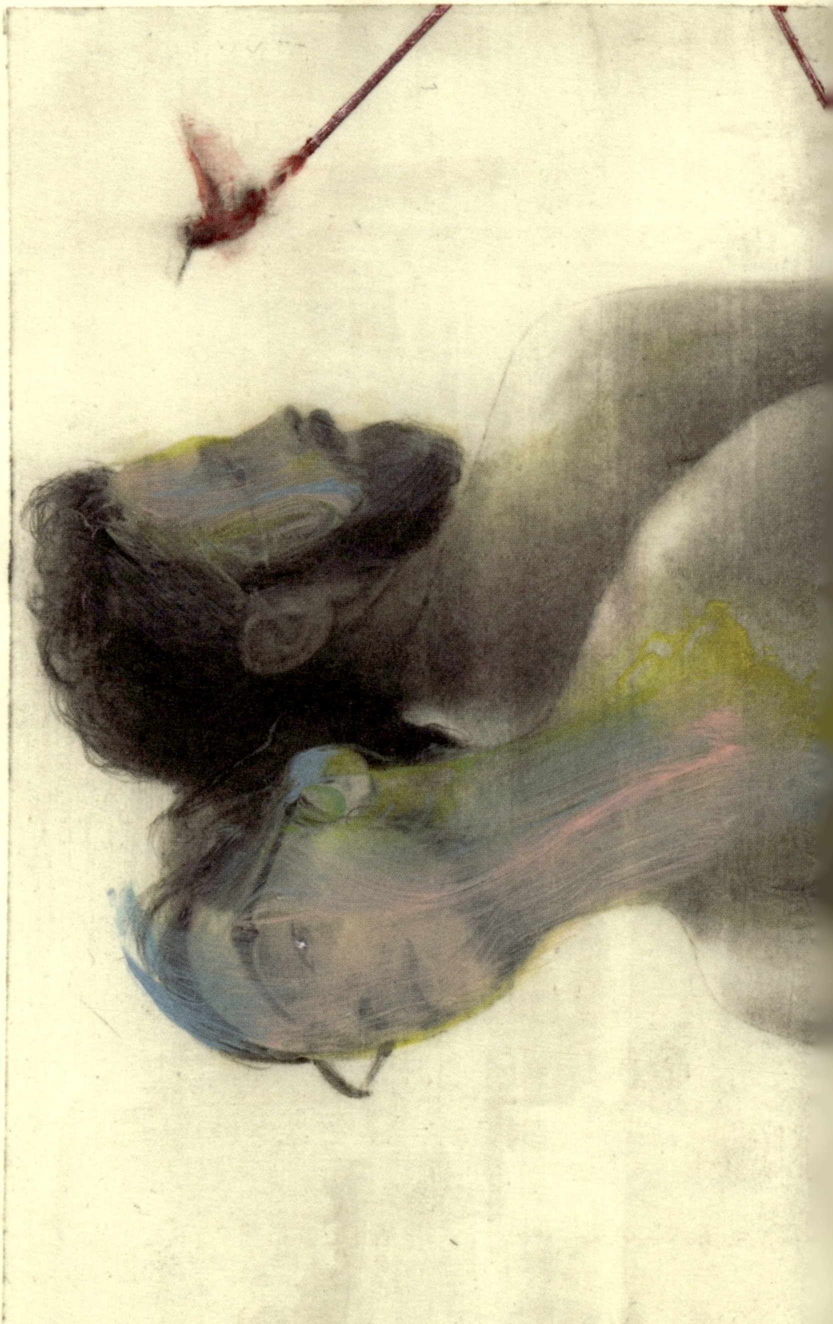

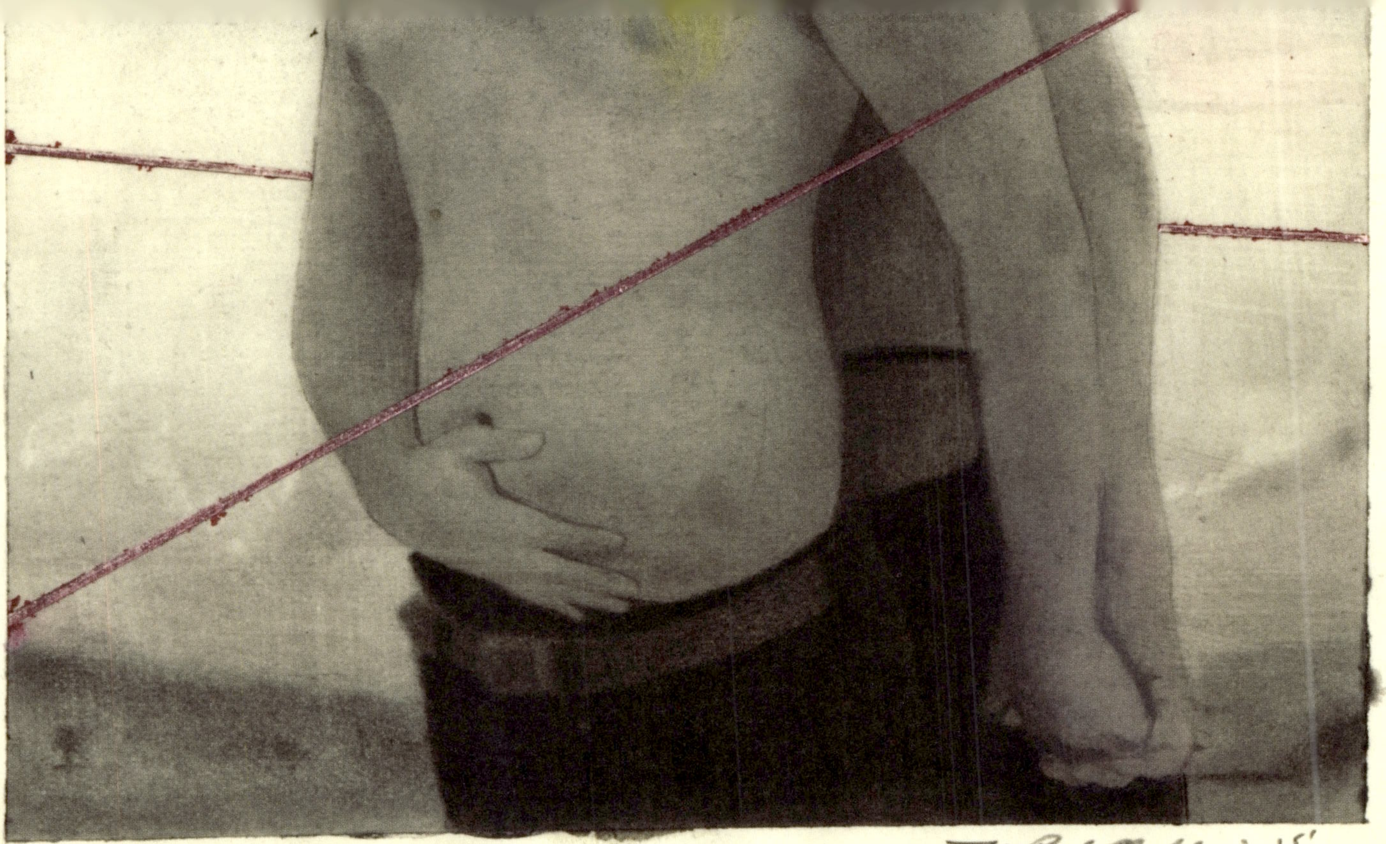

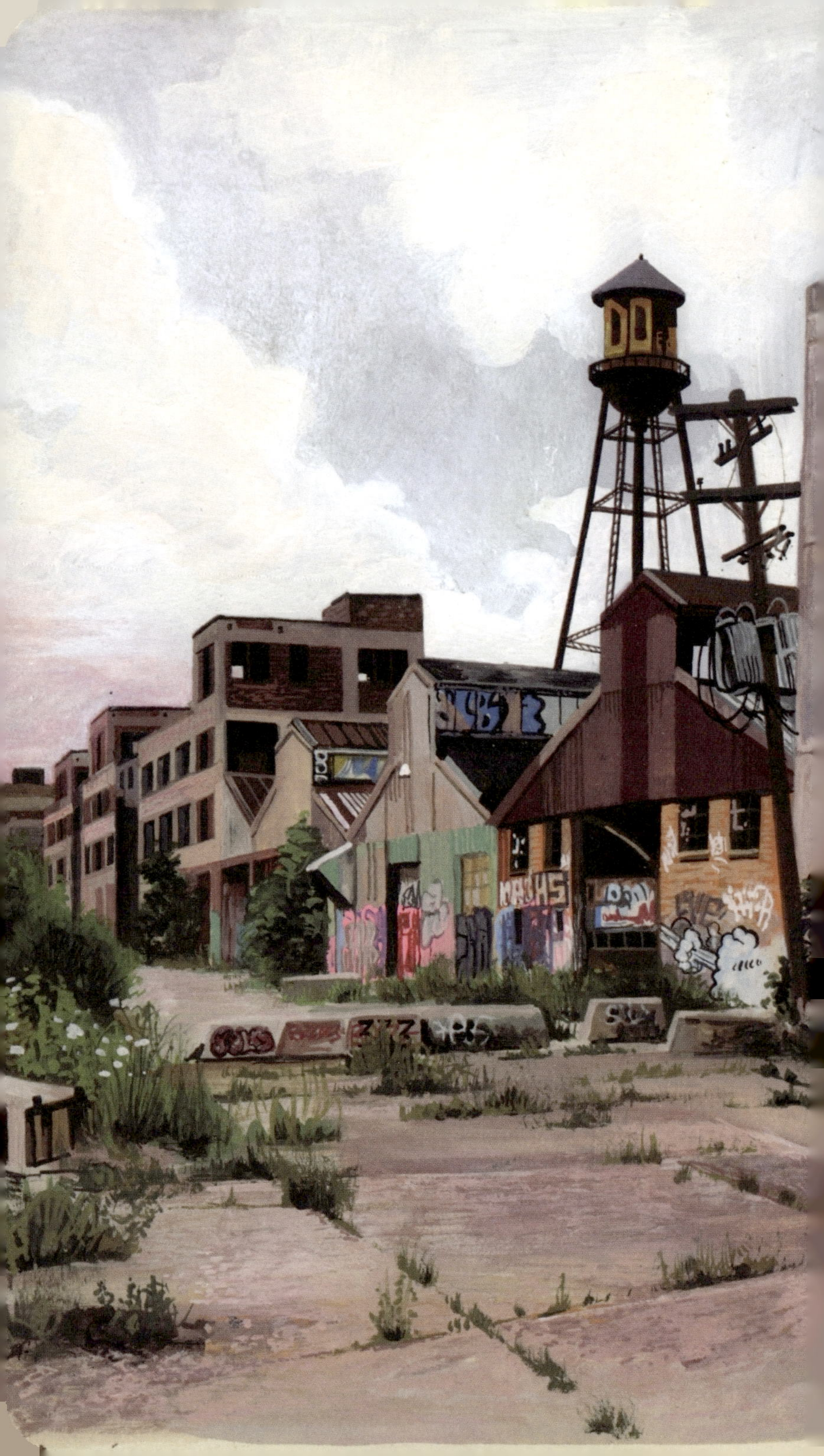

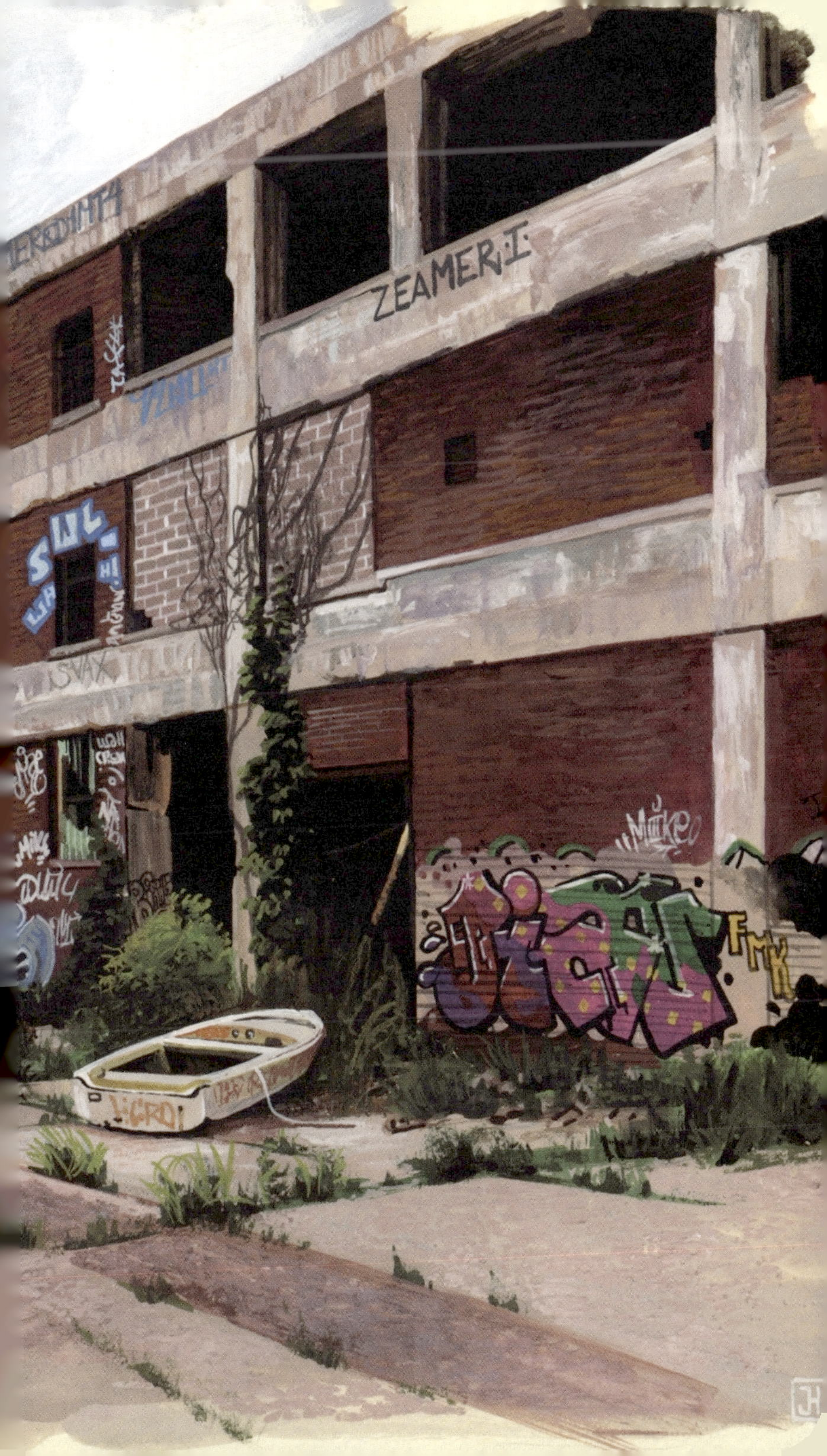
ZEAMER·I·
FMK

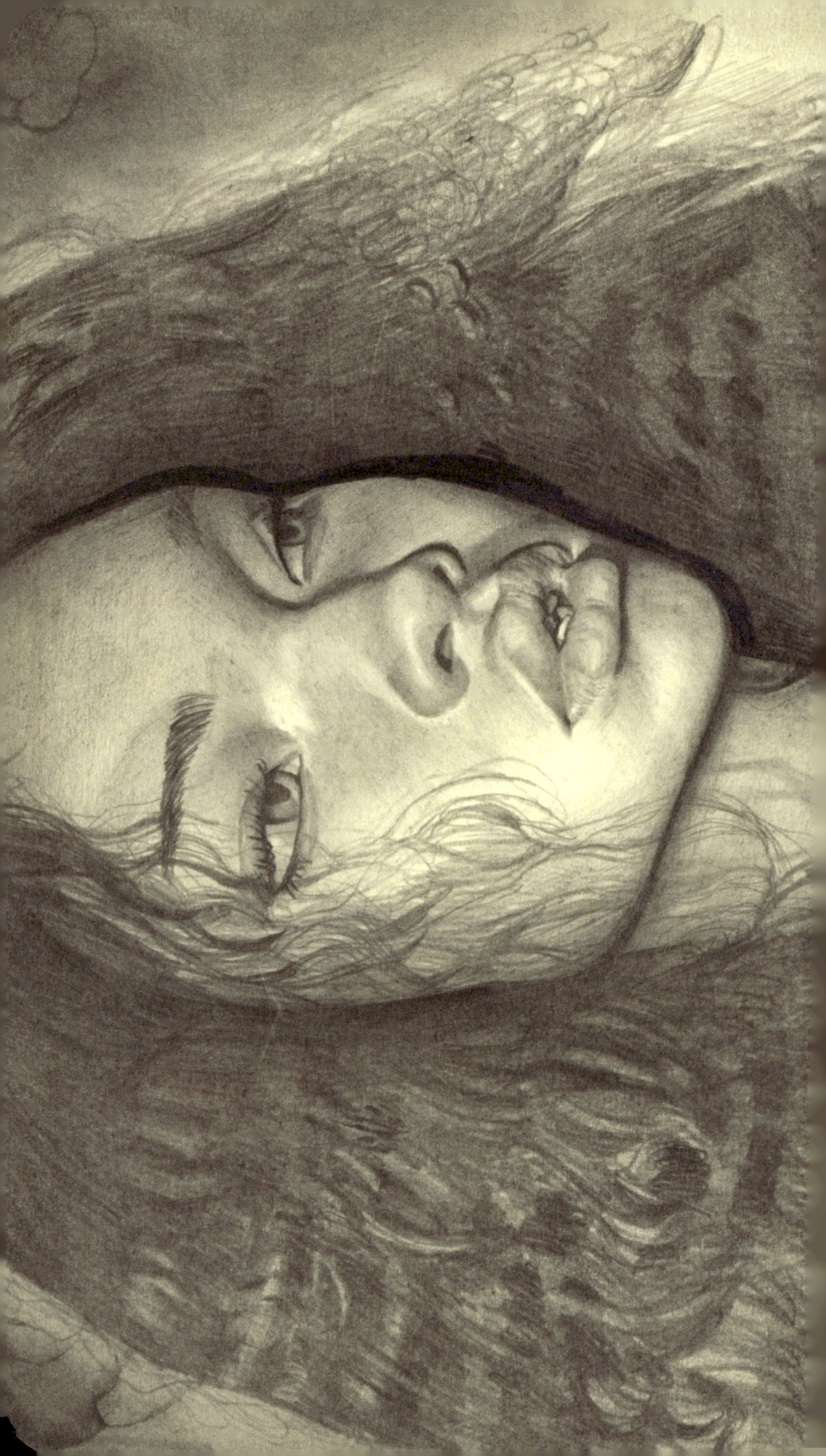

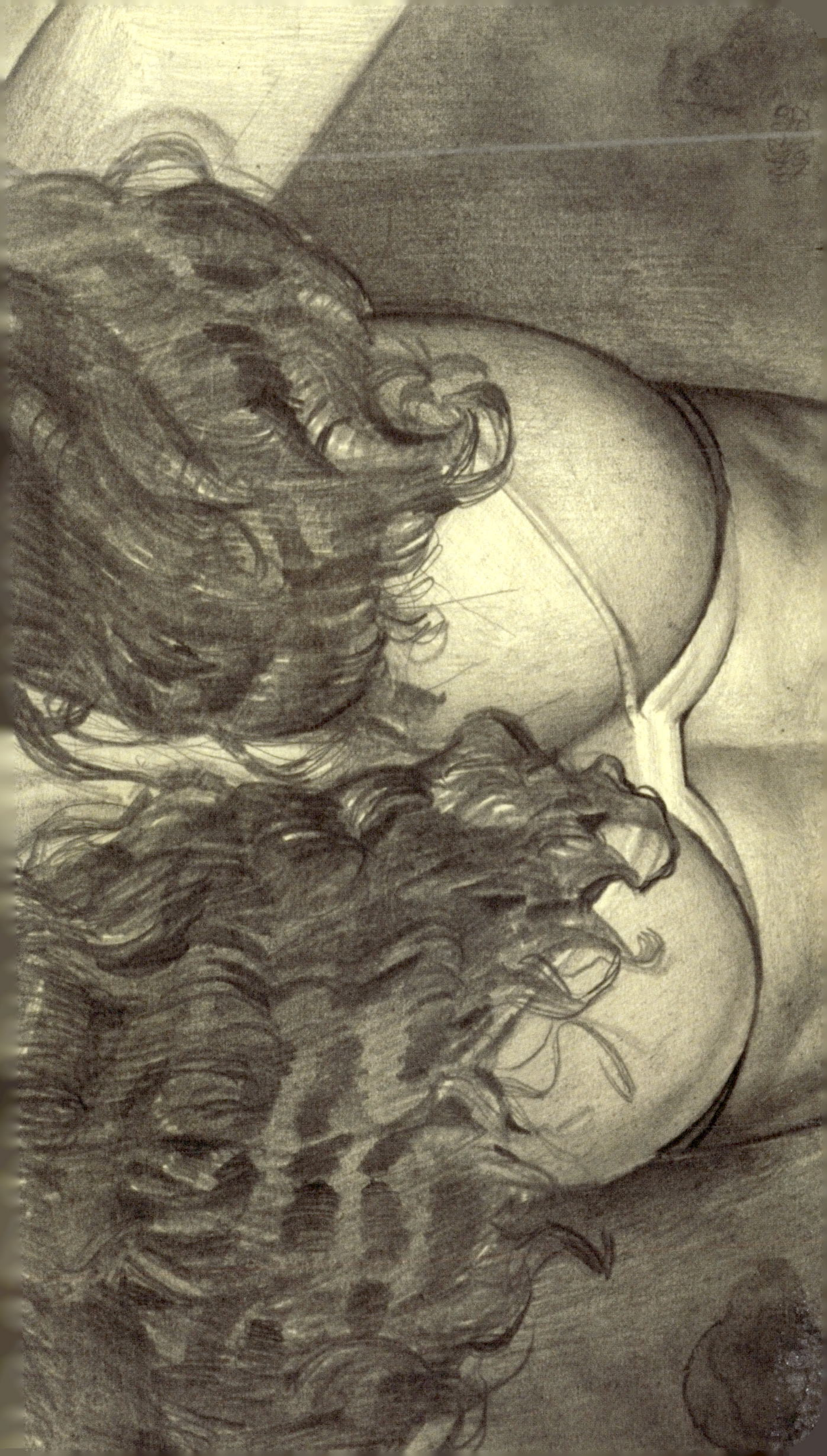

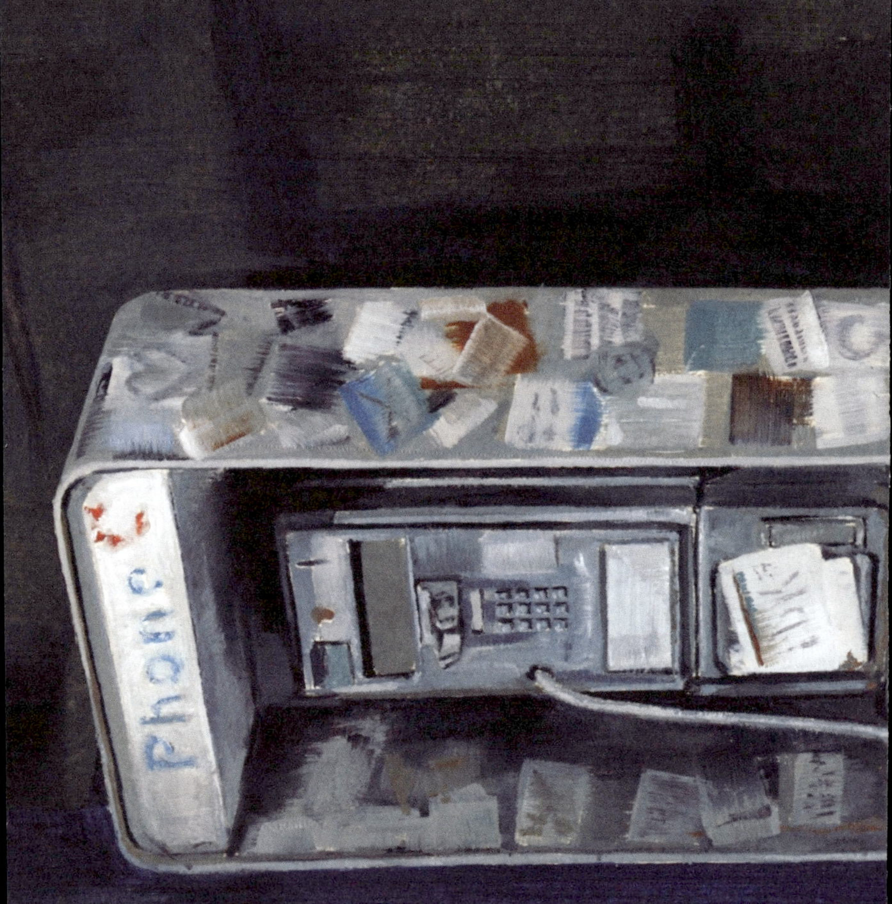
Phone

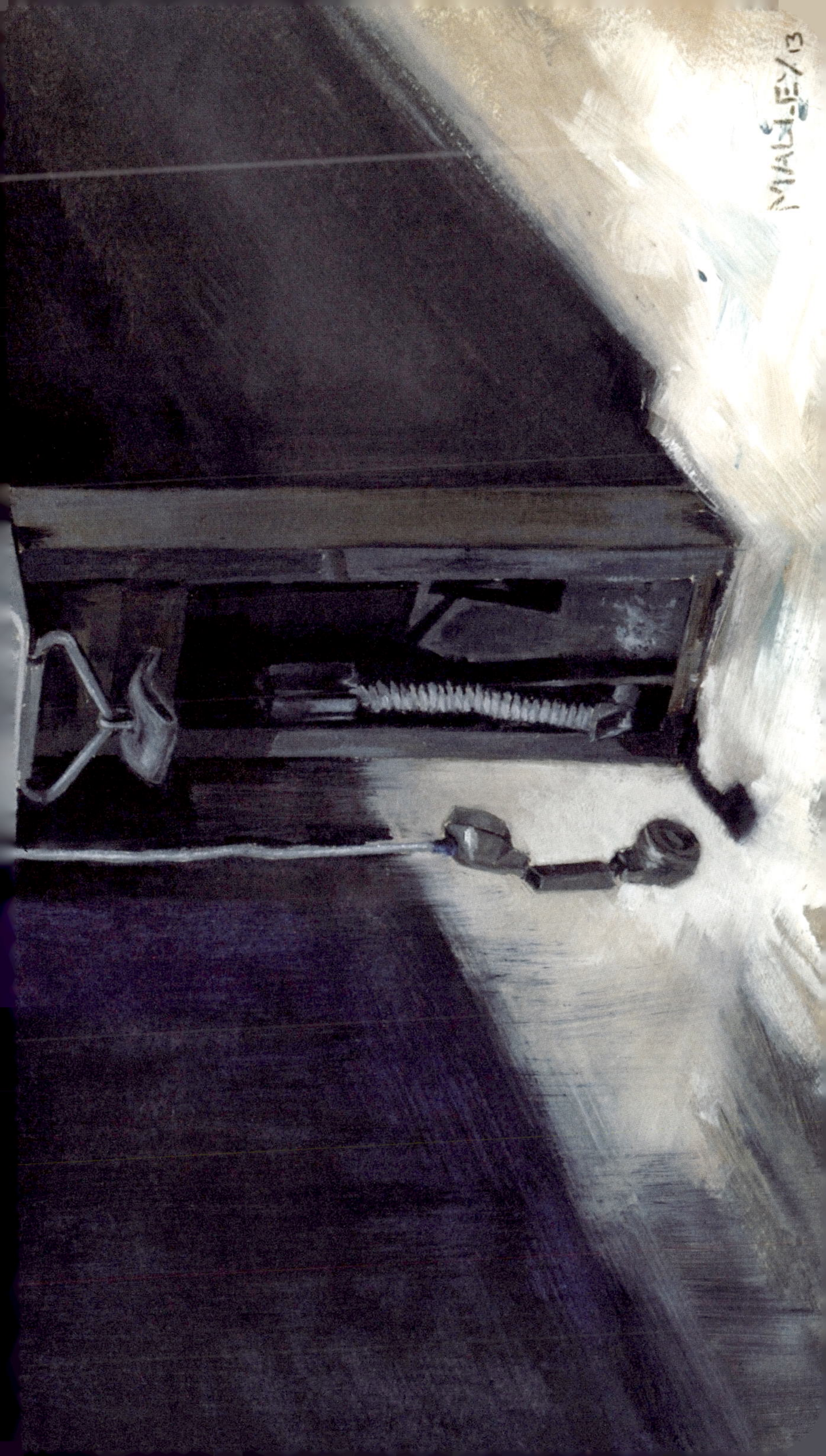

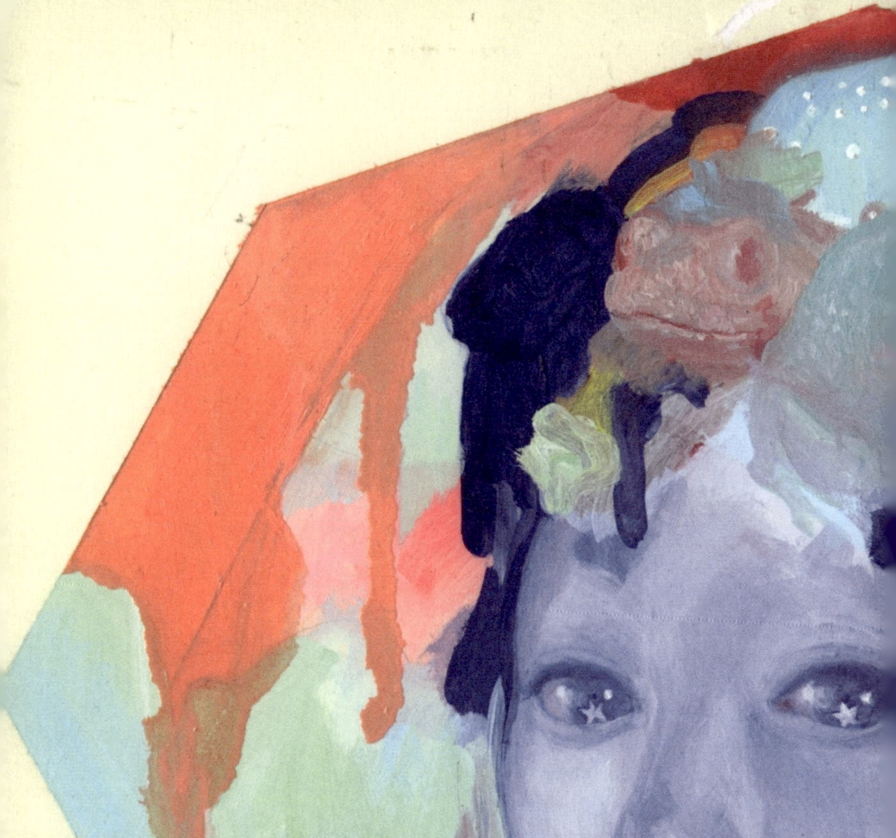

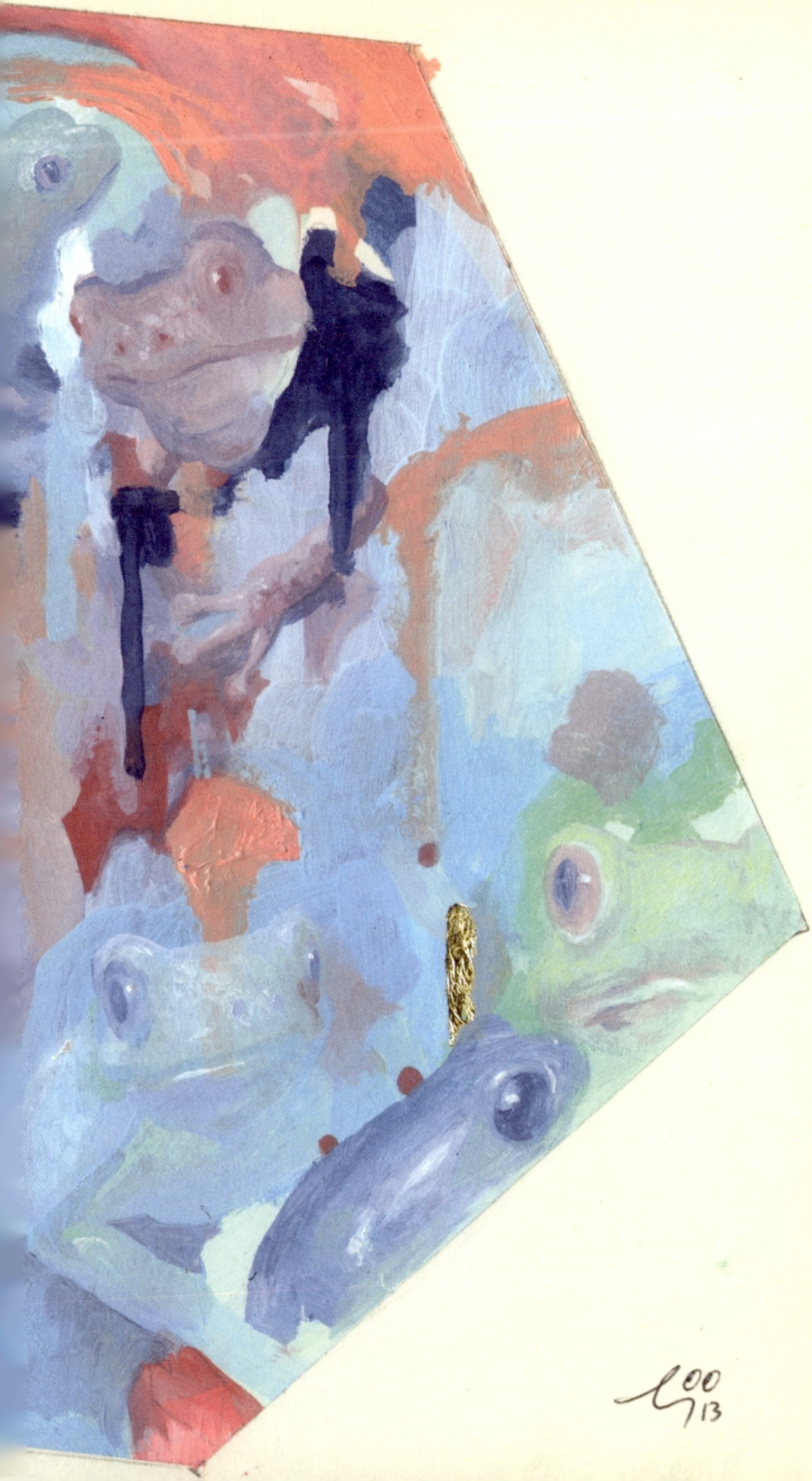

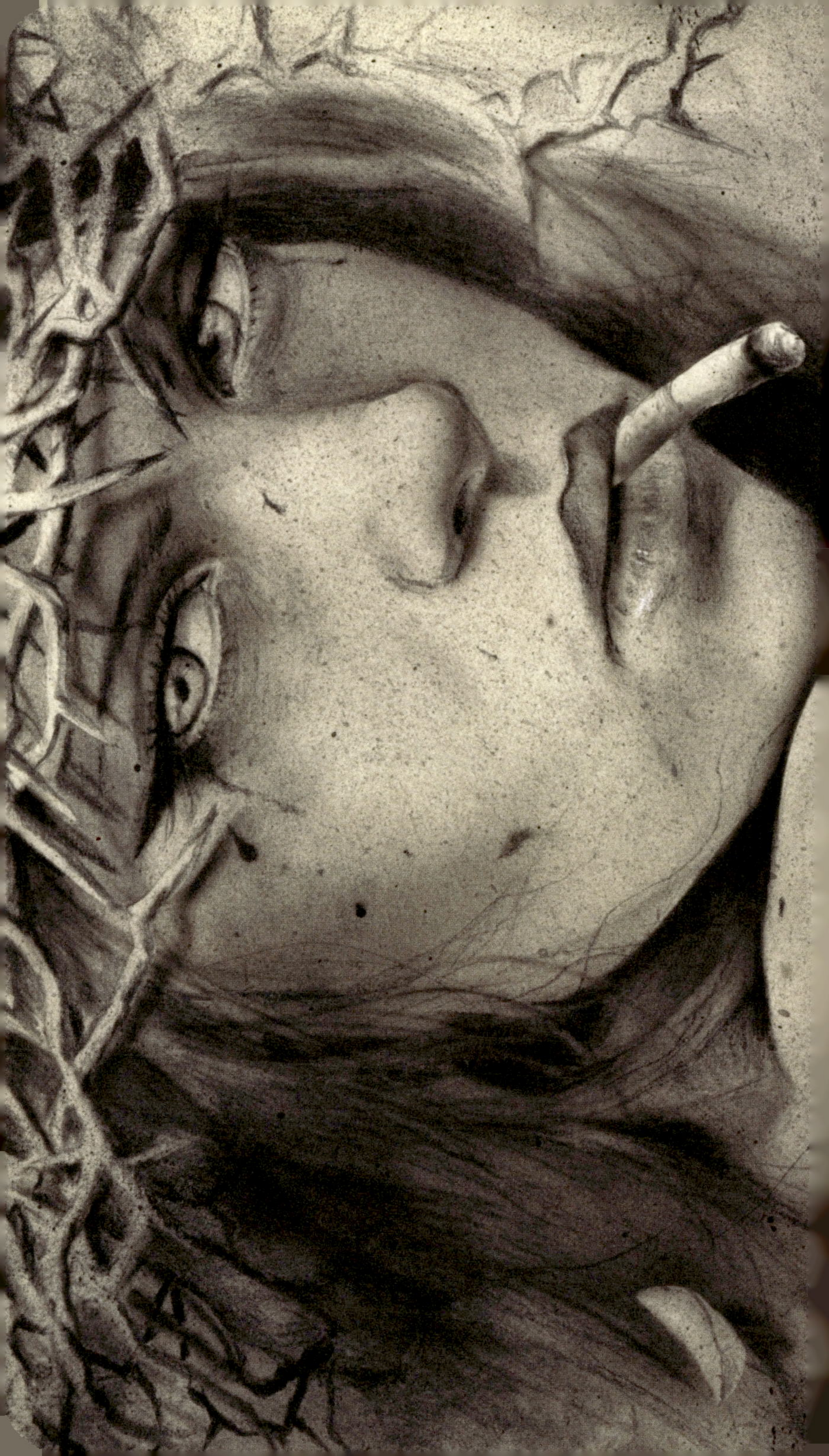

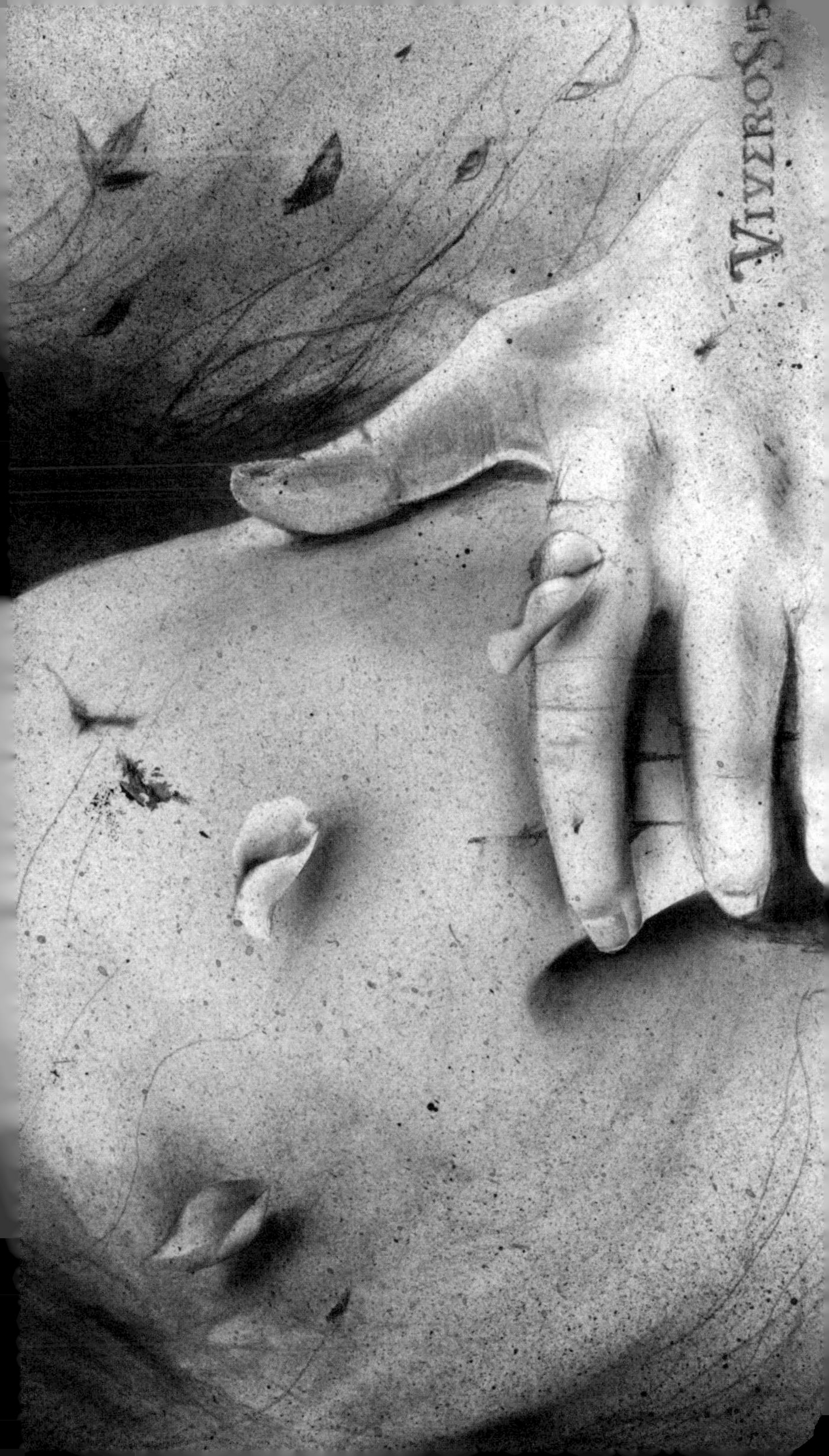

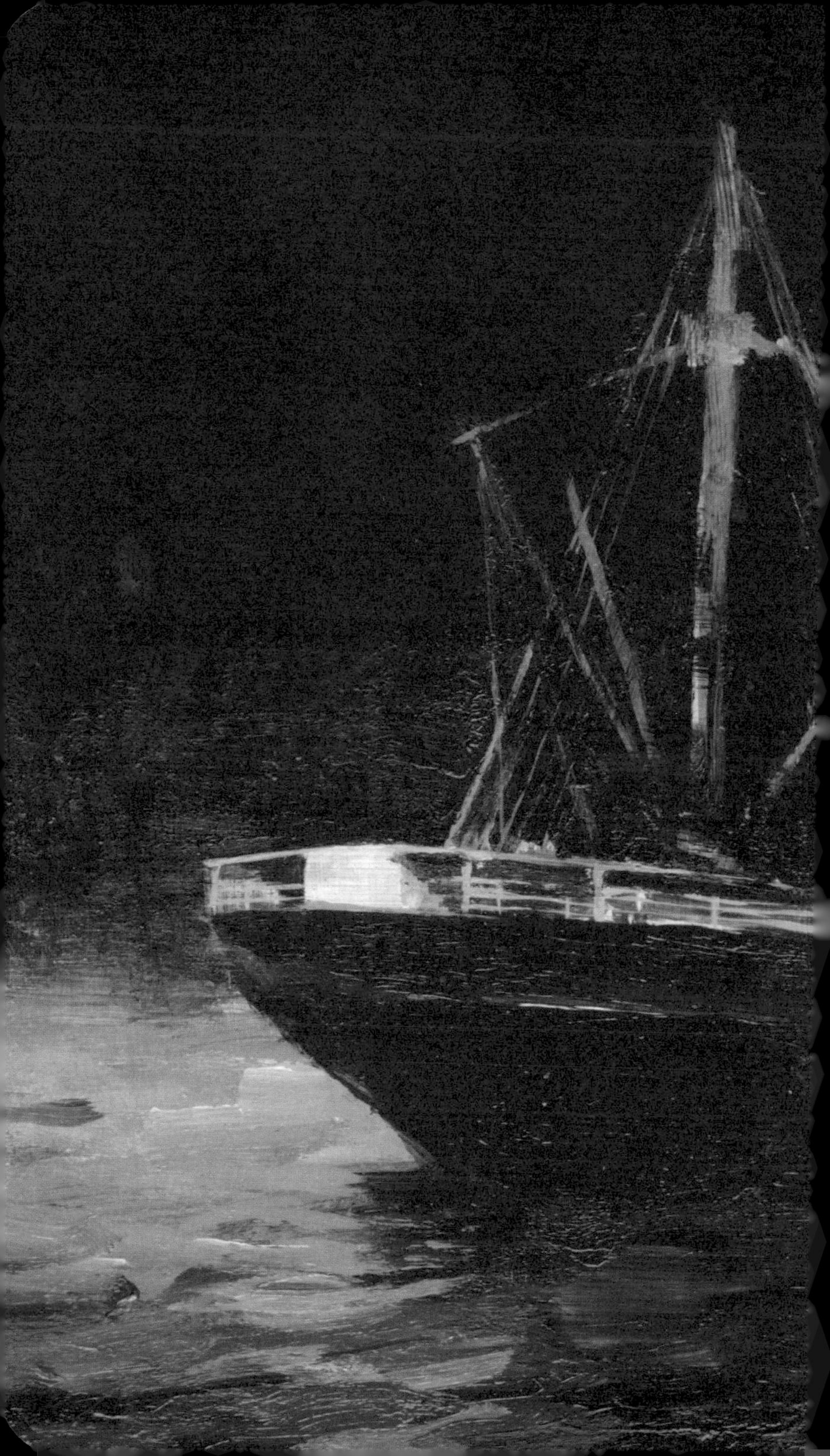

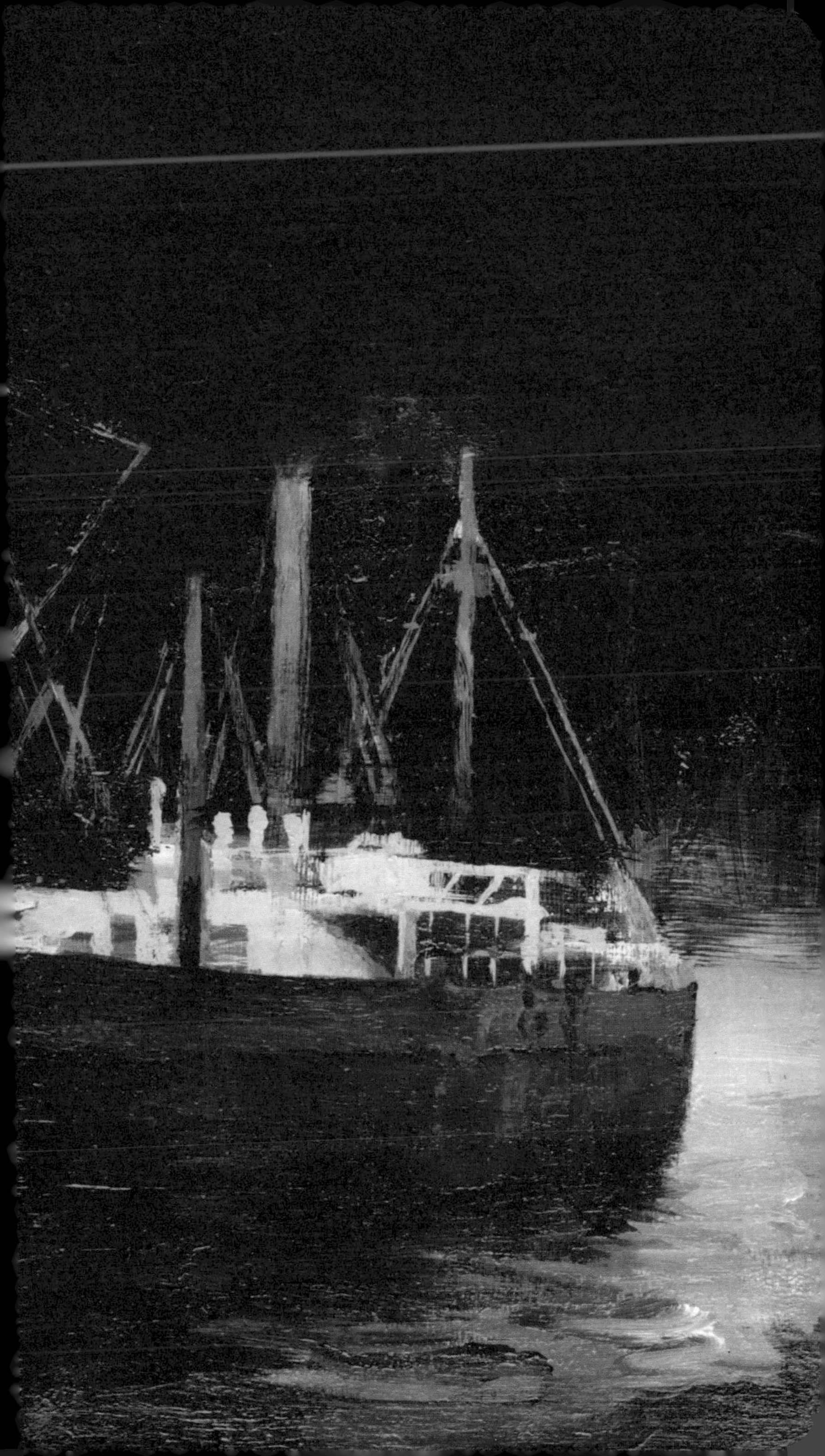

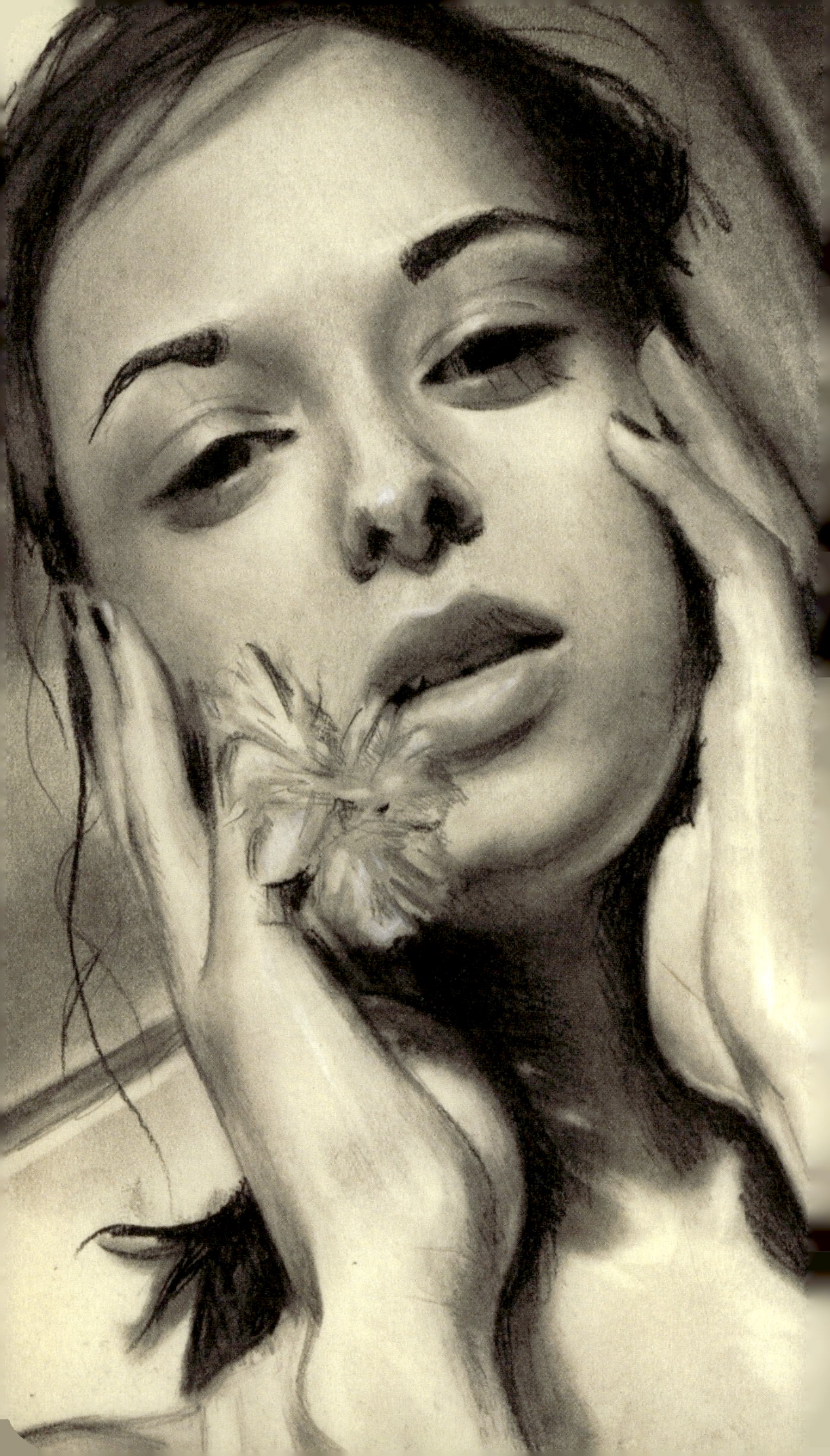

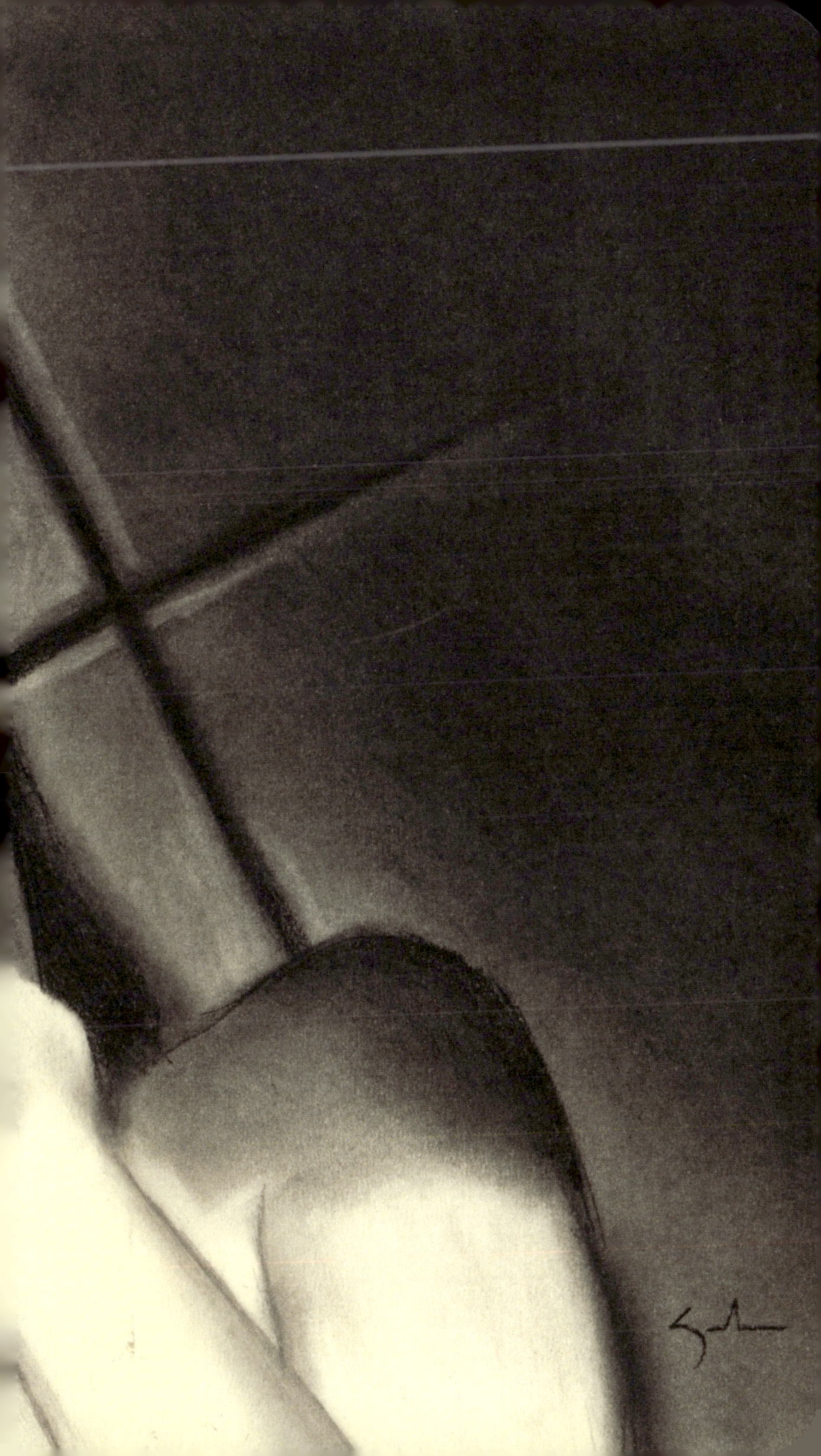

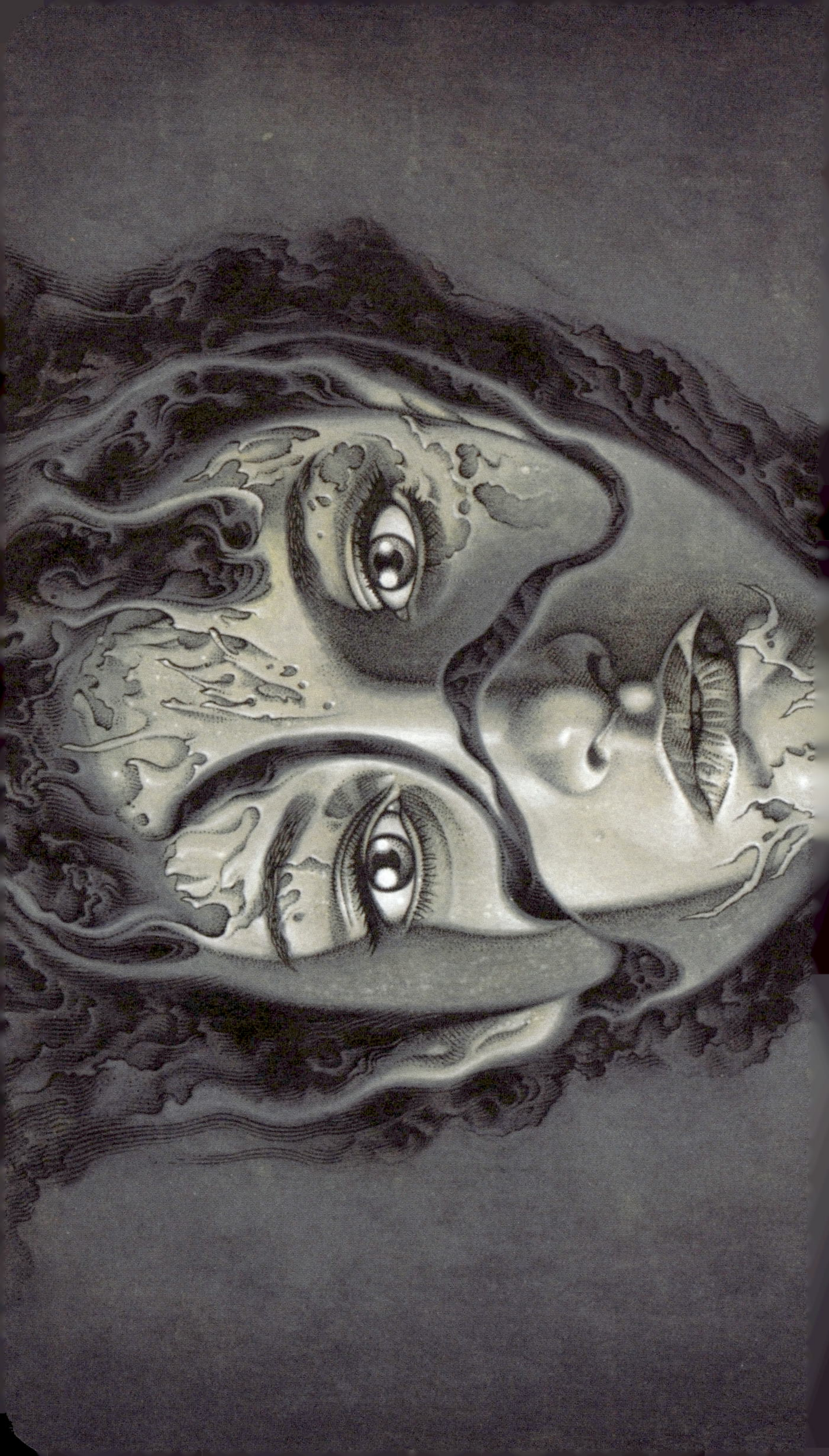

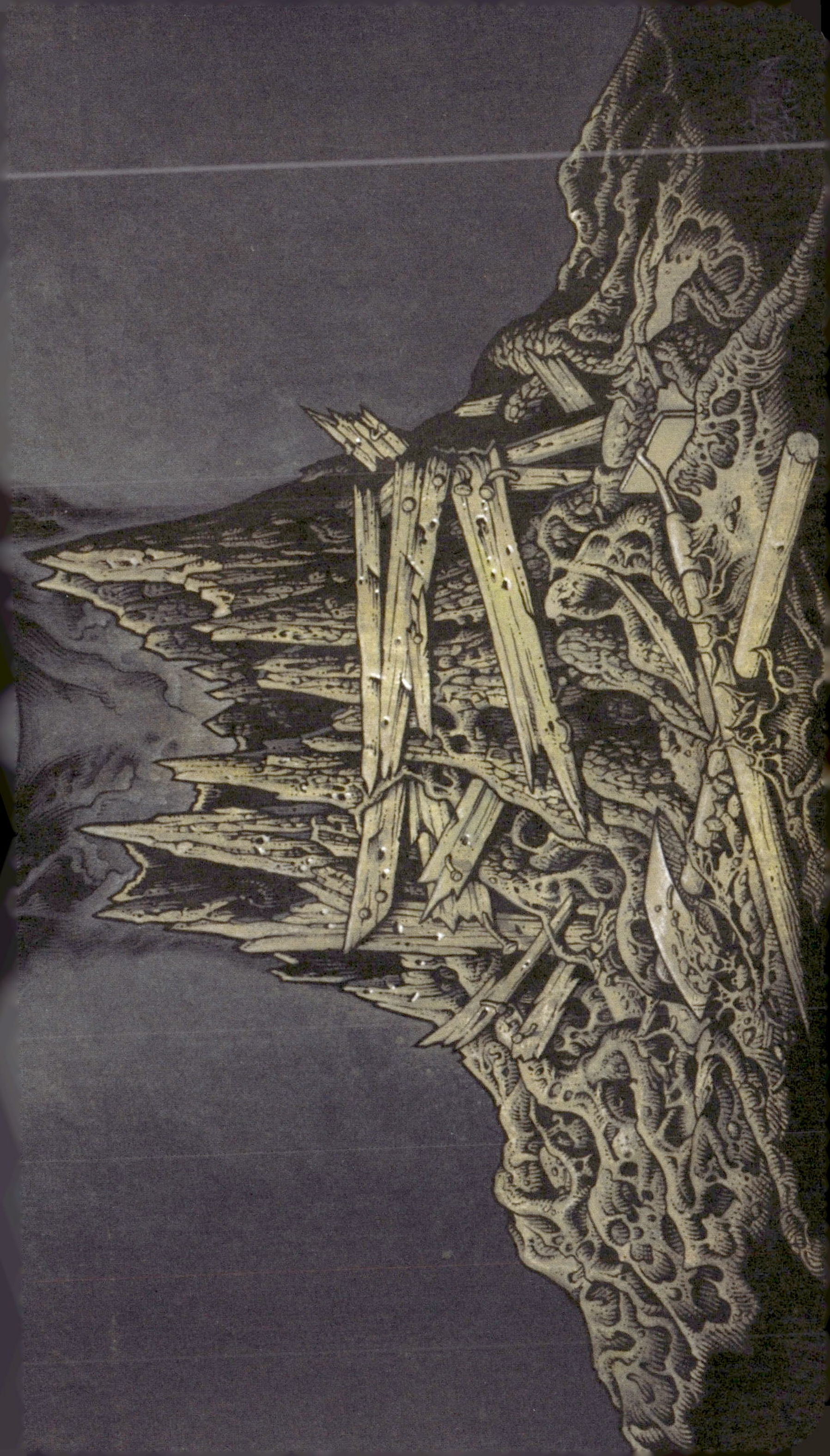

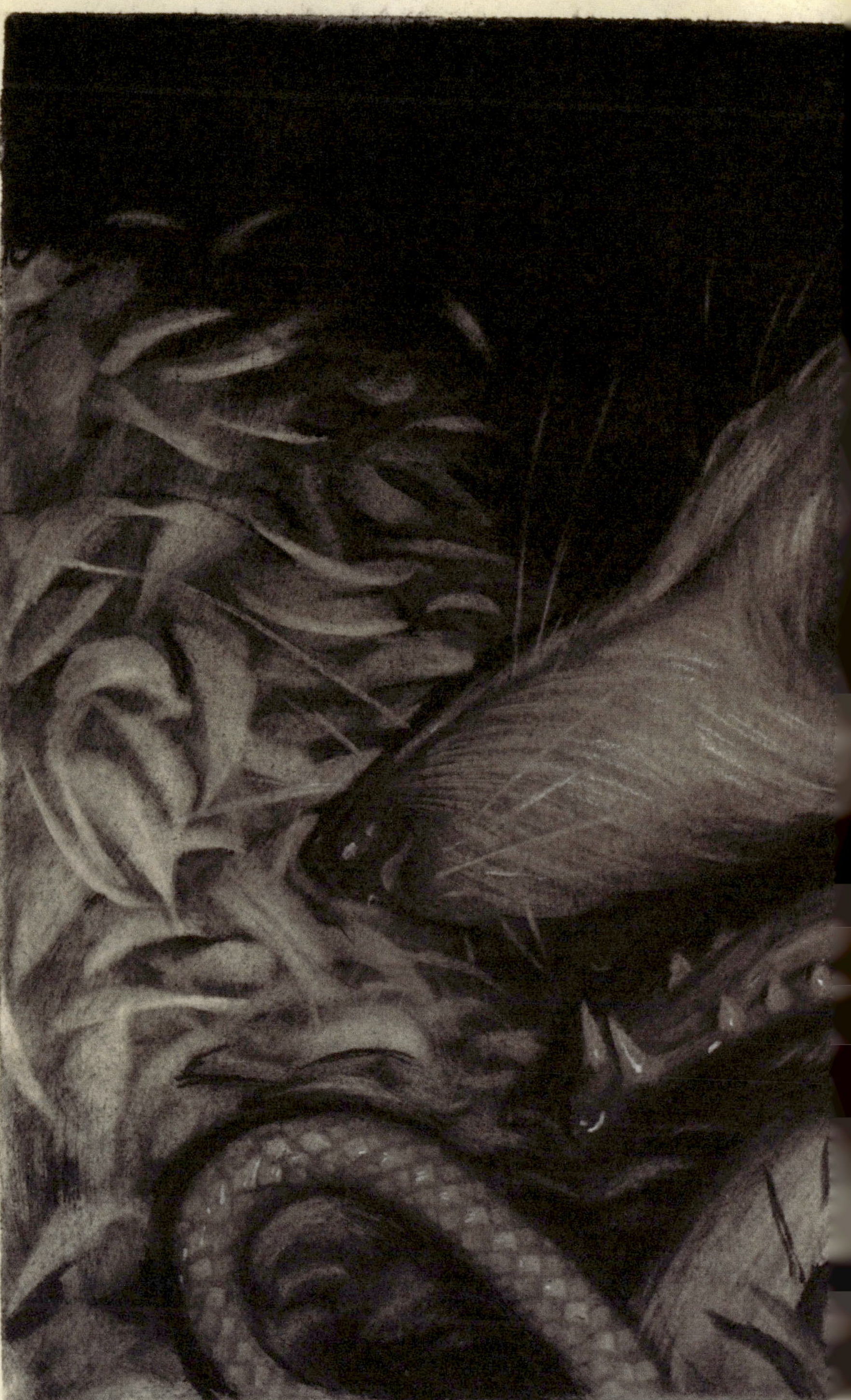

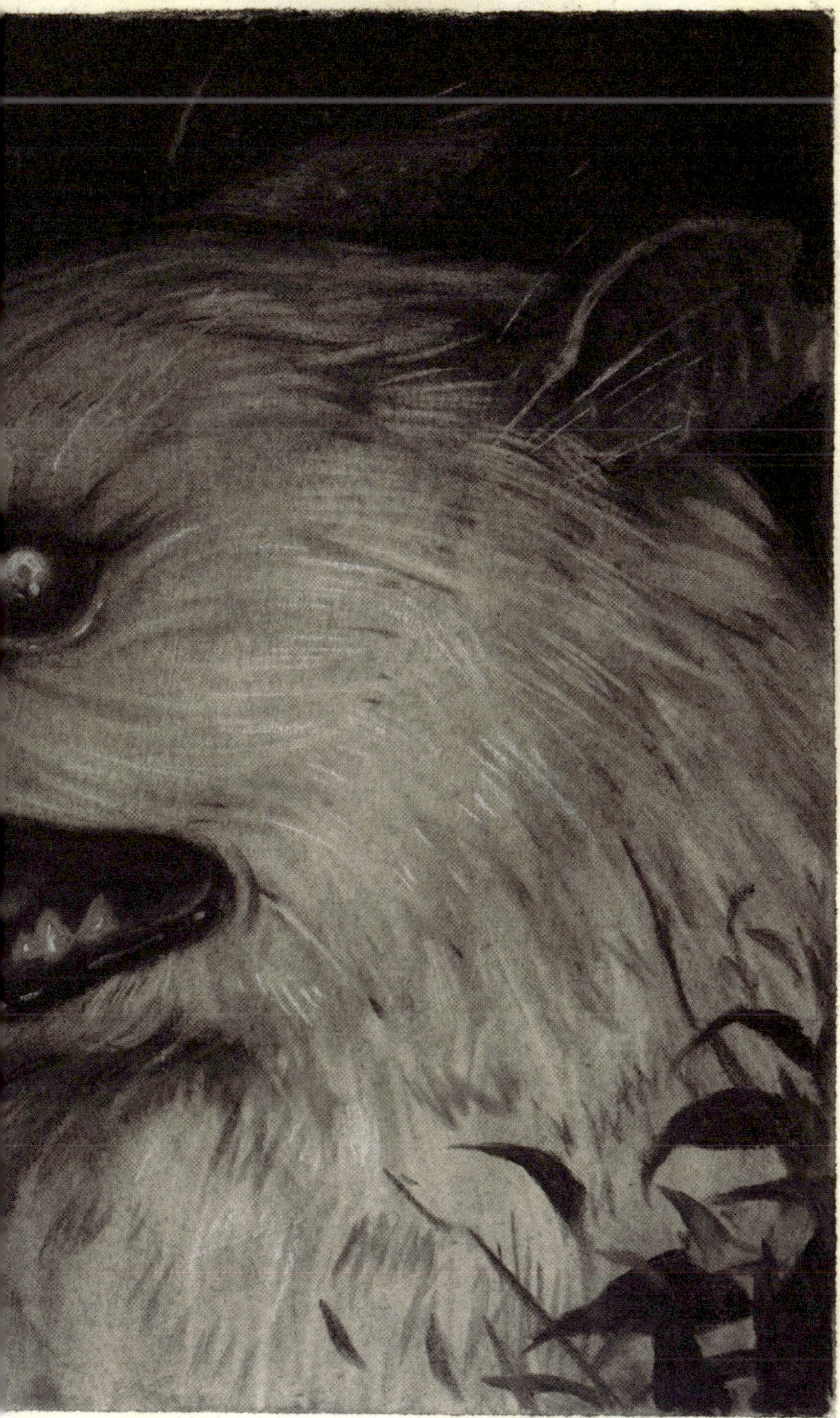

SAM WOLFF CONNELLY

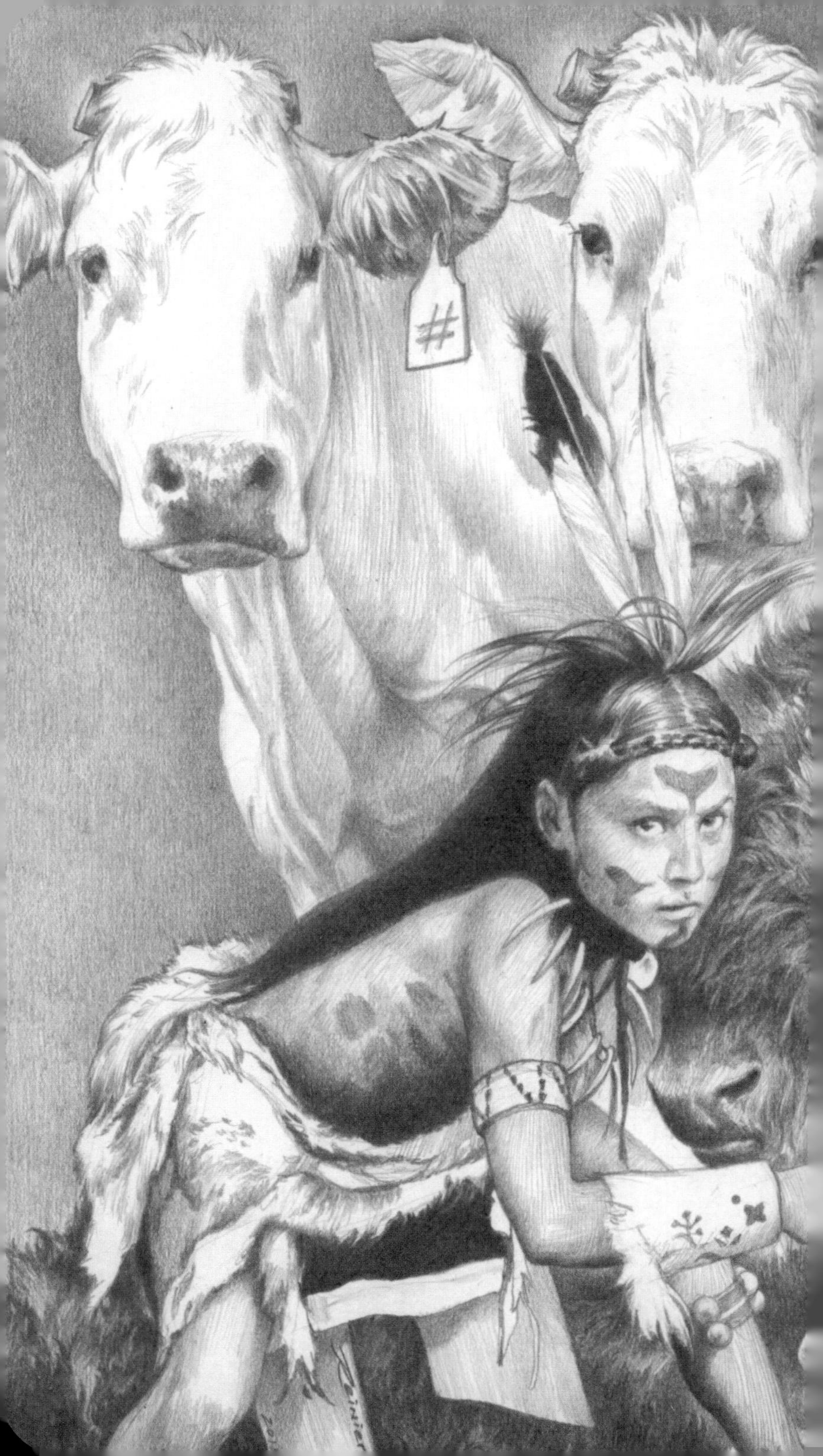

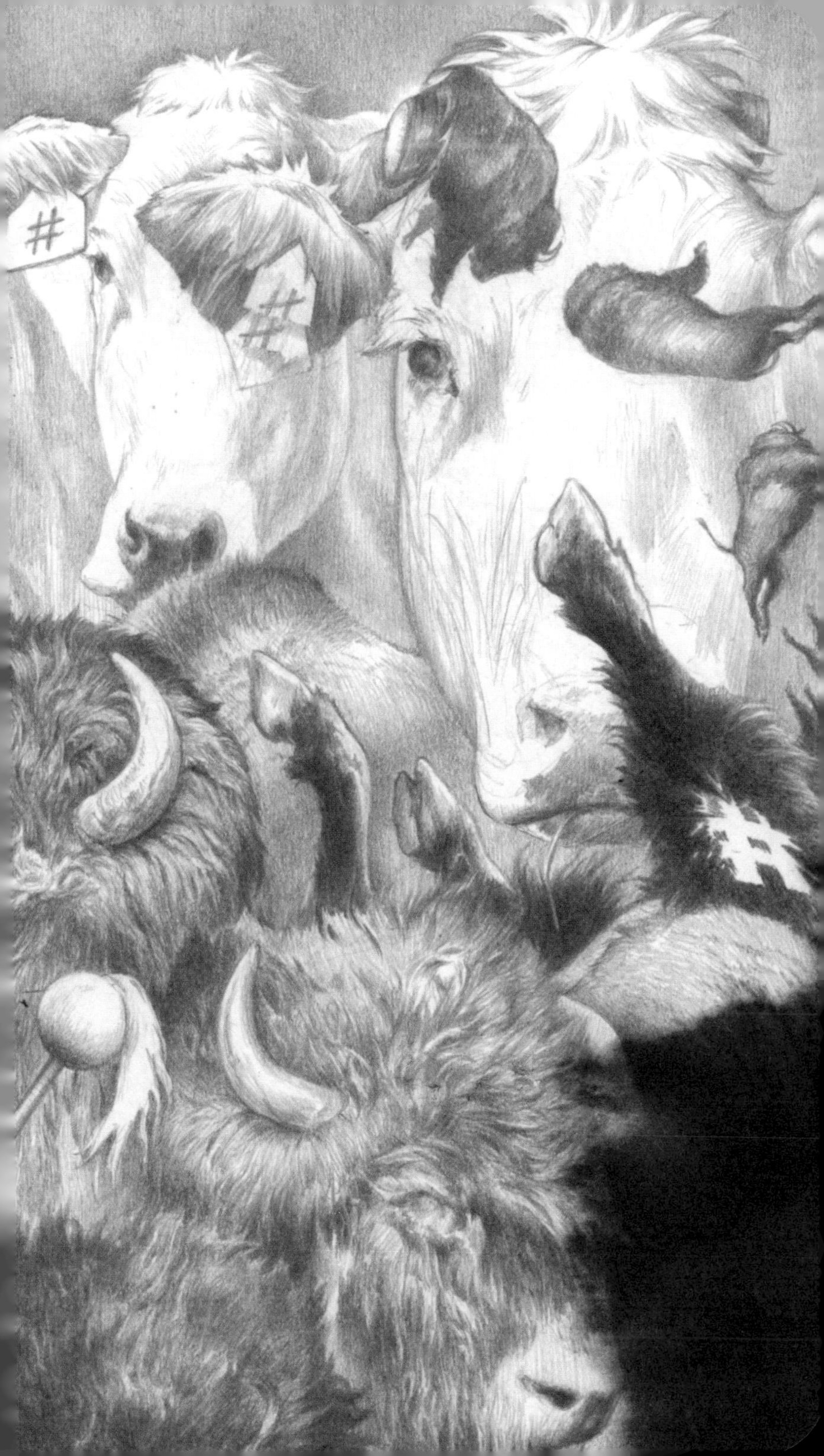

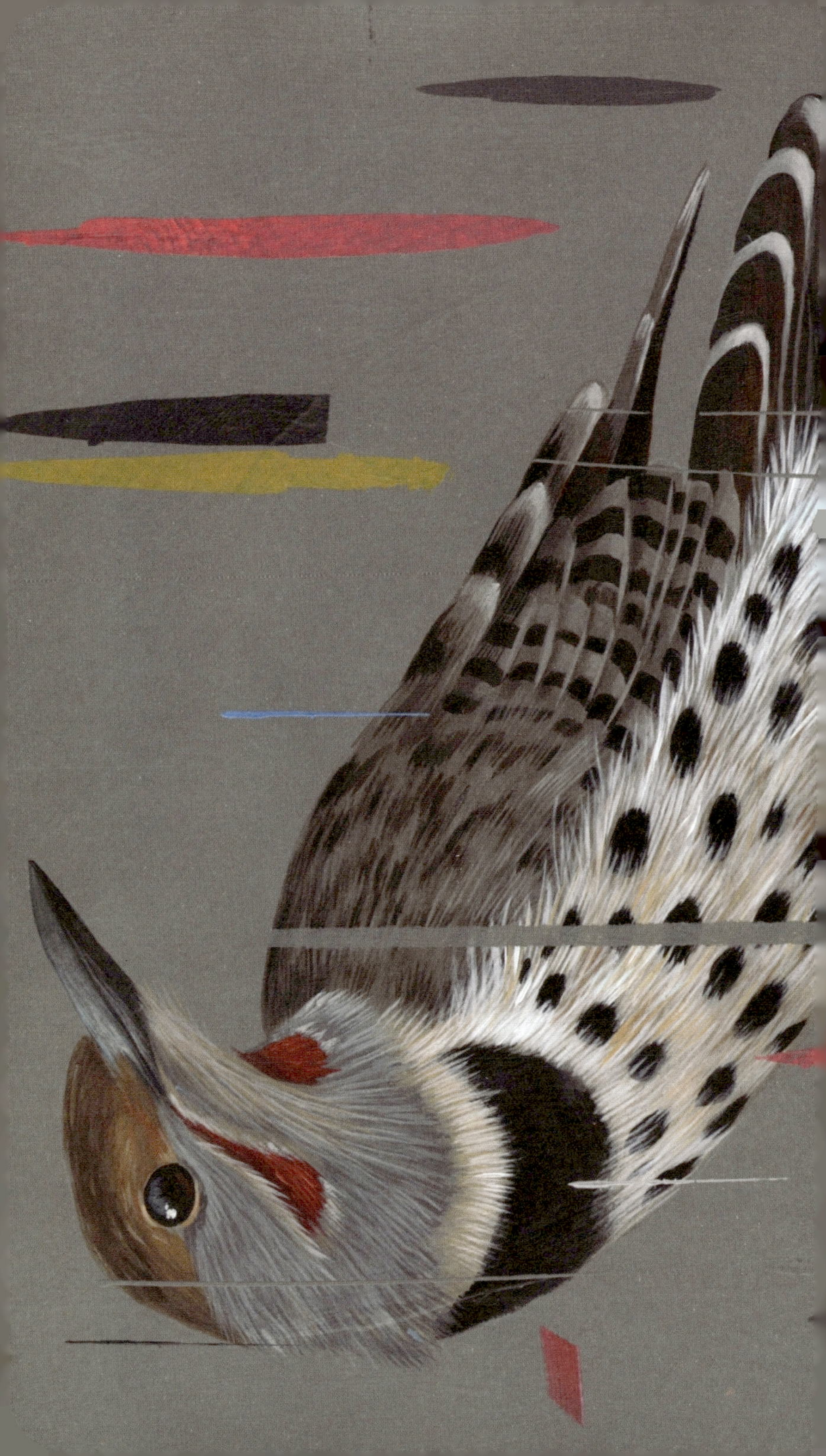

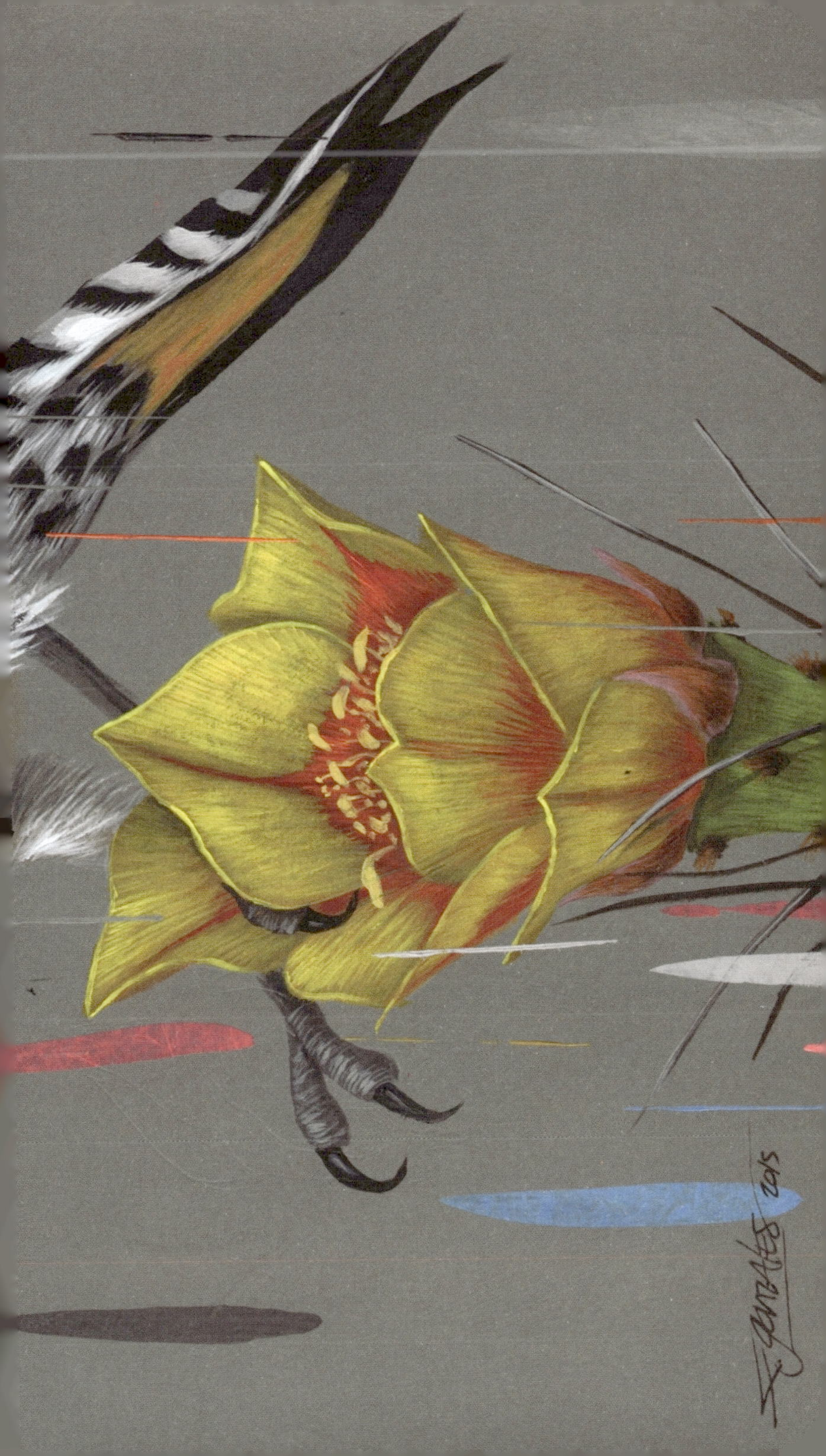

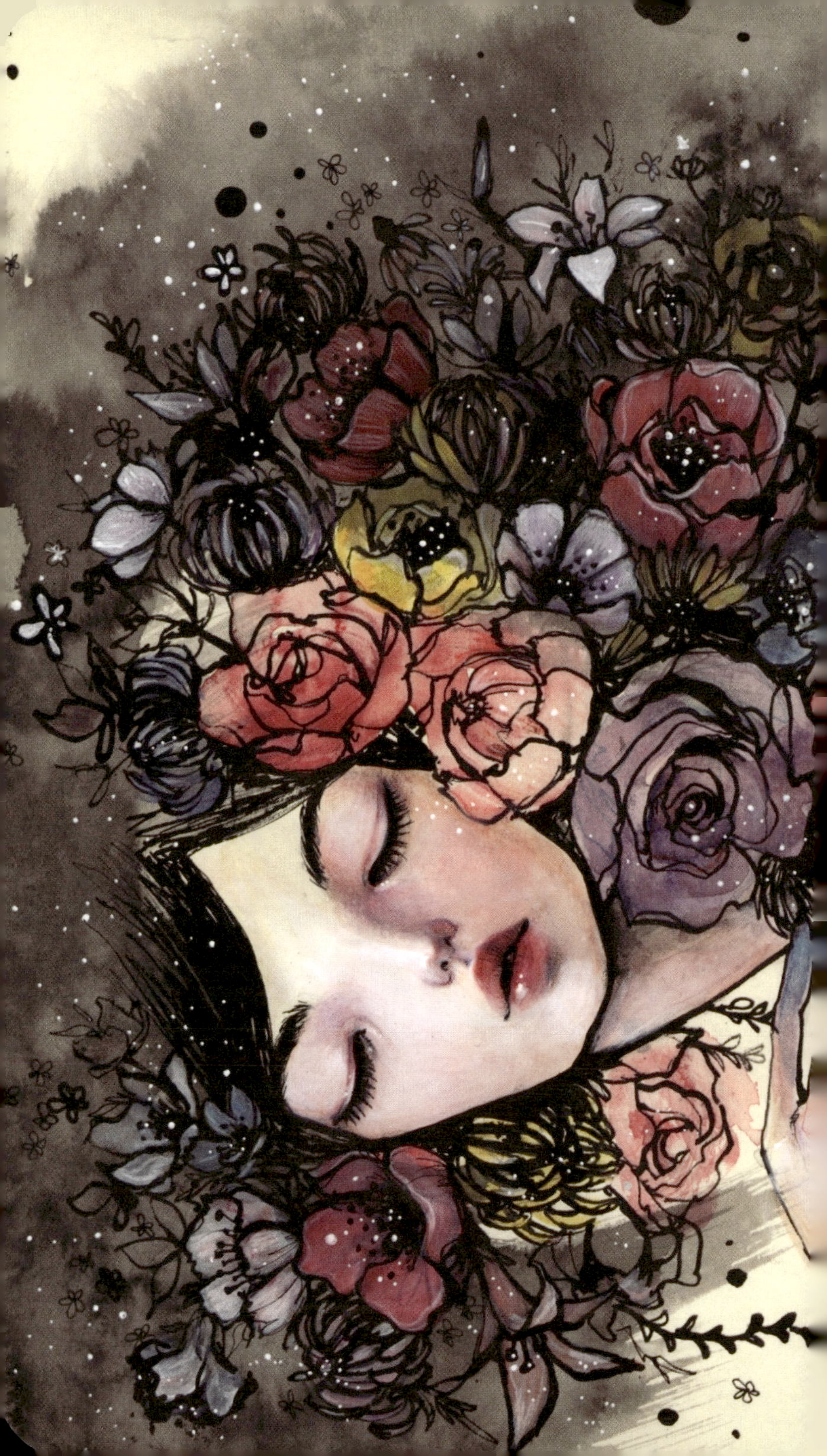

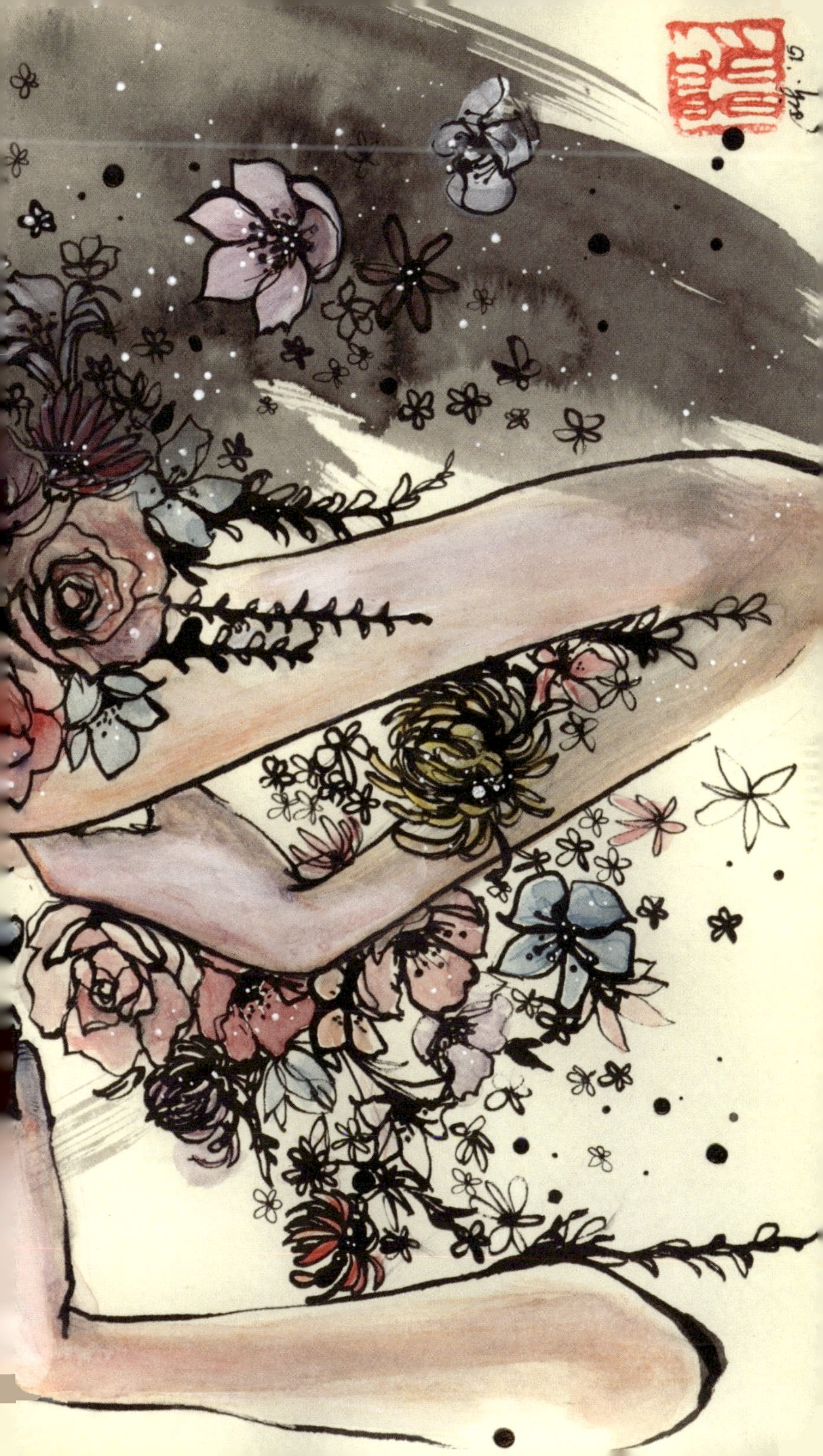

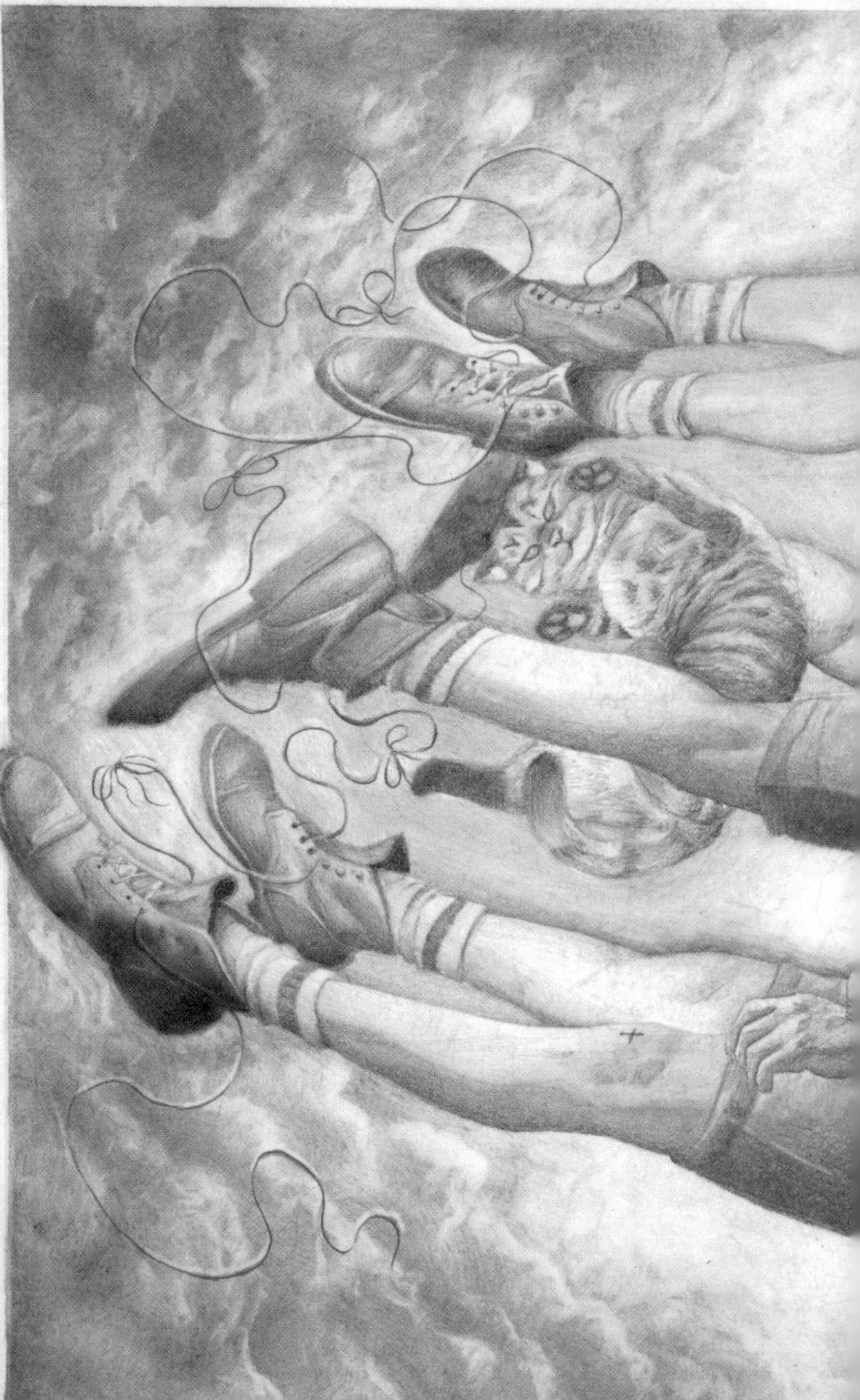

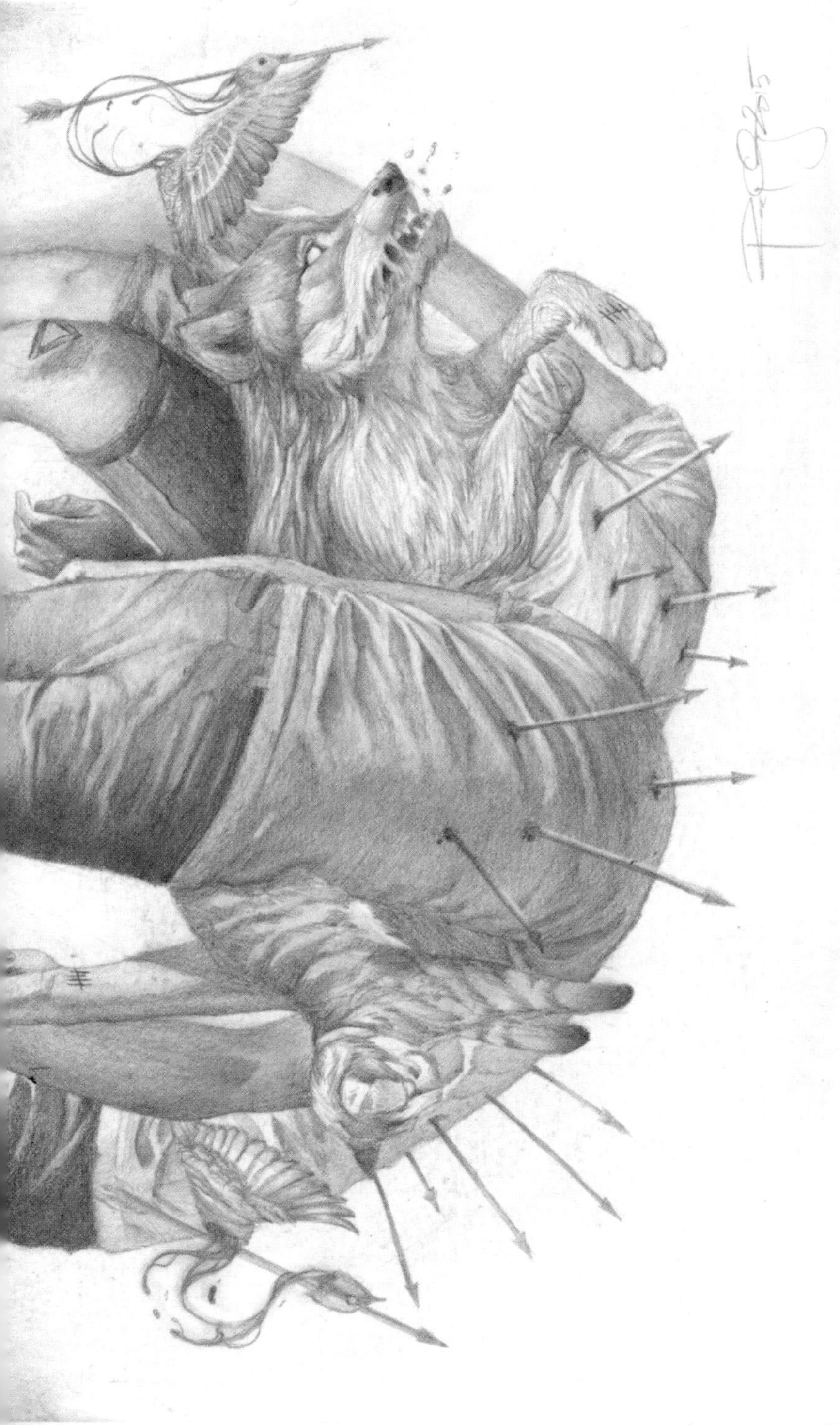

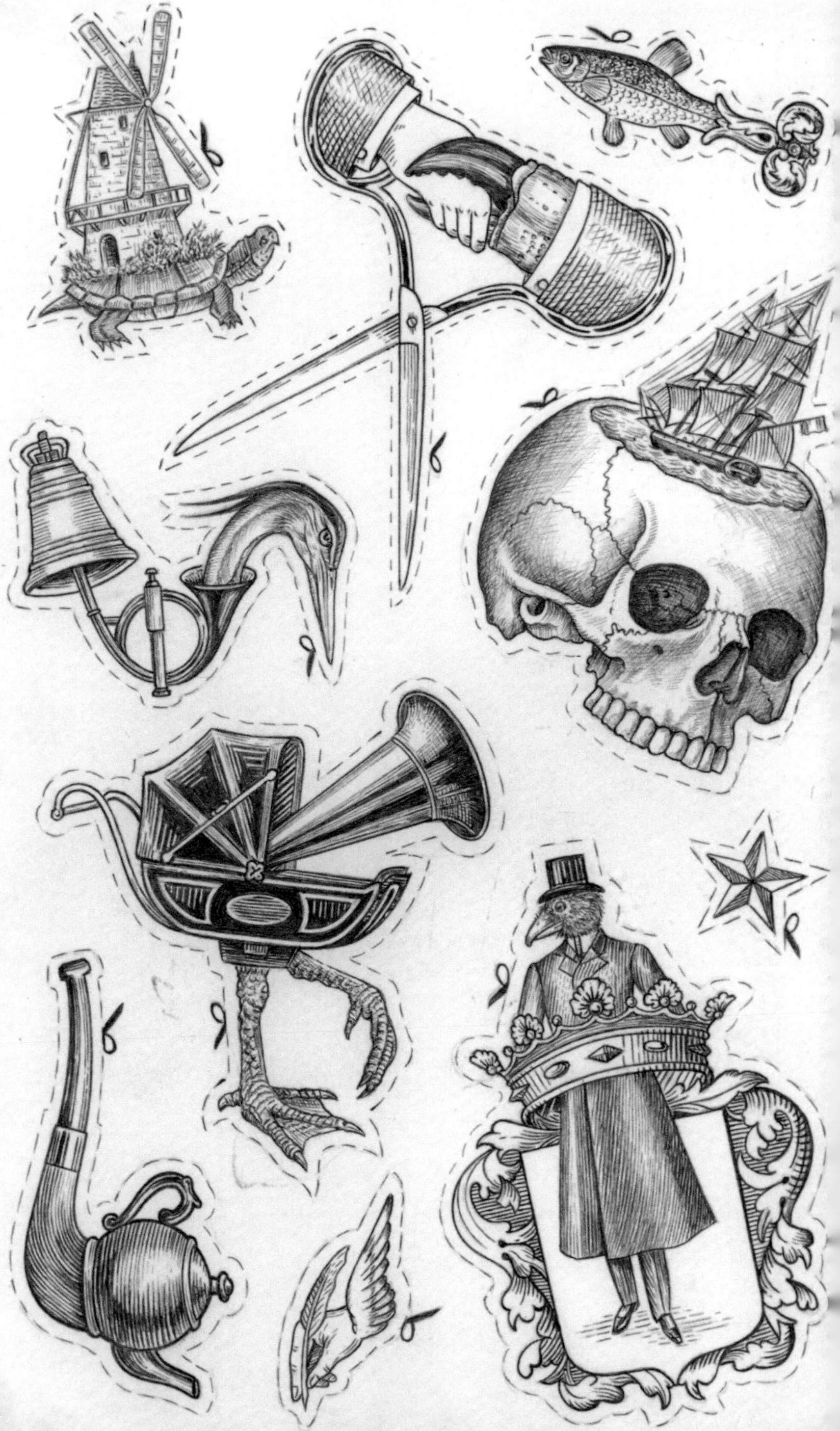

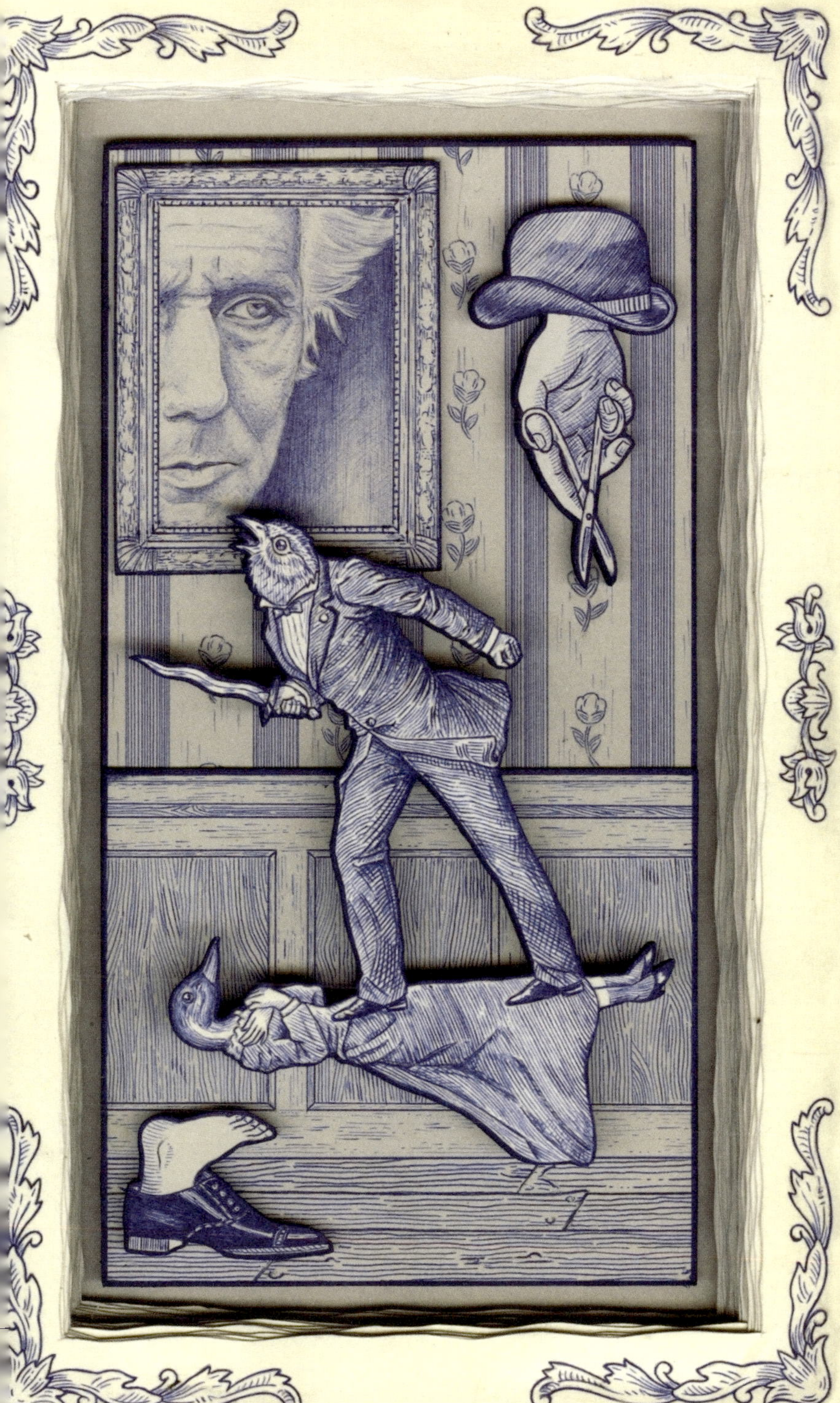

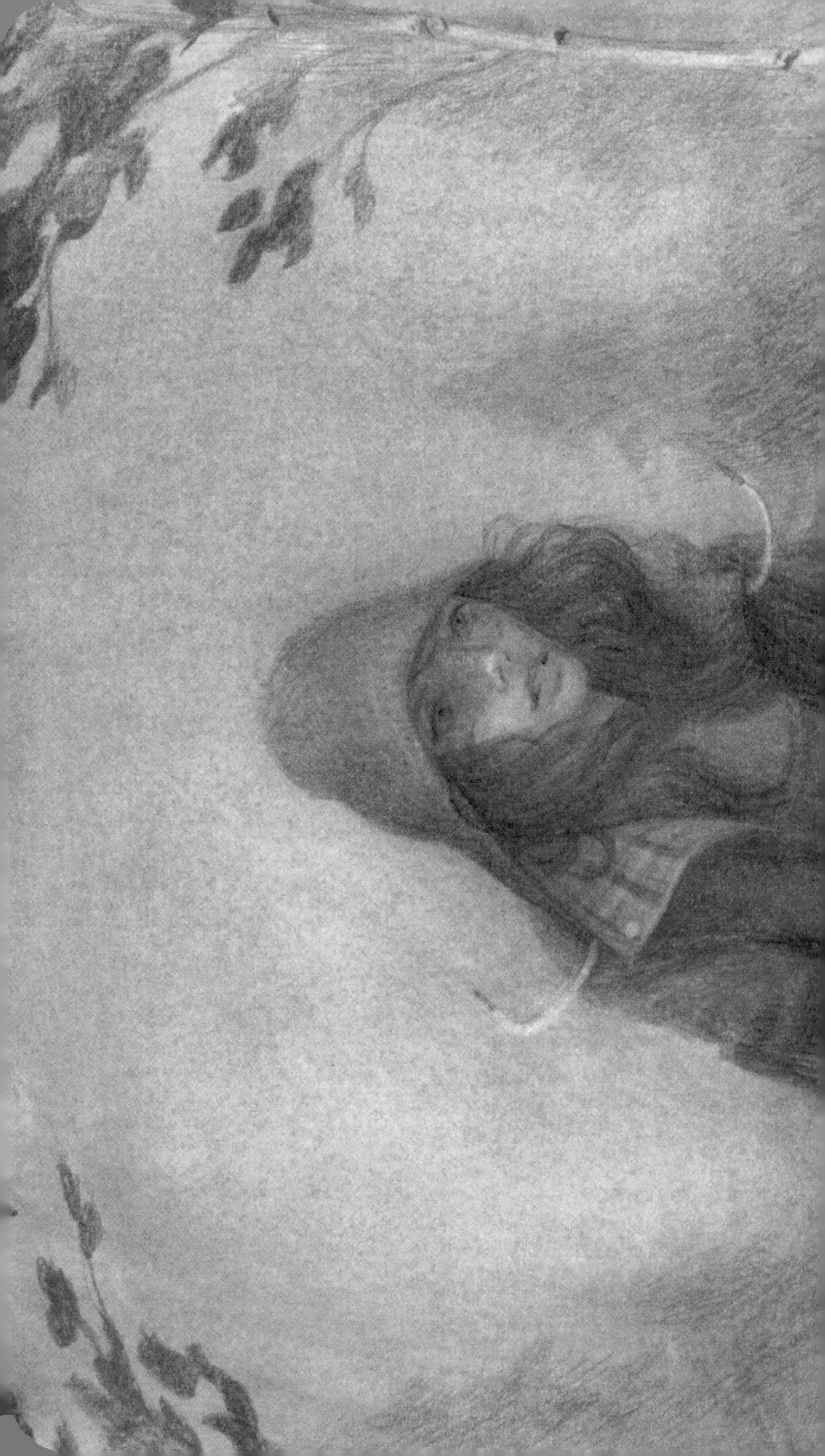

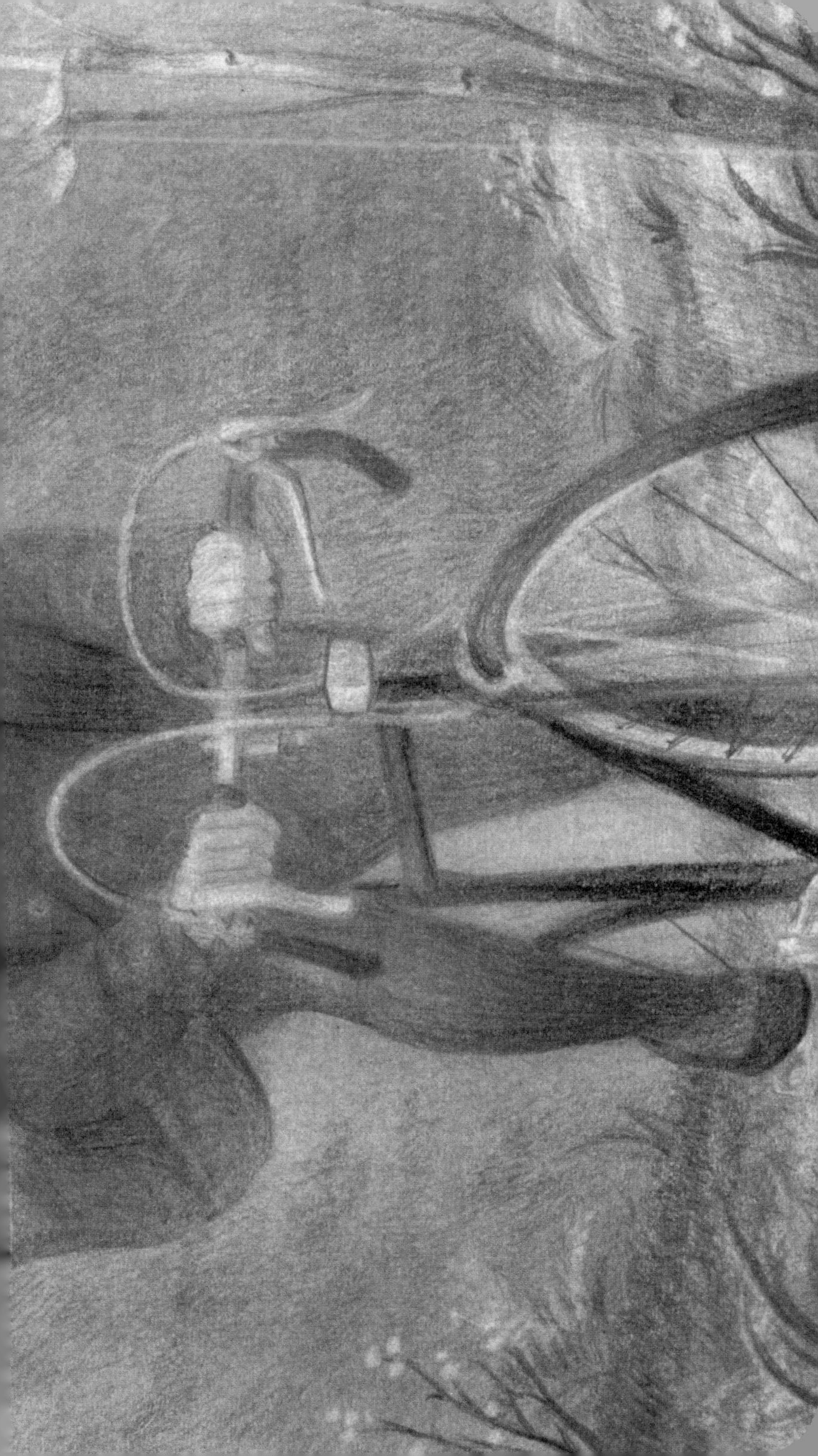

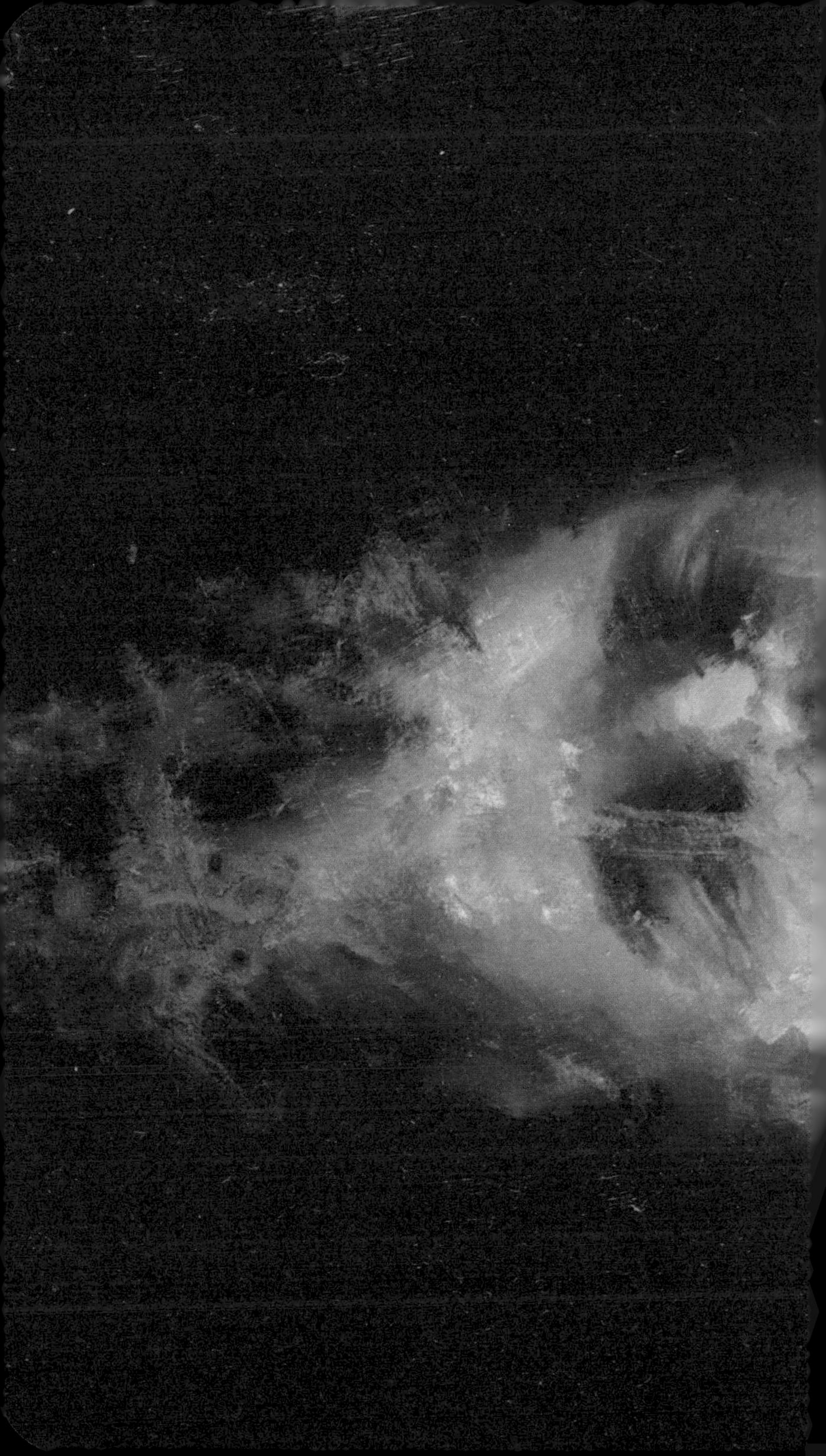

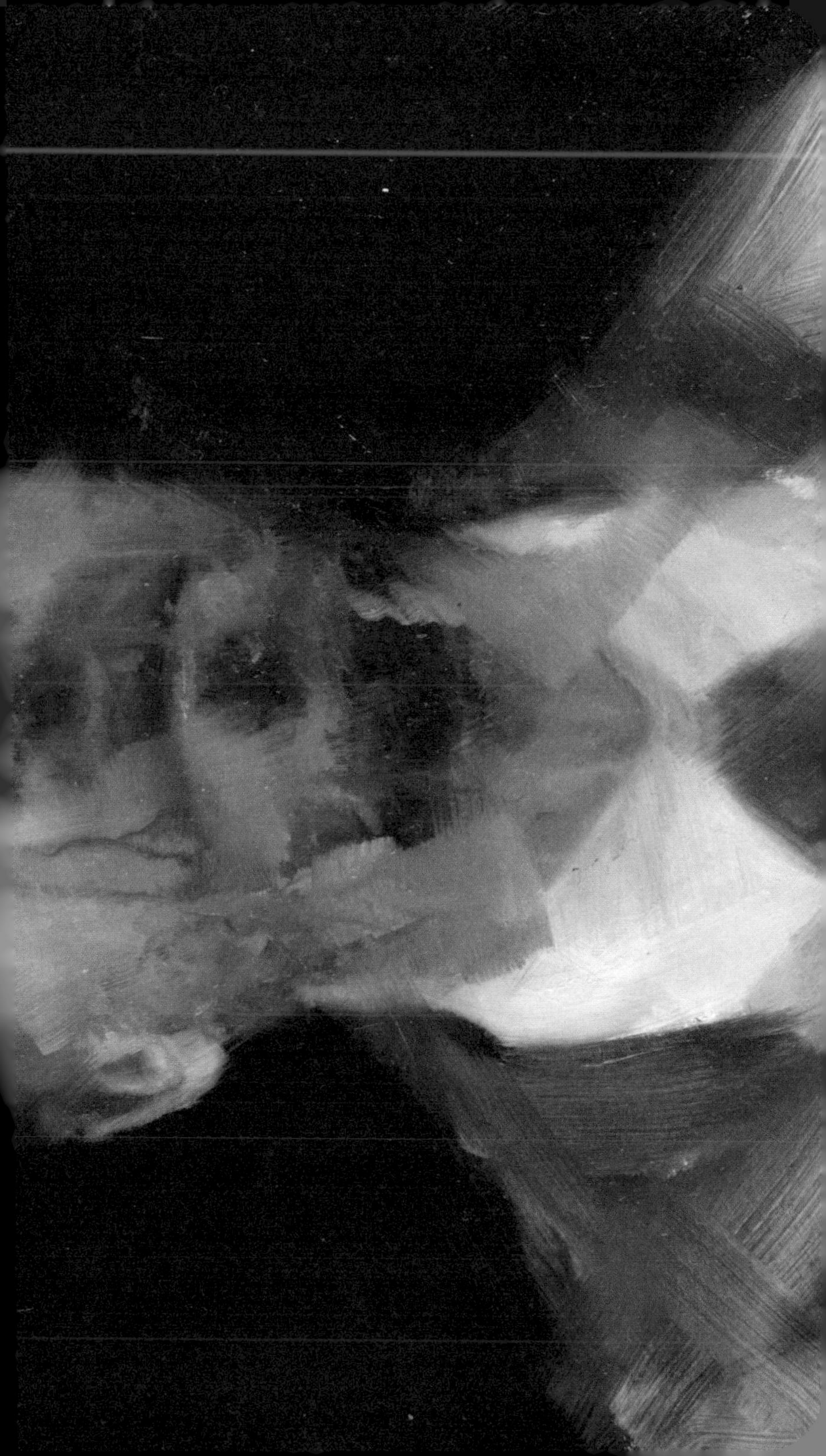

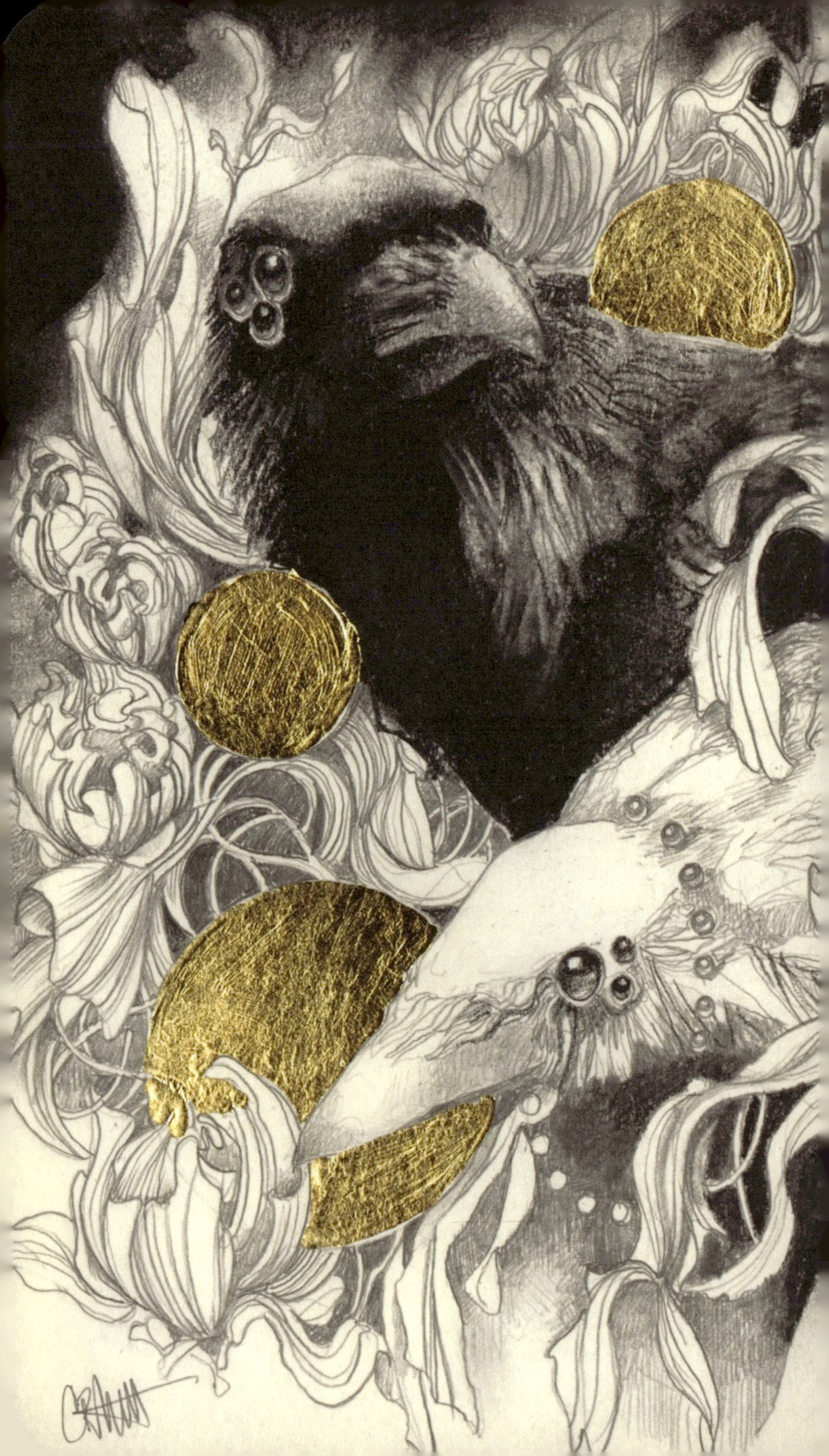

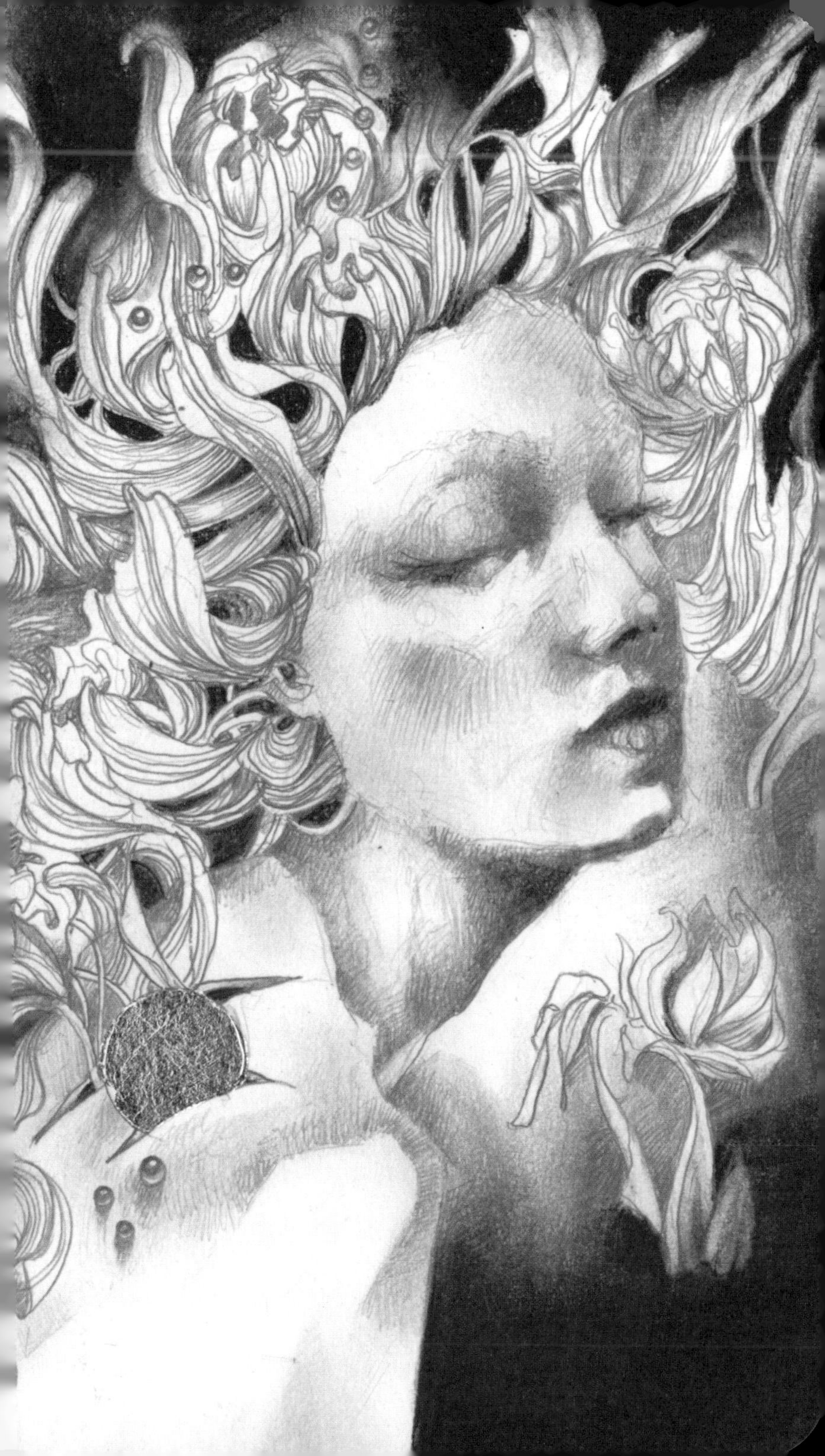

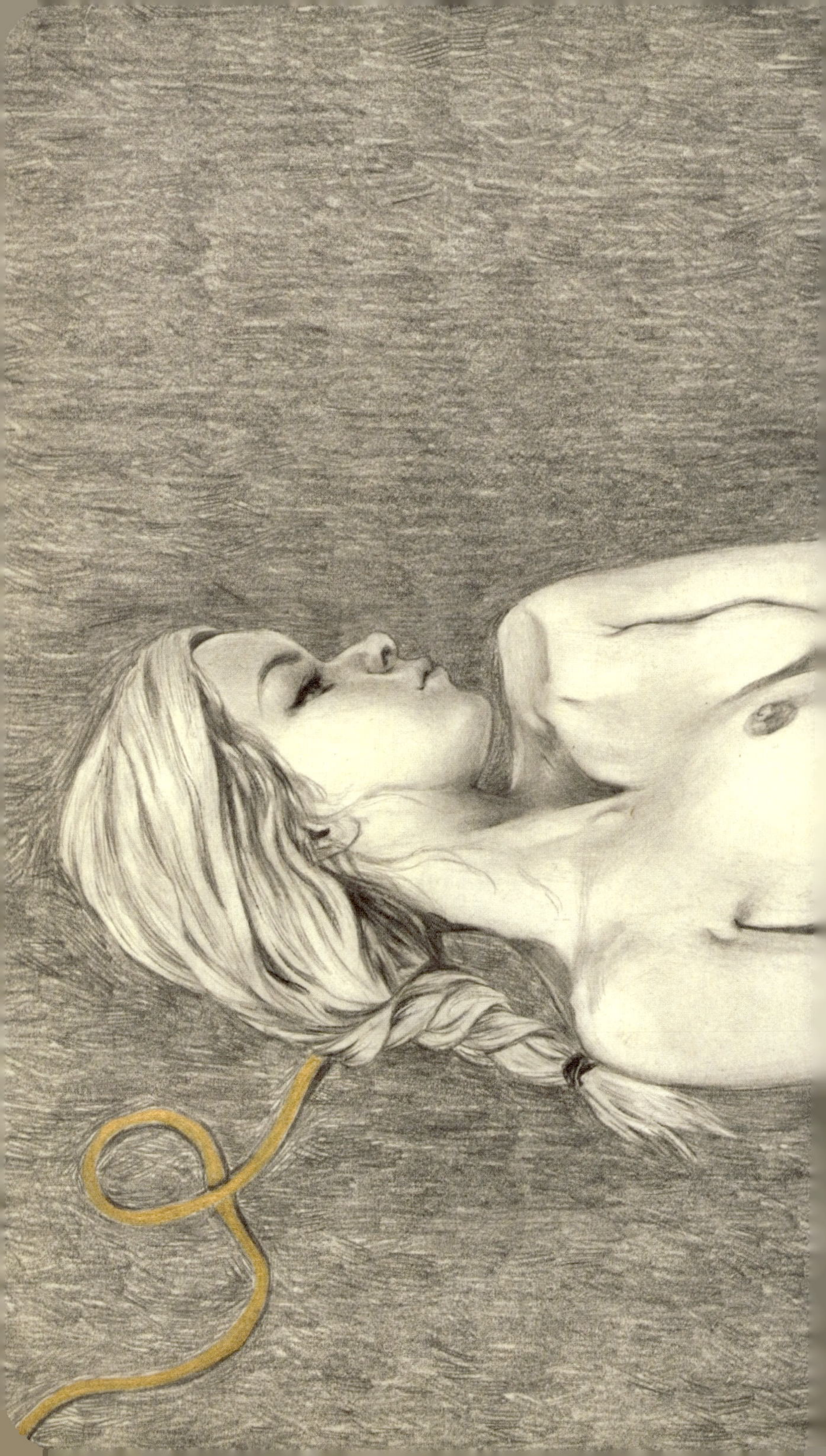

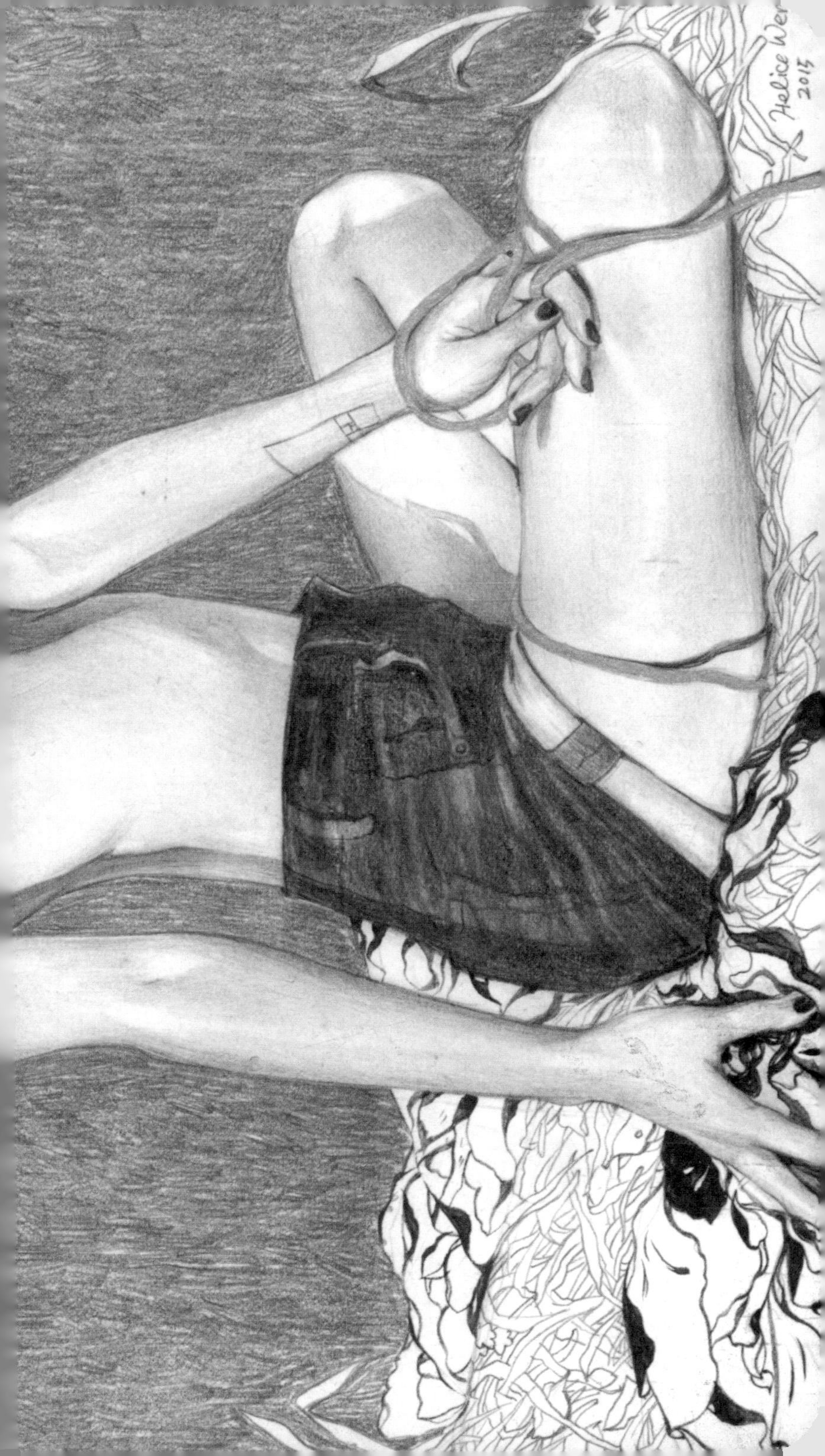

Helice Wer
2015

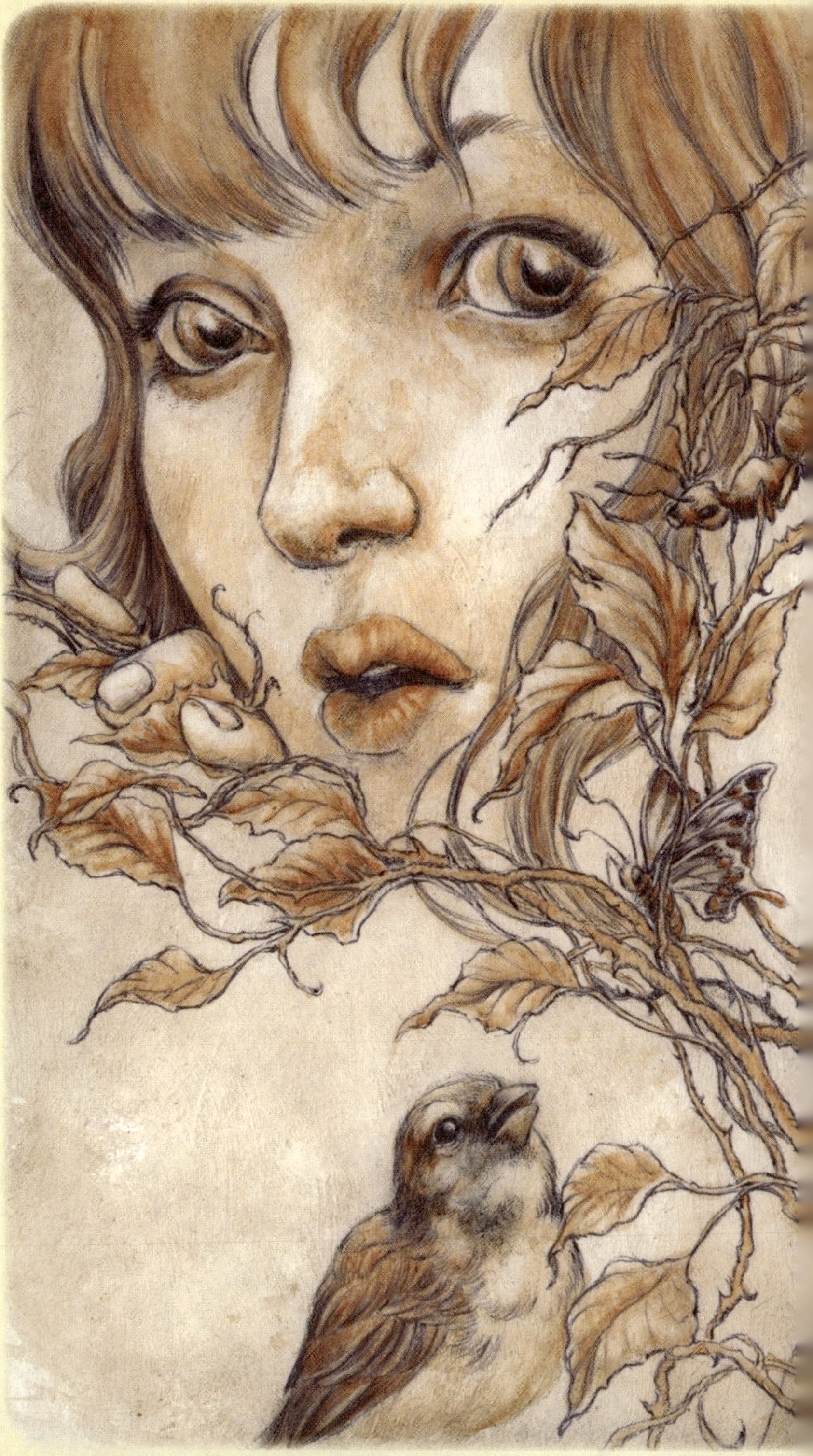

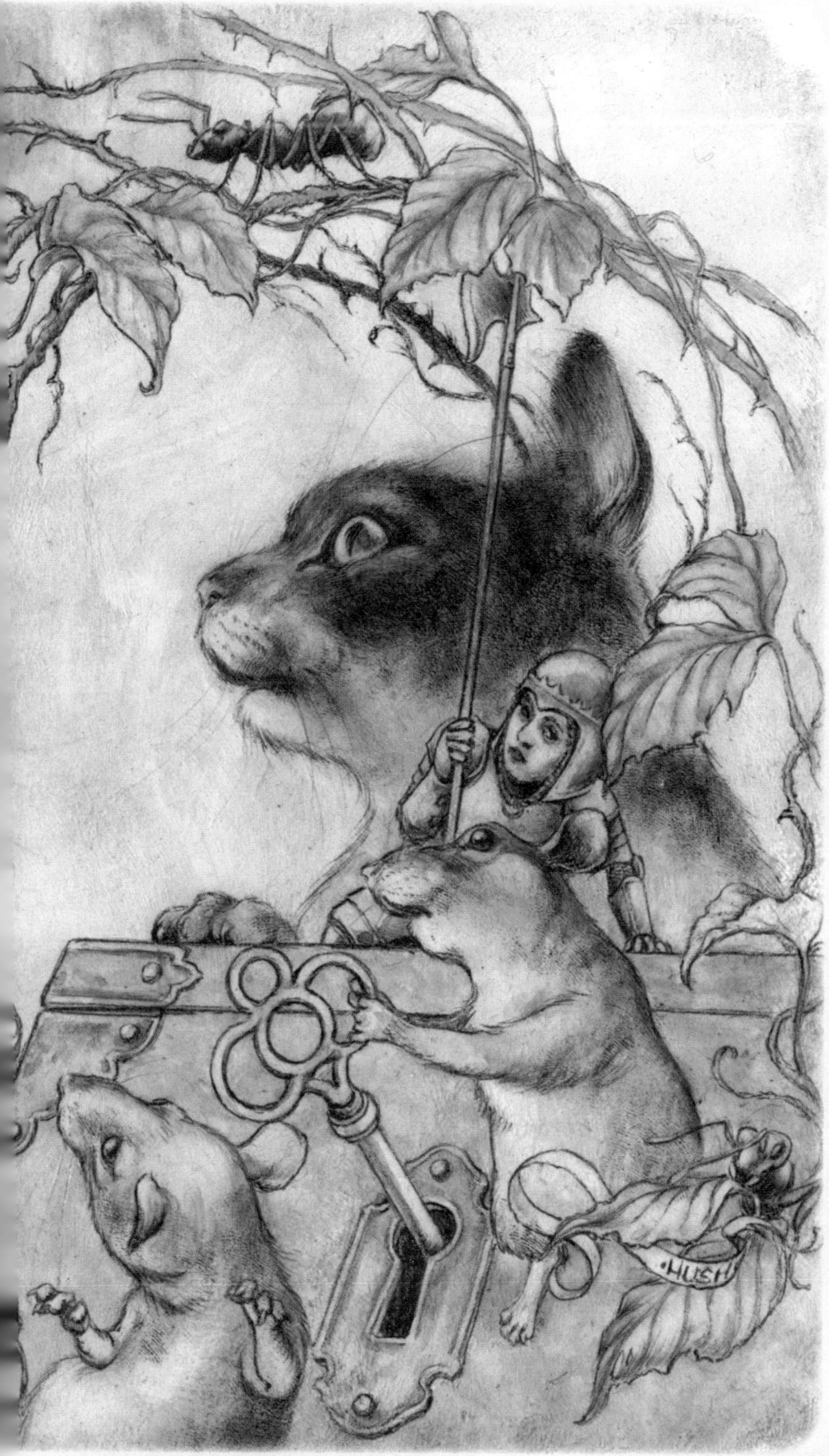
·HUSH

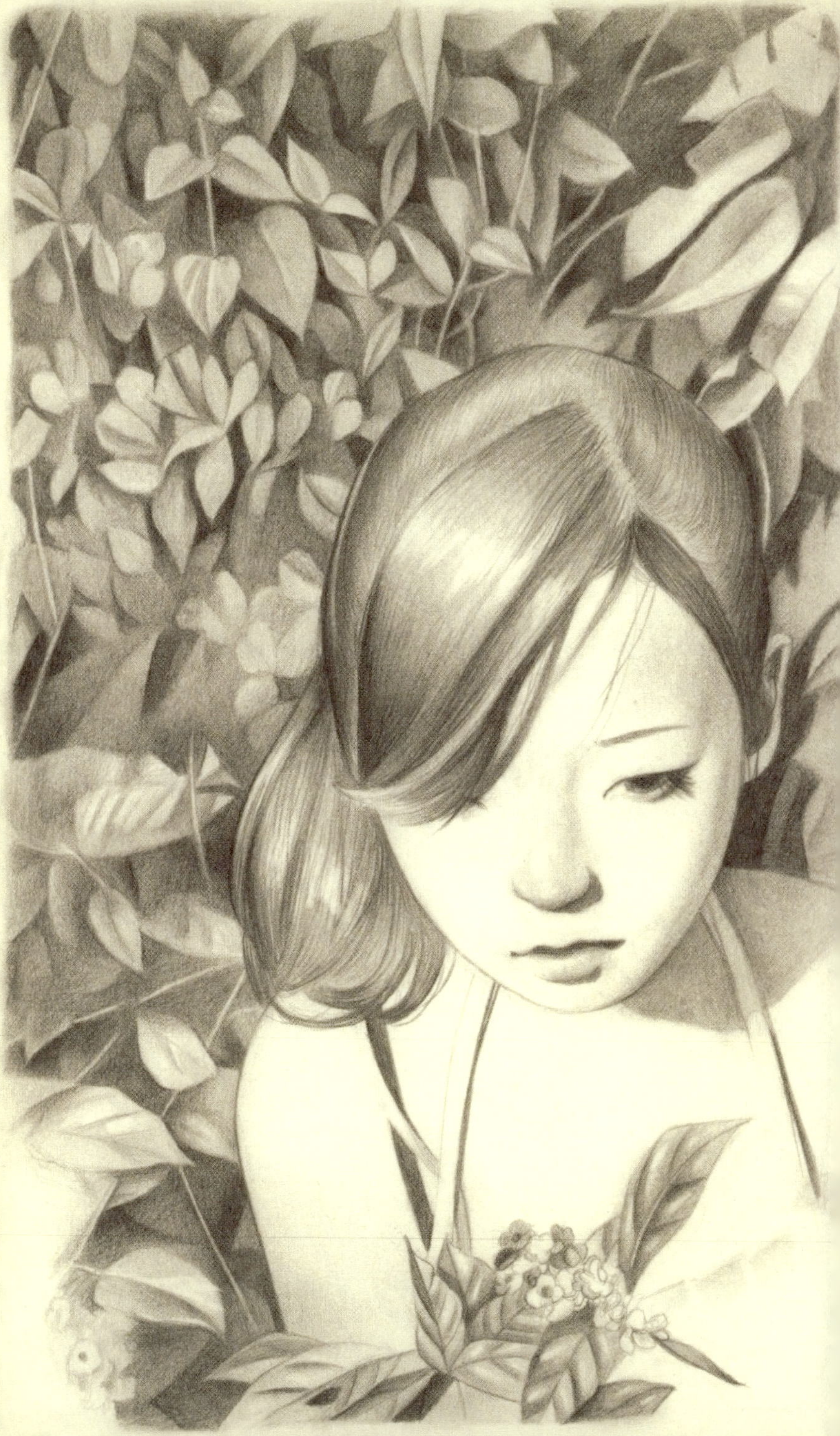

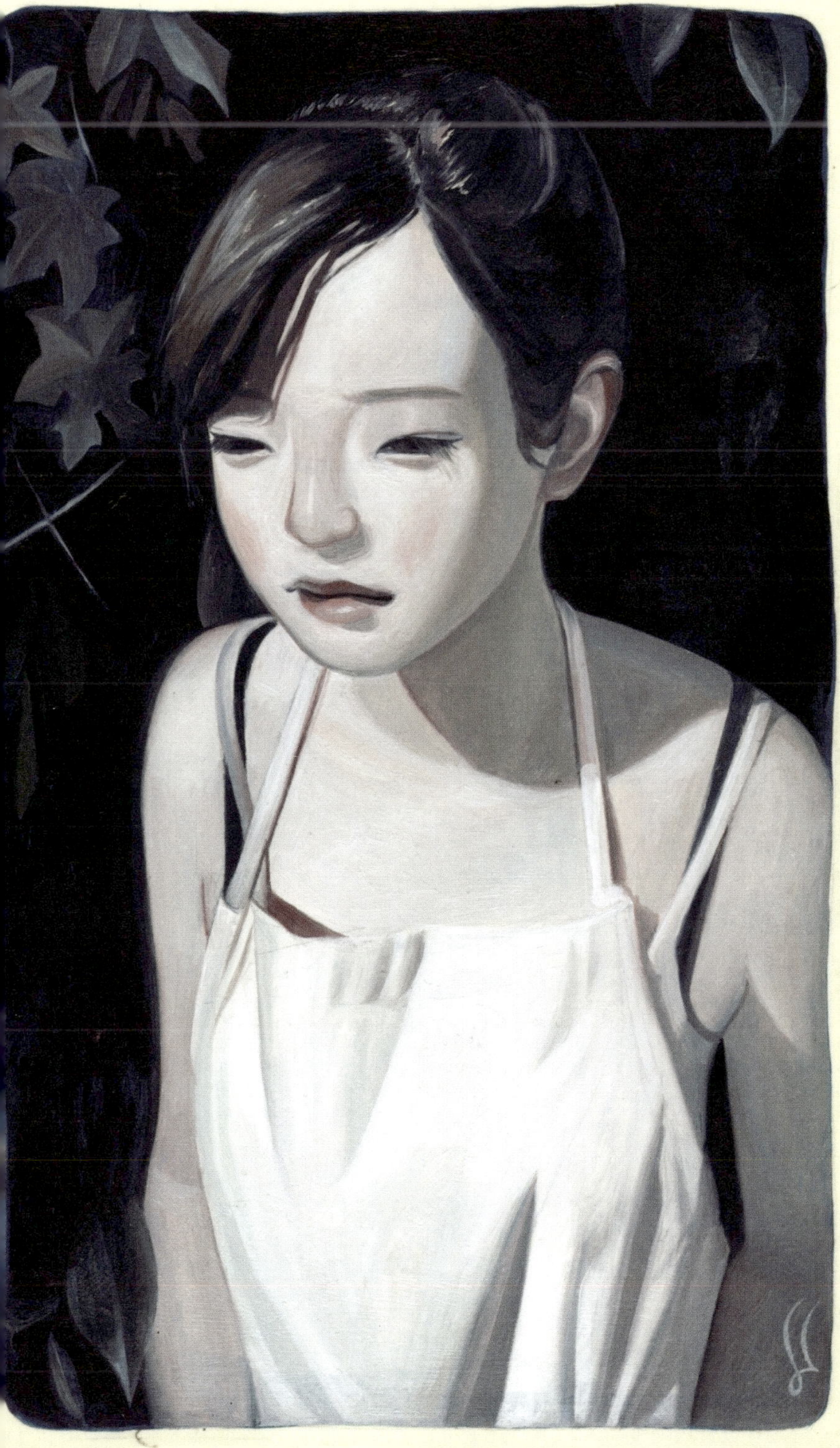

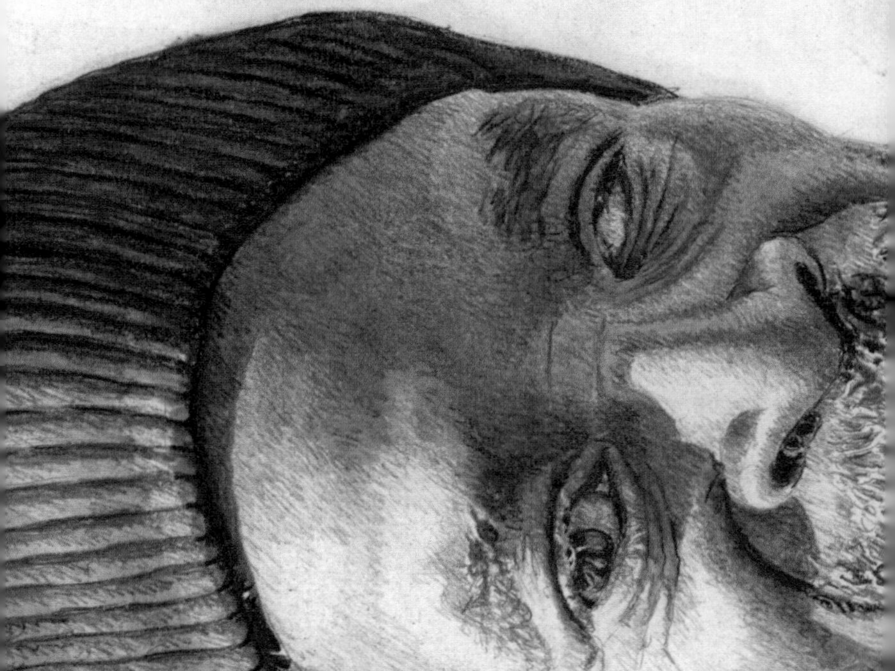

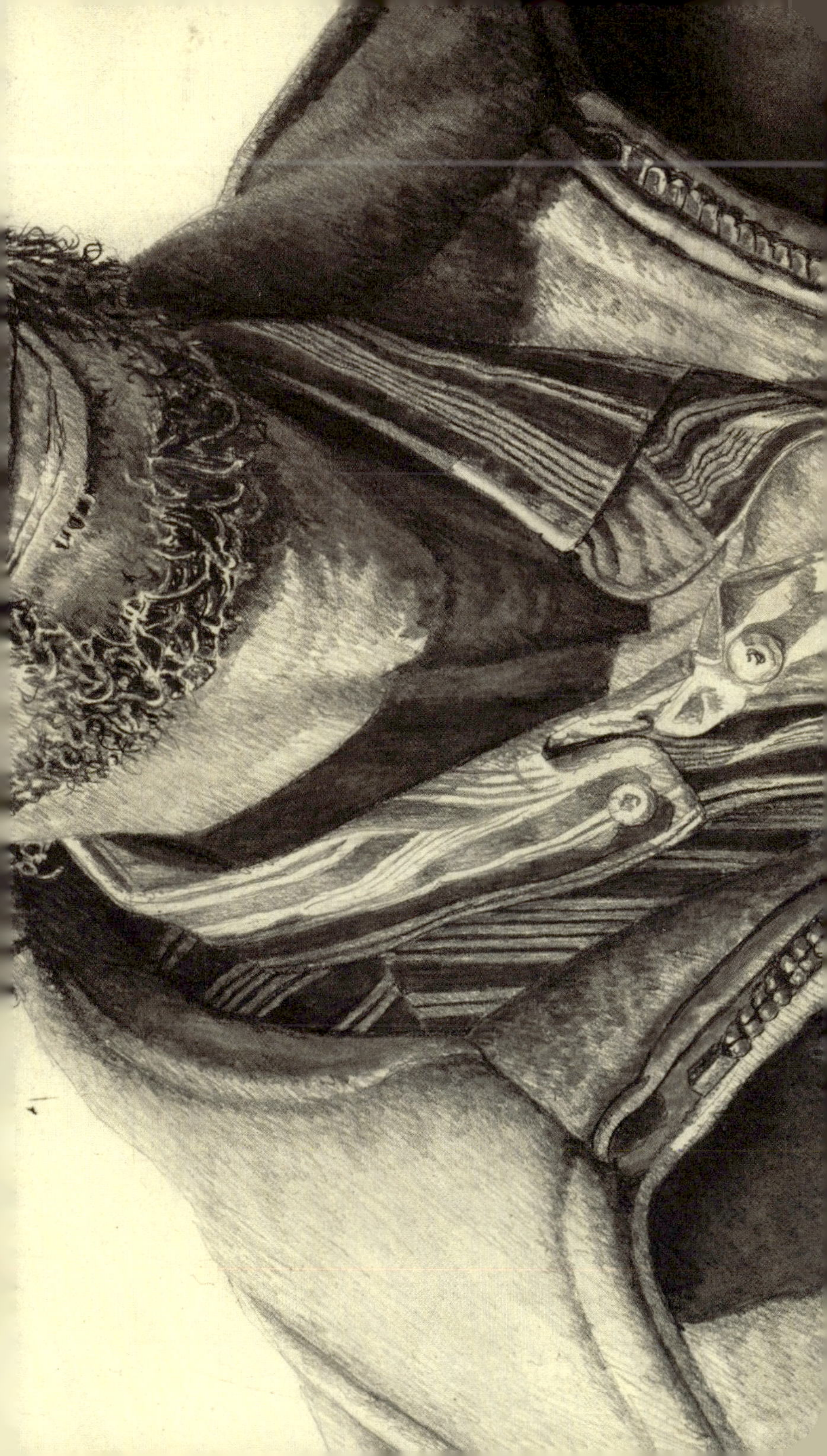

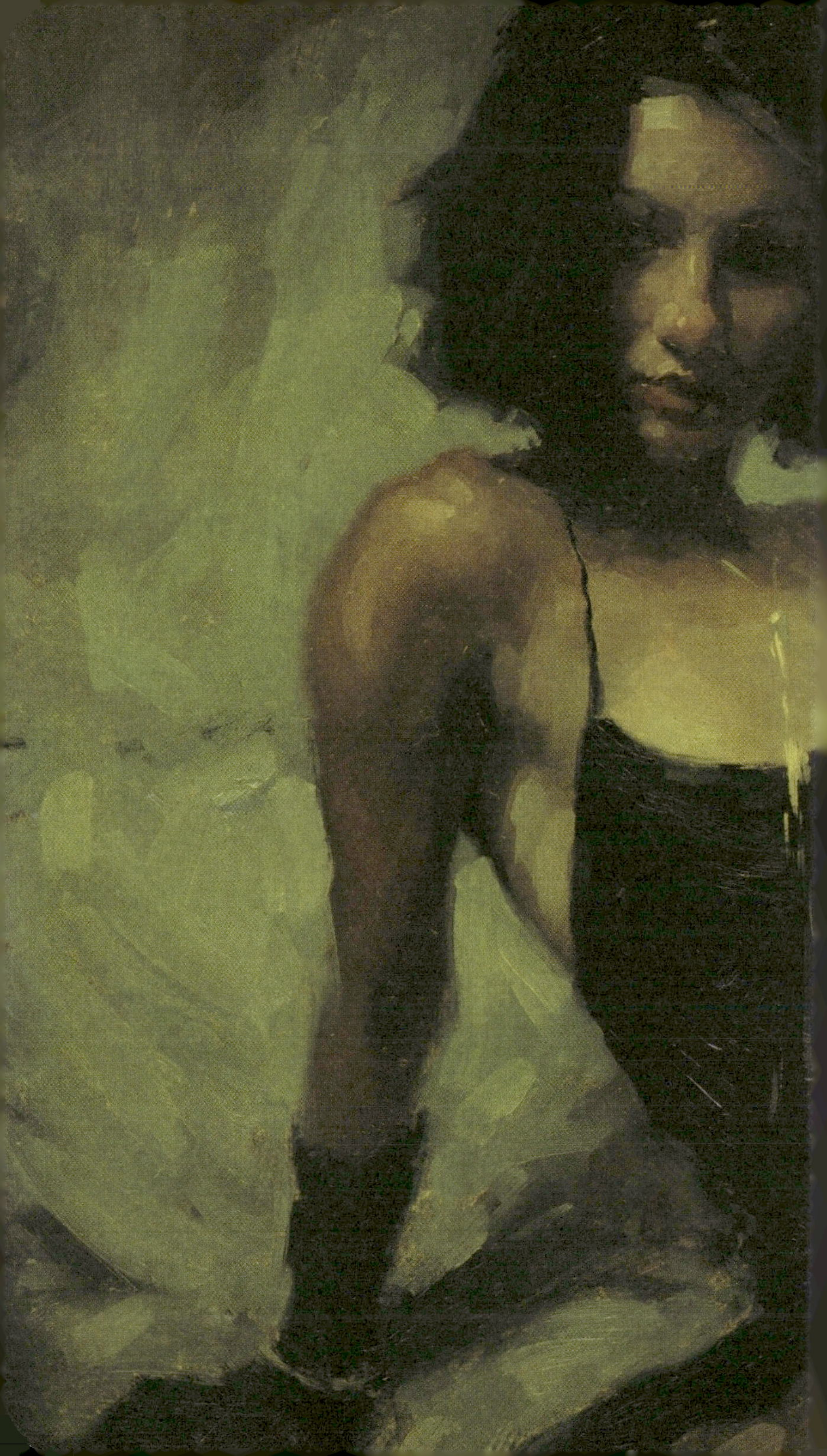

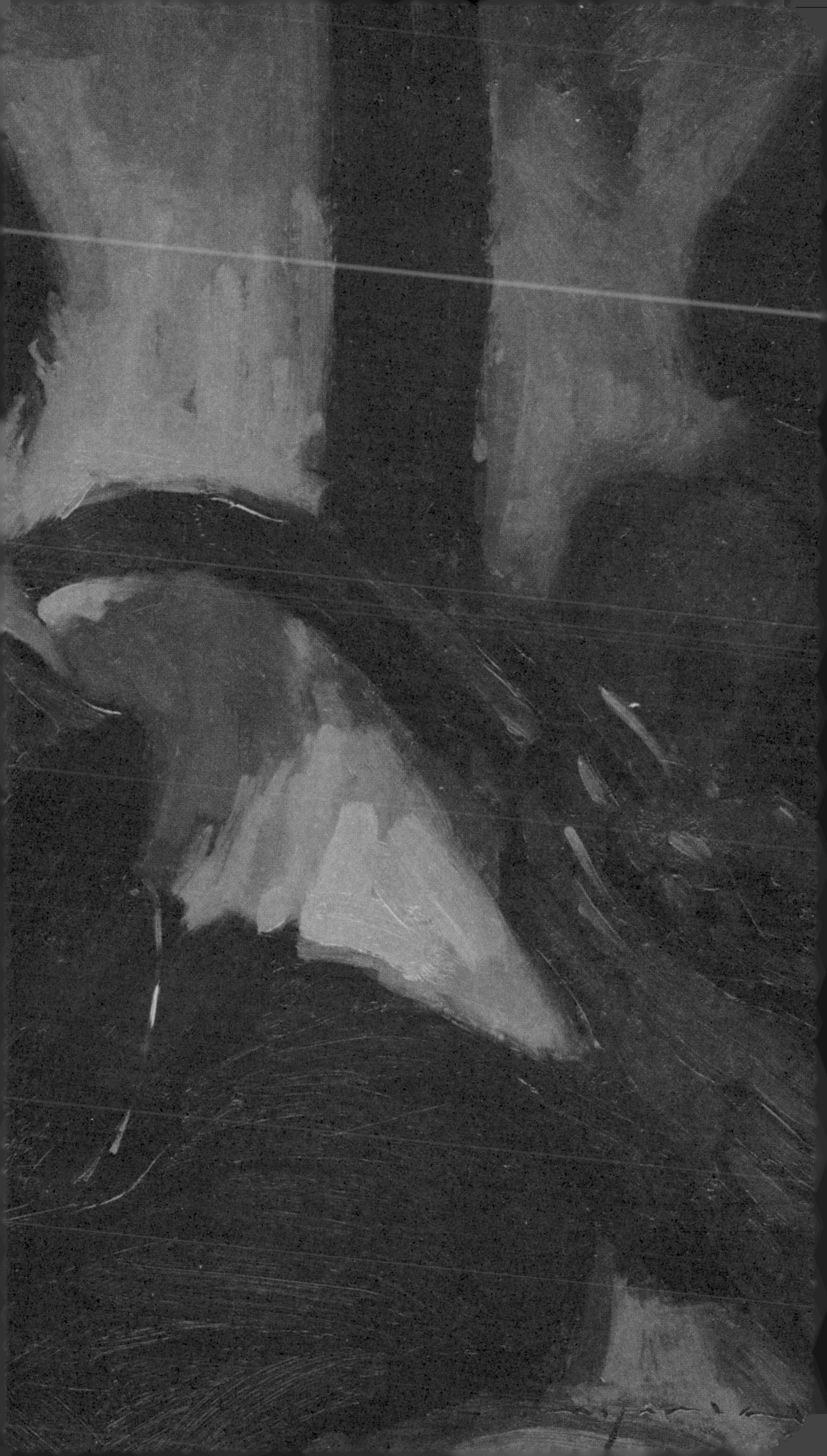

INDEX *of* ARTISTS

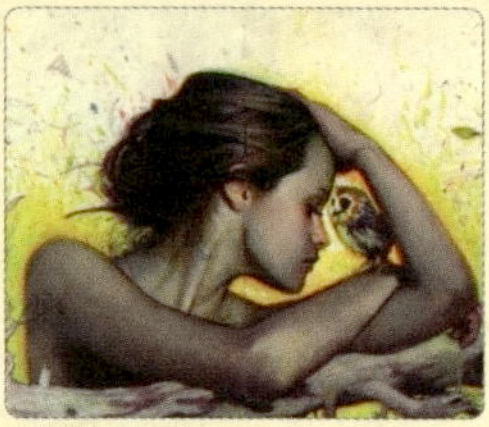

RODRIGO LUFF
Phantom
Pencil, color pencil, pastel, oil

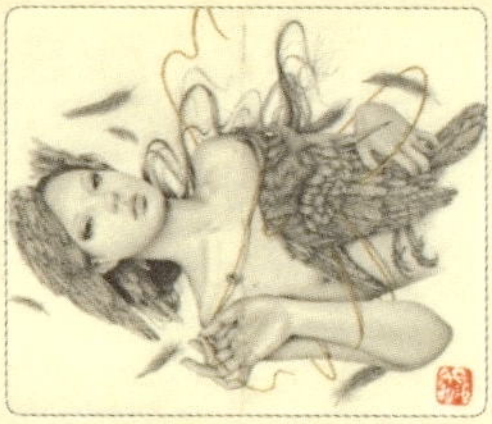

OZABU
Hedochi
Graphite and acrylic

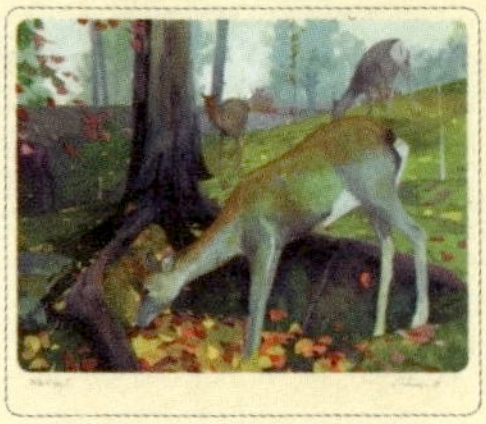

ANDREW HEM
Make It Rain
Acryla-gouache

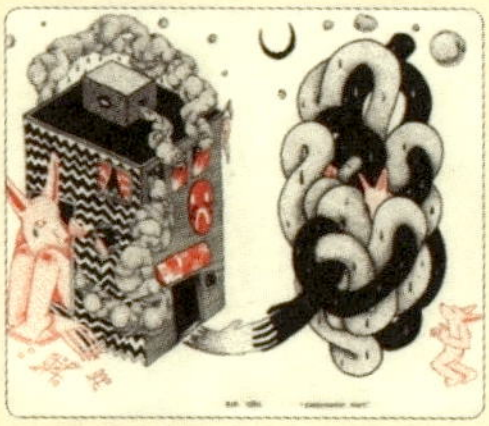

CANNON DILL
Impermanent Knot
Pen and ink

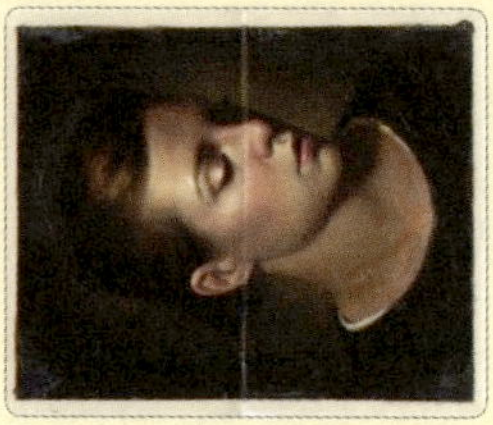

FREDRIK RATTZEN
Study of T
Oil

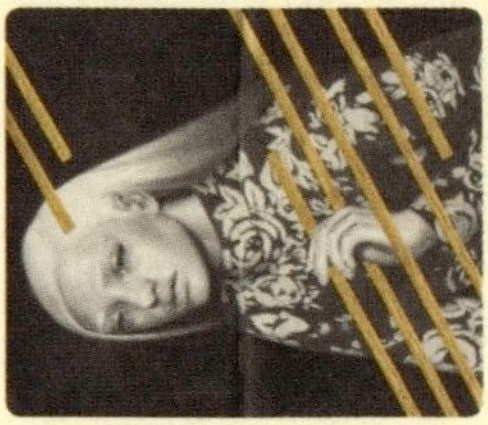

TRAN NGUYEN
A Linear Chasm
Acrylic and graphite

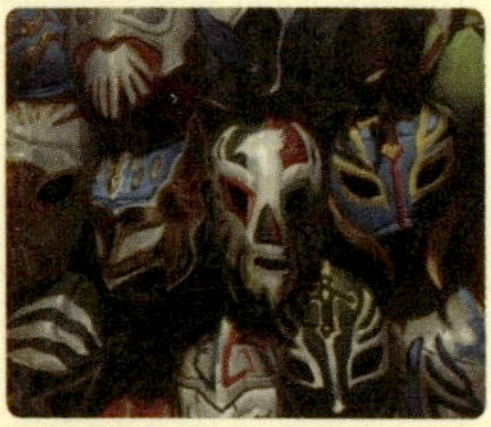

ZACH OLDENKAMP
Wall of Heroes
Oil

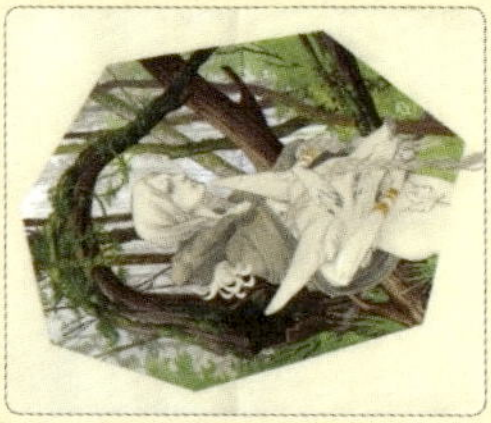

J.A.W. COOPER
Prowl
Gouache and graphite

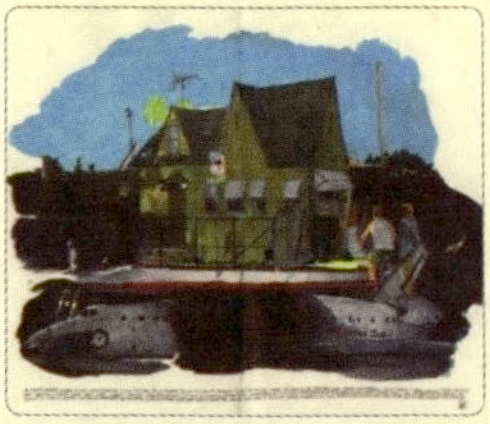

EDWIN USHIRO
Wesley, Higuera and Endeavor
Ballpoint pen and ink

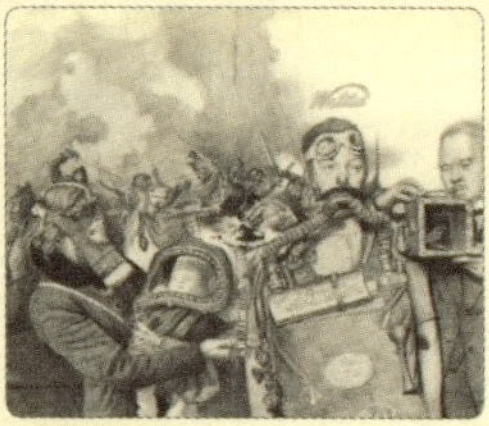

ADAM CALDWELL
Walita
Graphite

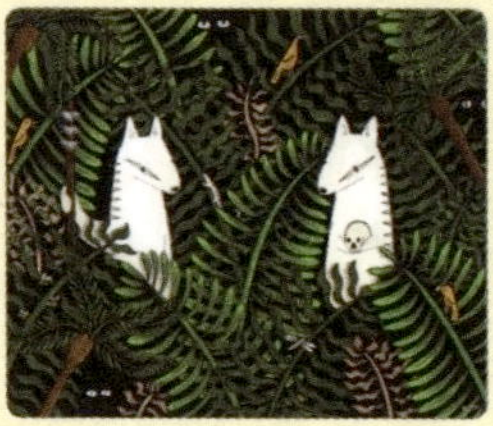

JAYDE FISH
May The Forest Be With You
Gouache

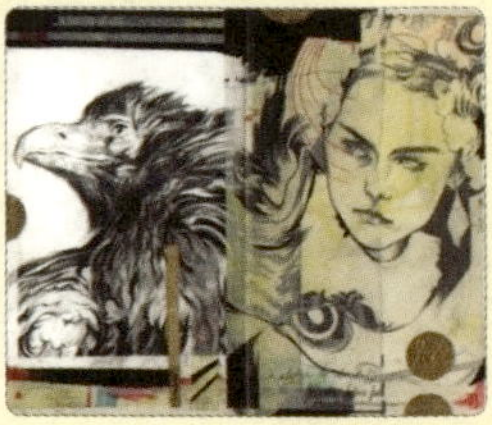

NIMIT MALAVIA
Born Amidst Thoughts of Empire
Graphite, carbon, ink, gold enamel, collage

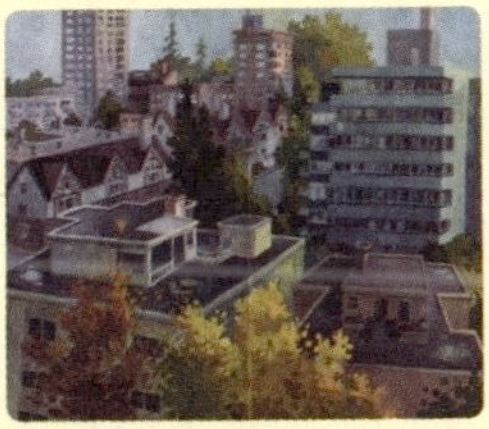

LAURA BIFANO
13th and Granville
Gouache

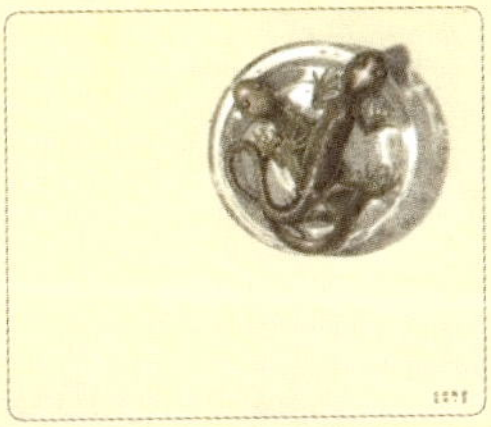

JUSTIN "CORO" KAUFMAN
Northwestern Salamanders
Ink

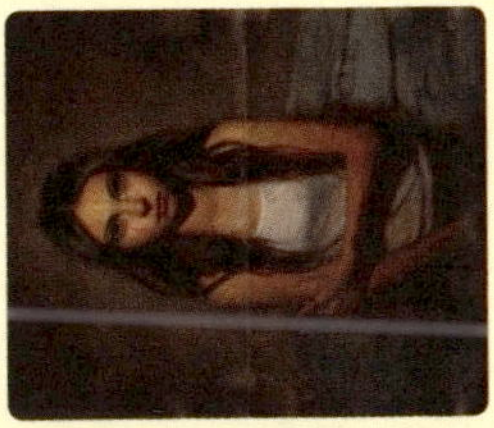

CHRYSTAL CHAN
The Earth and All of Its Efforts
Oil

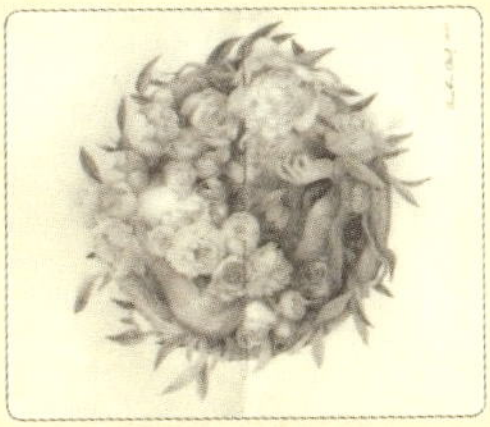

HSIAO-RON CHENG
Bloomy
Graphite

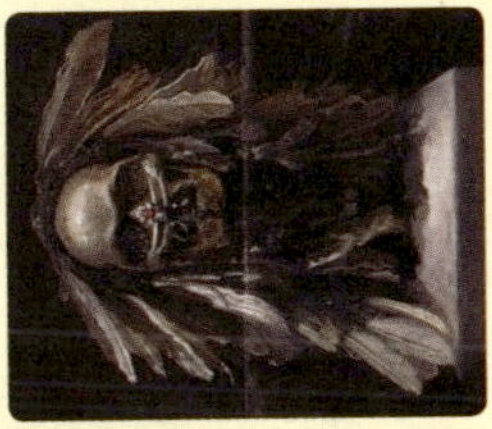

GREG GANDY
Study of Ancestor Skull
Oil

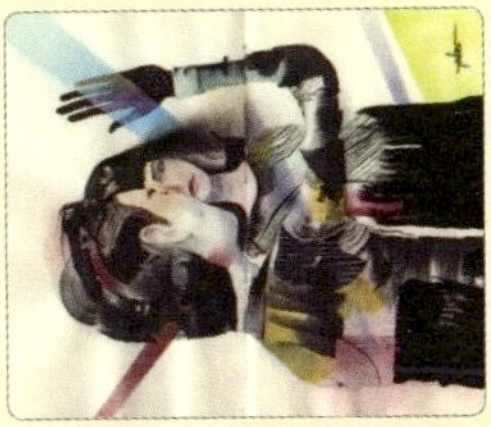

KEN GARDUNO
Phantom
Mixed media

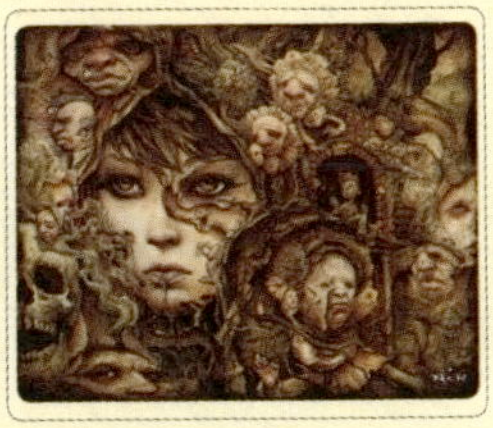

N.C. WINTERS
Broken Memories
Ink, varnished

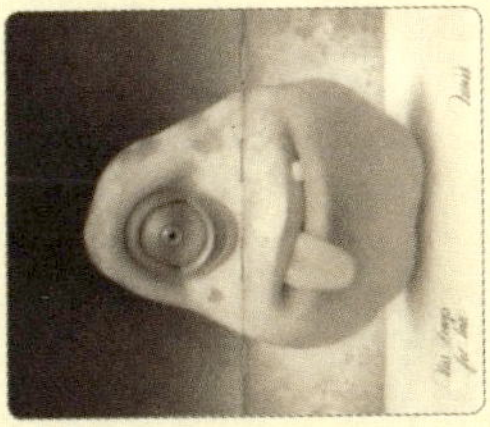

TRAVIS LOUIE
Curious Bump
graphite, Cretacolor Nero oil lead, acrylic wash

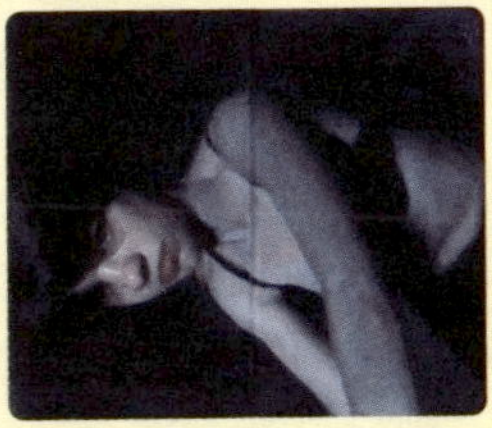

KEITA MORIMOTO
Blue Rhythm
Oil

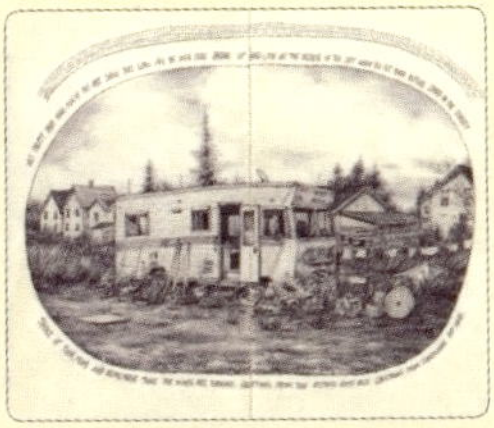

PAT PERRY
Untitled
Ink

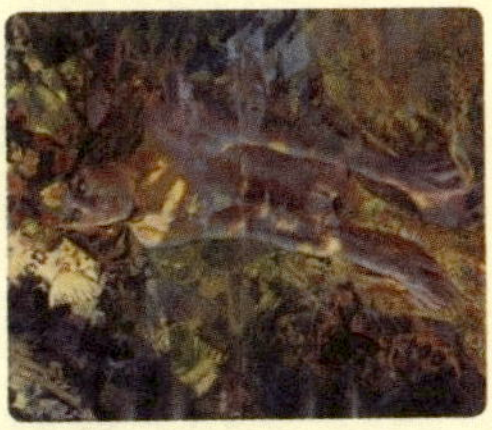

SERGIO LOPEZ
Parhelia
Acrylic

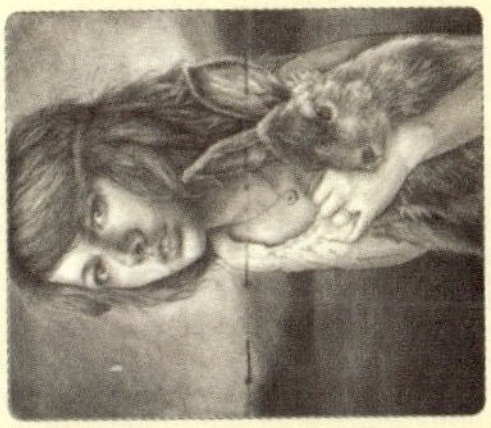

MICHAEL SHAPCOTT
Loom
Graphite

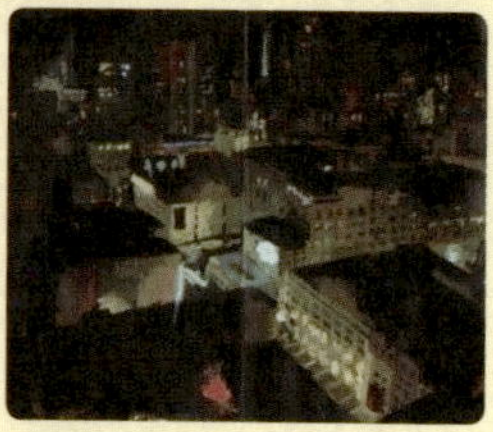

CHRISTIAN MacNEVIN
View From the Marriott 001
Ink and oil

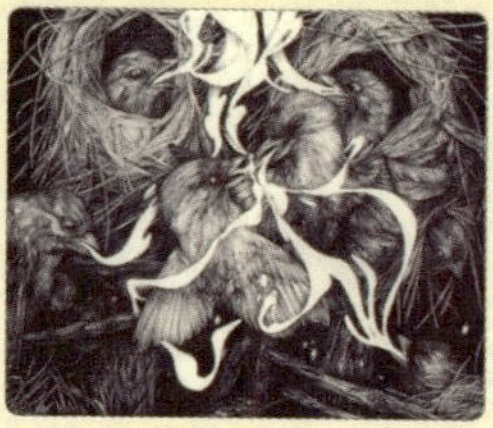

MARCO MAZZONI
The Square
Ink

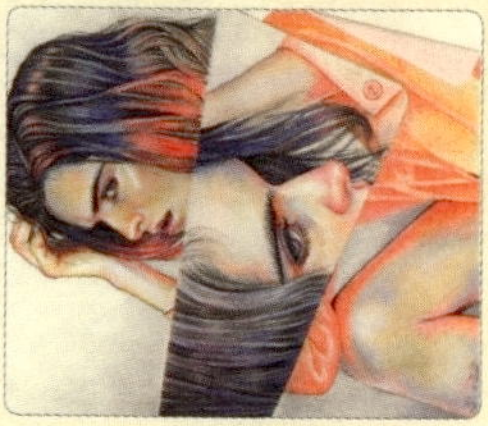

MARTINE JOHANNA
Afterglow
Colored pencil, ink and acrylic

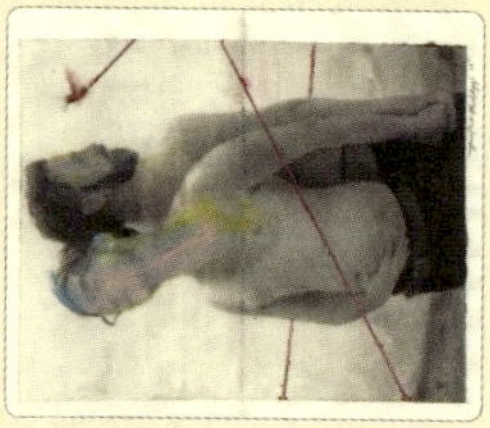

JEAN-PAUL MALLOZZI
Steadfast
Oil, graphite, iridescence

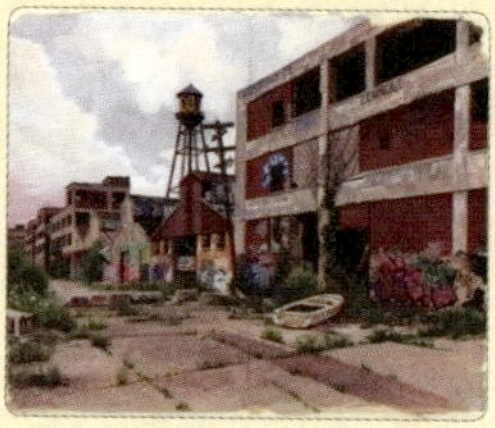

JESSICA HESS
Detroit II
Gouache

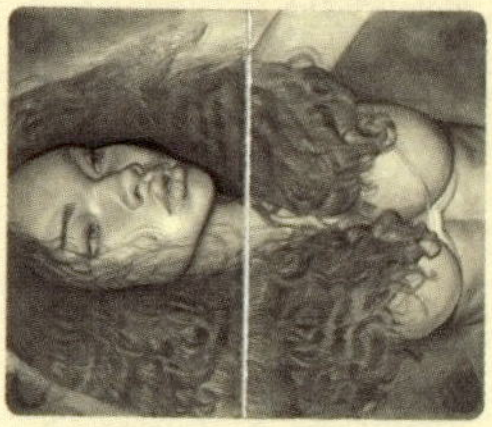

MARCO NELOR
A Portrait Study of Ashley
Graphite

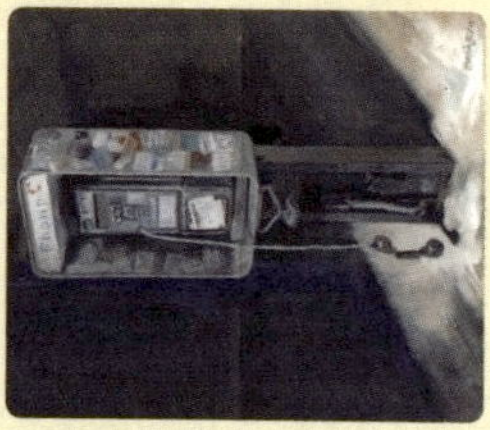

RYAN MALLEY
Phone (6th and Folsom)
Oil

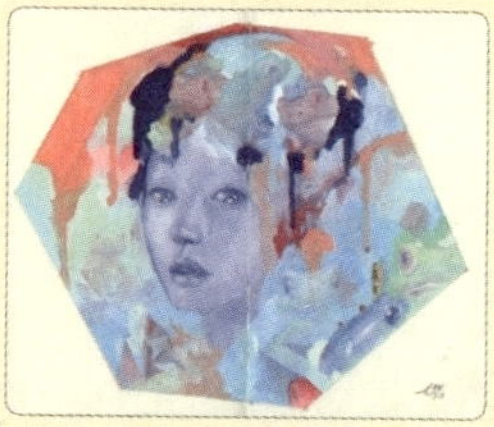

SO YOUN LEE
Stars
Mixed media

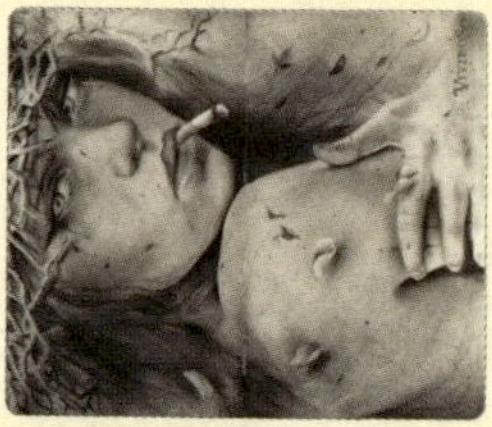

BRIAN VIVEROS
Sacred
Charcoal, watercolor, and airbrush

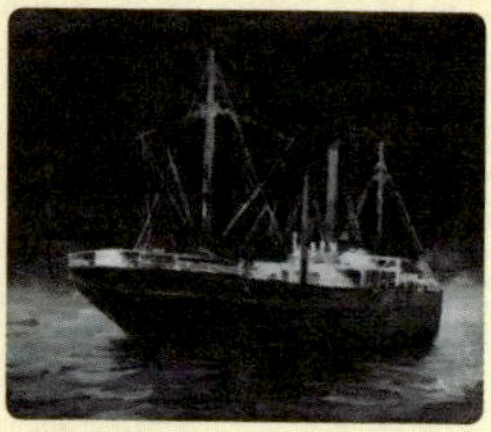

KIM COGAN
Sink or Swim
acrylic

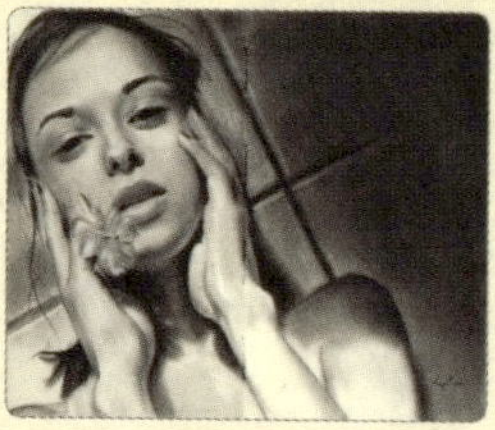

KATE ZAMBRANO
Obsidian
Charcoal

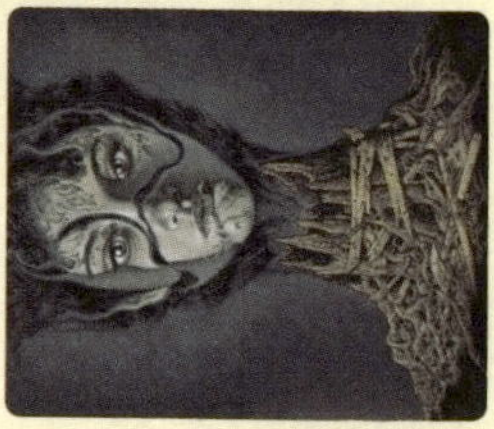

MIKE SUTFIN
Ghosts of Growth
Acrylic, ink and colored pencil

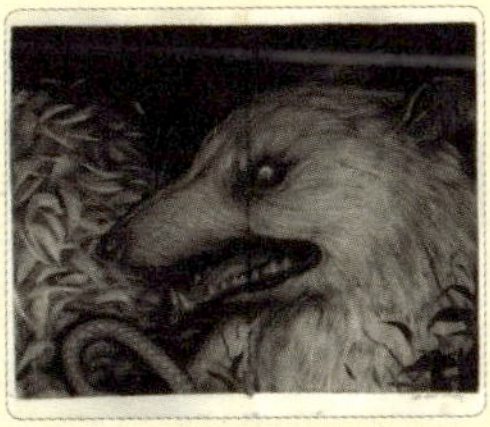

SAM WOLFE CONNELLY
Skittering Burrow
Conté crayon

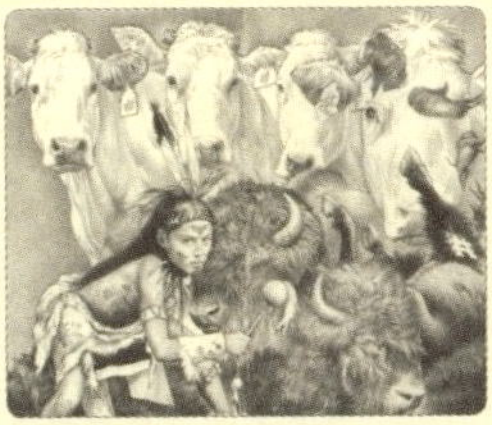

REINIER GAMBOA
White Bull
Graphite

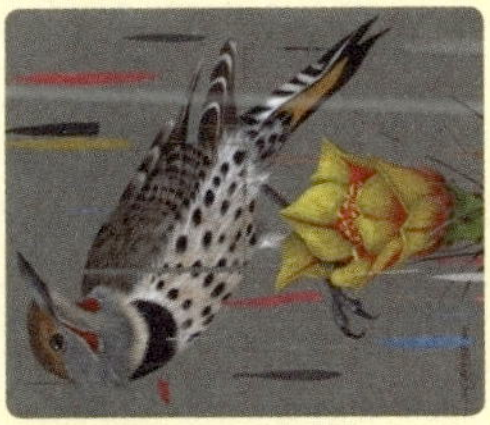

FRANK GONZALES
Northern Flicker and Opuntia Bloom
Acrylic

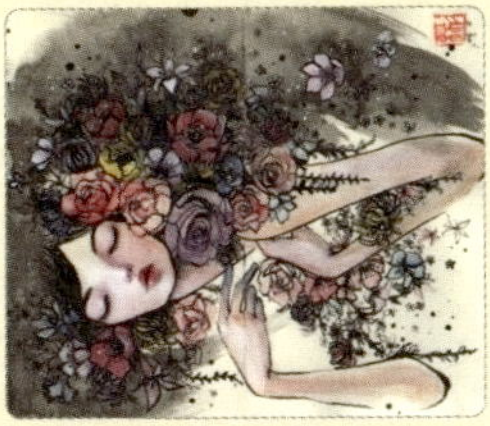

STELLA IM HULTBERG
Only Love Can Break Your Heart
Sumi ink, watercolor and acrylic

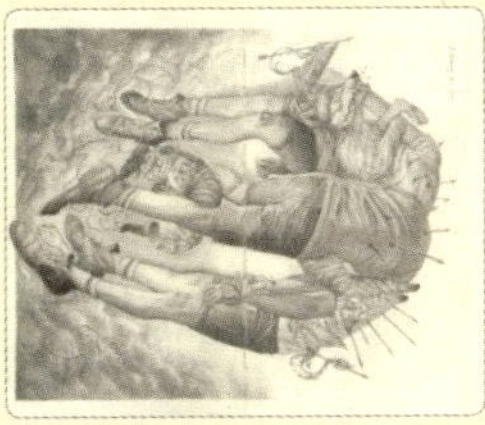

RANDY ORTIZ
Natura Non Contristatur
Graphite and charcoal

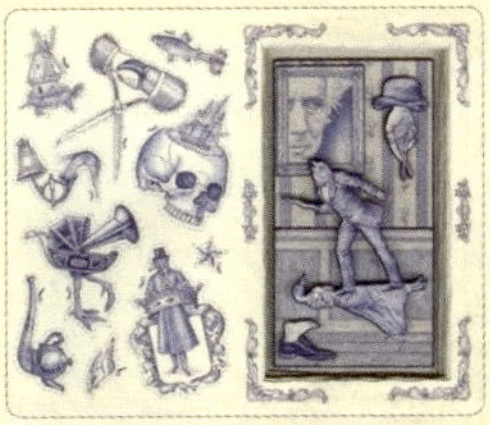

MATT RITCHIE
Une Heure de Bonte
Ballpoint pen and wood

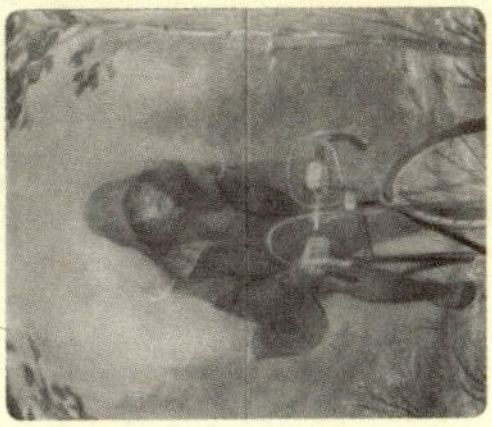

ZACH MONTOYA
North
Graphite

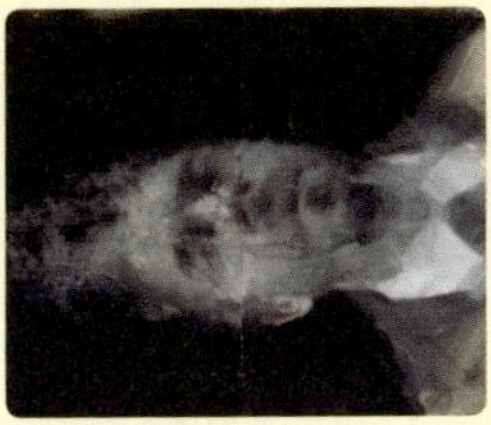

HENRIK ULDALEN
Cede
Oil

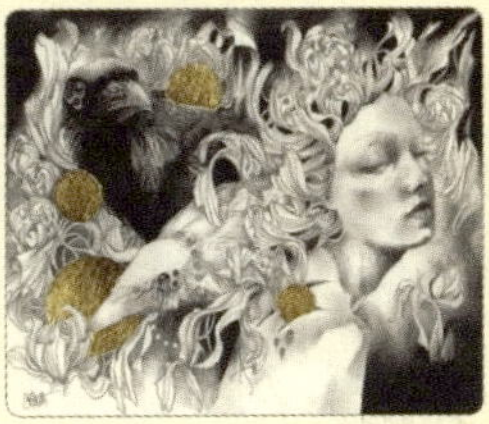

CRAWW
Coronis
Graphite, charcoal and gold gilding leaf

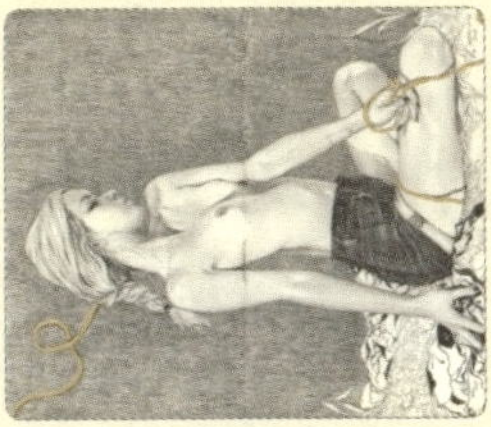

HELICE WEN
A Garden Within
Graphite and gold pigment

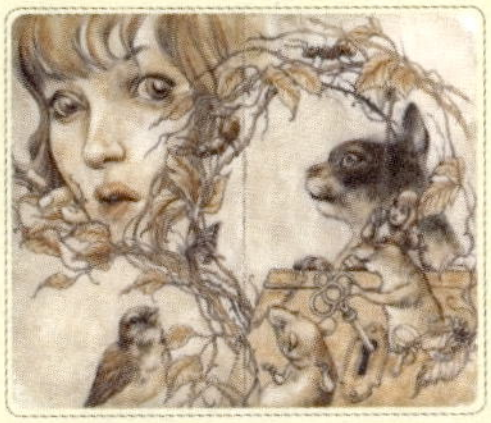

JEREMY HUSH
Nature of Secrets
Ballpoint pen and watercolor

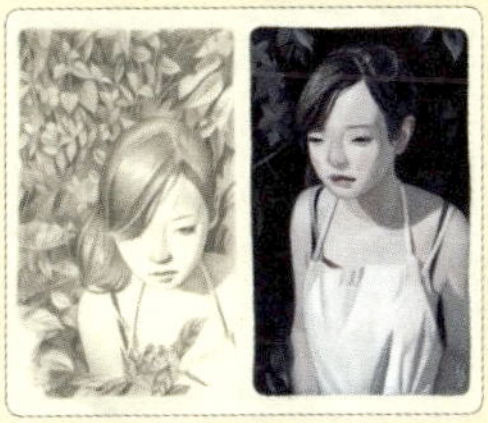

JOANNE NAM
Sisters
Graphite and oil

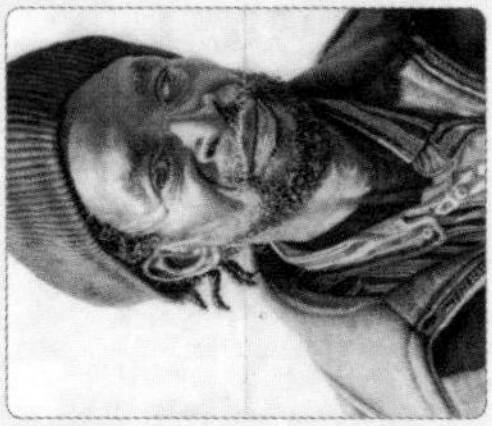

JOEL DANIEL PHILLIPS
Nate #5
Charcoal and graphite

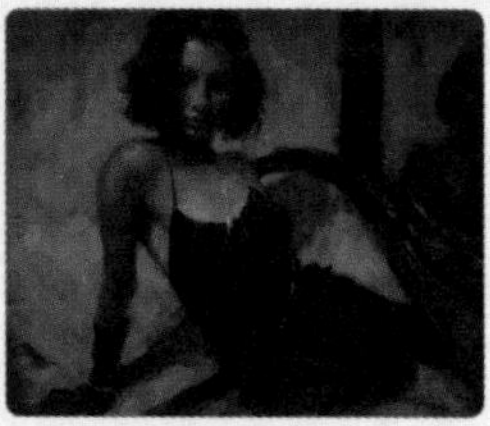

JEREMY MANN
Note in Green No.1, Nadia
Oil